STAR AND KEY

OLIVIER HEIN

Star and Key

The Historical Adventure of Mauritius

HURST & COMPANY, LONDON

First published in the United Kingdom in 2025 by
C. Hurst & Co. (Publishers) Ltd.,
New Wing, Somerset House, Strand, London, WC2R 1LA
© Olivier Hein, 2025
All rights reserved.

Distributed in the United States, Canada and Latin America by
Oxford University Press, 198 Madison Avenue, New York, NY 10016,
United States of America.

The right of Olivier Hein to be identified as the author of
this publication is asserted by him in accordance with the
Copyright, Designs and Patents Act, 1988.

A Cataloguing-in-Publication data record for this book
is available from the British Library.

This book is printed using paper from registered sustainable
and managed sources.

ISBN: 9781805262923

www.hurstpublishers.com

Printed and bound in Great Britain by Bell & Bain Ltd, Glasgow

This book is dedicated to all the people of Mauritius, past, present and future.
This is your story.

CONTENTS

List of Illustrations	ix
Preface	xiii
1. The Nameless Island	1
2. Explorers in the Sea of Zanj	11
3. The Dutch Century	21
4. Terror on the Open Seas	37
5. Îsle de France	55
6. The Man Who Changed Everything	65
7. The Calm Before the Storm	81
8. Revolution and Corsairs	91
9. The Battle of Grand Port	109
10. Mauritius Once More	121
11. The Seeds of Identity	135
12. Transition	149
13. The Noisy Neighbourhood	163
14. Consolidation	181
15. Progress	197
16. The Long and Rocky Road	213
17. The Miracle	229
18. Friction	247
19. Here and Now	263
Bibliography	273
Index	279

LIST OF ILLUSTRATIONS

1. Portuguese explorer Dom Pedro de Mascarenhas (1480–1555). CC0, via Wikimedia Commons.
2. One of the earliest maps of Mauritius ever drawn: a 1603 rendering by Dutch sailor Reijer Cornelisz. Public domain, via Wikimedia Commons.
3. Dutch sailor Johann Theodor de Bry's early seventeenth-century sketch of life in the Mauritian colony. Public domain, via Wikimedia Commons.
4. Raouf Oderuth's rendition of the arrival of the first Malagasy slaves on Mauritius in 1640 aboard a VOC ship. Courtesy of Raouf Oderuth.
5. François Leguat (c.1639–1735)'s 1708 map of his pioneer colony on Rodrigues. Public domain, via Wikimedia Commons.
6. Legendary pirate Olivier Levasseur (c.1690–1730)'s infamous cryptogram. Public domain, via Wikimedia Commons.
7. Bertrand-François Mahé de La Bourdonnais (1699–1753), the man who turned Mauritius from a colony into a permanent settlement with a bright future. Rijksmuseum, CC0, via Wikimedia Commons.
8. A bust of Pierre Poivre (1719–1786), Mauritius' intendant from 1767 to 1772. Benoît Prieur, CC0, via Wikimedia Commons.

LIST OF ILLUSTRATIONS

9. A drawing of Virginie from Jacques-Henri Bernardin de St Pierre (1737–1814)'s novel *Paul et Virginie*, in Mauritius' most famous shipwreck, the *St Géran* (1744). CC0, via Wikimedia Commons.

10. English explorer Matthew Flinders (1774–1814), famous for his outrageous captivity on Mauritius from 1804 to 1810. The History Trust of South Australia, CC0, via Wikimedia Commons.

11. Captain Nesbit Willoughby, the chief provocateur in the epic 1810 Battle of Grand Port. Chronicle / Alamy Stock Photo.

12. Robert Surcouf (1773–1827), the most notorious of the corsairs in Mauritius. Public domain, via Wikimedia Commons.

13. A late nineteenth-century poster of various Mauritian stamps. CC0, via Wikimedia Commons.

14. The Séga dance. Courtesy of Vintage Mauritius.

15. French missionary Jacques-Désiré Laval (1803–1864), who converted thousands of Mauritians to Catholicism from 1841 onwards. Public domain, via Wikimedia Commons.

16. Sailing ships in Port Louis' harbour, 1899. Courtesy of Vintage Mauritius.

17. Indentured labourers, late nineteenth century. Courtesy of Vintage Mauritius.

18. The path around the Trou aux Cerfs volcano in Curepipe, concretised in 1937. Courtesy of Vintage Mauritius.

19. Marcelle 'Didi' Lagesse's 1976 painting of Le Morne. Author's personal collection.

20. The Piat family in the village of Moka, 1945. Author's personal collection.

21. The Champ de Mars racecourse, the site of the celebrations of Mauritian independence in 1968. Author's personal collection.

LIST OF ILLUSTRATIONS

22. Le Réduit, which has been the official home of many Mauritian leaders. Courtesy of Vintage Mauritius.

23. Raouf Oderuth's painting of labourers in sugar cane fields. Courtesy of Raouf Oderuth.

24. Destruction left behind after Cyclone Carol in 1960. Courtesy of Vintage Mauritius.

25. The 'Father of the Nation', Sir Seewoosagur Ramgoolam (1900–1985). Public domain, via Wikimedia Commons.

26. The Chinese New Year Festival, 1950s. Courtesy of Vintage Mauritius.

27. The Mauritian *pirogue*, 1946. Author's personal collection.

28. A political gathering on Royal Road in Rose Hill. Courtesy of Vintage Mauritius.

29. The island of Diego Garcia in the Chagos Archipelago. NASA, Public domain, via Wikimedia Commons.

30. The Pink Pigeon, one of Mauritius' nine endemic bird species. Public domain, via Wikimedia Commons.

31. Mauritius' national park at the Black River Gorges. Public domain, via Wikimedia Commons.

32. Mauritius' worst ecological disaster: the bizarre shipwreck of the oil tanker *MV Wakashio* in 2020. CC BY 2.0, via Wikimedia Commons.

PREFACE

History is fun. Some people may question this, but invariably it's because they had an uninspiring experience during their schooldays. In reality, history is like life: adventurous, exciting, unpredictable, dangerous, sad, funny and all the rest.

To that end, I have chosen to write and present this book on the history of Mauritius a bit like an adventure story. To be clear: this is most certainly *not* historical fiction; it is solidly grounded in abundant primary and secondary sources to enrich the detail and help shape the narrative, including Dutch, British and French archives as well as Mauritius' very own repository in Coromandel. That is on top of numerous academic papers and scholarly studies in English and French. However, what I wanted to get away from was having lots of footnotes and sources within the text itself, as some more scholarly historical tomes are wont to do. Whilst this offers some histories a veneer of gravitas, I find that it also distracts the reader from getting immersed in the story.

To that end, the challenge I set myself whilst writing *Star and Key* was to present the kind of story one can read on the beaches of the island—much as you would a novel—whilst also acting as a secondary reference book for those studying more deeply. And the fact remains that Mauritius' story is immersive and exhilarating, and the focus should be on what happened and why, rather than on constantly quoting the (sometimes contradictory)

PREFACE

sources. For those who insist on knowing where I have looked to pull all these strands together, or who would love to know more about particular aspects of this tale, take heart in the fact that I have compiled a bibliography of books and articles at the end.

It is equally worth pointing out that compiling this book has been something of a balancing act, in that just as important as deciding what to include and how to present it has been making the tricky decisions about what to leave out. Including every iota of information captured so far in one colossal and all-encompassing volume would be a pointless feat, as it would be deathly dull to read. Consequently, the story has been compressed into a manageable size that neither daunts the reader by its sheer number of pages, nor underwhelms by its lack of detail. Ultimately, I hope that I have captured the salient issues that really mattered in shaping the wonderful, heart-warming, idiosyncratic, contradictory and unique island that is the ever-changing Mauritius of today.

Finally, a note regarding ethnicities. As in most countries, the external naming of ethnic groups is a sensitive subject: that Mauritius presents particular challenges in this respect is no surprise. In any case, these naming conventions have a habit of changing and morphing over time according to preference and shifting social attitudes. That said, one cannot write about Mauritian history without referring to the various components of the famed Mauritius 'rainbow'. The official categories mentioned in the Constitution of Mauritius are Hindus, Muslims, Chinese and 'General Population'.

Among the General Population, there are certain specific subgroups worth spelling out. It is common usage to refer to Franco-Mauritians—also nicknamed 'Blanc Mau' (white Mauritians) in recent years—as a specific subgroup. Another subgroup of the General Population are the 'Creoles'. This term can have a wider definition—for example, persons of mixed par-

PREFACE

entage (African-European, African-Indian, European-Indian, Sino-African-European-Indian, etc)—but in line with other authors on this subject, I will use the term here in the more restricted sense, as referring to those who descend more or less directly from African ancestors. Within the wider Hindu group, it is also sometimes found appropriate in certain contexts to distinguish the Tamils as a specific subgroup. In short, I have tried to use wording that is as neutral and unpolitical as possible and to avoid anything that can be deemed offensive, inaccurate or pejorative. If I haven't succeeded in this, I can only apologise. Ultimately, this is an island and a people that are part of me, and by the time you have finished reading this I hope that—one way or another—the Dodo will have gently bitten you too.

As with every big project, you can never do it alone. Lots of people have been incredibly helpful and generous and I can't name everyone, but I would like to single out Philippe Hein and Susanna Dalais and give them massive thanks for their invaluable feedback and advice in helping me shape this narrative. Second, I would like to thank Michael Dwyer and all the amazing team at Hurst, both for their constant expert help and encouragement as well as their support in general. And a final huge thank you to my children, Alexander and Beatrice, and especially my wife Natasha, for being so patient and supportive in letting me indulge myself in undertaking this long-gestated project.

1

THE NAMELESS ISLAND

One indeterminate day, nearly 10 million years ago, some colossal basalt rocks underneath the vast stretch of water latterly known as the Indian Ocean decided that they had had enough.

Slowly but remorselessly, in a hitherto featureless location nearly 500 miles east of Madagascar, the huge slabs rose up from their watery prison and committed themselves instead to feeling the burning tropical sun on their reflectionless black backs. That same sun rose and set an unimaginable number of times as those volcanic stones climbed further and further, eventually forming a huge dome.

Volcanoes randomly pockmarked the island, and in their angry infancy they spewed lava and ash repeatedly, as though throwing tantrums against their new open-air home. After countless millennia of this behaviour, one of these volcanoes conjured up a monstrous explosion, resulting in some chunks of the island slipping back into the waves and others being launched so far that their remnants helped form offshore islands, like a string of wonky pearls, to the north.

It wasn't the end of their show. They continued to belch out a few further eruptions that helped shape the idiosyncratic

STAR AND KEY

mountains, which themselves soon punched the clouds and saluted the huge and stunning coral reef that had simultaneously formed and that nearly surrounded the island.

A constant wind likely blew, its origins in unseen distant shores, and hitching lifts within it—on certain rare occasions—were the flightiest of seeds and the tiniest of insects. Most would end up perishing in the merciless ocean, but if the stars of fortune aligned just so, these life forms would land safely on the island. And there they settled and evolved, often in ways unknown anywhere else. Human eyes were not there to witness what nature had dreamed up, but had they been, they would have scanned those forest-clad mountains and volcanoes, sparkling lagoons and untouched beaches, and soon proclaimed it a tropical perfection.

And then came the birds.

A mere wind would not have blown them here; what was needed was a huge cyclone. The cyclone—the Southern Indian Ocean name for the North Atlantic hurricane—is an annual event in this part of the world, kicking off the calendar year with lashing rains and terrifying winds, and always turning in a clockwise direction, the inverse of its North Atlantic cousin. Only in certain years, though, will a monstrous one appear, and only some of these have the capacity and force to carry birds with them against their will.

But time was on the island's side.

A pair of Fruit Doves were likely the first victims, dragged away from their homeland in Southeast Asia around 8 million years ago, to land shaken, but still in breeding condition, on the now 714-square-mile island. Over the generations, their ancestors would adapt to their novel surroundings and morph slowly into the magnificent red, white and blue Dutch Pigeon, so named—millions of years later—as its colour scheme resembled that nation's flag. By the mid-nineteenth century, it would disappear forever.

THE NAMELESS ISLAND

Two species of parrot would soon join them, both in terms of co-existence and subsequent extinction. The Mascarene Grey Parakeet and the Broad-Billed Parrot were also revealed in recent times to be taxonomically and genetically related to Southeast Asian species, with a mighty tropical storm again likely to have been the culprit for dumping their ancestors here. They in turn were joined by a kind of Scops Owl, whose distant ancestry has never been fully proven. The version that developed here never ended up going anywhere else before dying out. The owl—modest in size though it was—claimed top seat as the island's principal predator alongside another endemic species, a perfectly proportioned speckled-brown kestrel, for by now lizards and other small reptiles had found their way to this green oasis, most likely via large branches floating hopefully, rather than purposefully, on the currents.

Two much larger species of reptile were also colonising the island in their inimitably slow way. Both were Giant Tortoises, one domed and one saddle-backed, and each one dwarfed even the largest tortoises of today. When humans did eventually discover the island, they found that two adults could easily sit on the back of the domed species. The saddle-back was no smaller, but with the lack of land predators, it had evolved a shell merely 1 millimetre thick and very few of the scales that would normally be typical of a reptile. With distant Madagascar—a much older island—already nurturing its own tortoises, we can only surmise that the first specimens to reach this speck of land did so using their incredible ability, despite their bulk, to float on the current with their heads held high like slow-motion periscopes and to survive for six months off their fat reserves, without the need for food or fresh water.

A mammal made it too, this time having the advantage of wings. Where the ancestors of this huge bat—known as the Flying Fox—originally came from still cannot be determined, but

3

as a megabat species it was—and still is—only interested in eating the bounteous fruit on offer in the emerald canopy.

Nearly sixty bird species either found their way here by accident or design, or evolved from those that had. For the most part, their stories fall beyond the scope of this story, although one more immigrant *is* worth mentioning. At a date still difficult to pinpoint, but certainly millions of years ago, a pair of Nicobar Pigeons—or that pigeon's ancestor—found their way to the island. With the Nicobar Islands thousands of miles to the northeast, it is possible that they too were cyclone victims, but equally likely, from fossil records found around the Indian Ocean, that they had island-hopped their way around the vast rim of the Indian Ocean. Either way, they stayed, bred and gradually increased in size over the generations to fill an empty ecological niche. When they called out to each other, it sounded like 'doo-doo', which—Occam's razor suggests—was the most likely origin of the simple, evocative, but fateful name assigned to it when humans eventually arrived. With no land predators to disturb them, they were naturally selected to dispense with flight and to roam and forage instead on the goodness of the forest floor.

And what a forest it was. Its average canopy height was nearly 80 feet, with only a few trees poking significantly beyond that. With an average diameter of 3 feet, the trunks were robust without being massively sturdy. As evolution strutted its stuff, many of the trees became endemic—having developed here and nowhere else—including the Bois Jaune, Marbled Ebony, Brown Palmiste, Bois de Pomme, White Fig and many more. Some developed leaves as thick as leather, and many were conjoined by the climbers and lianas that seem to define so many tropical jungles. A dozen species of orchid appeared, some native also to neighbouring islands, others finding their one and only home here. The forest gripped tight to almost all the land, even reaching and conquering, in the southwest, the highest peak (2,720

THE NAMELESS ISLAND

feet) that the island's forces had mustered. The roots of those countless trees constantly gorged themselves on the incredibly rich and fertile volcanic soil.

Thus, the outsized and flightless descendants of those Nicobar Pigeons had everything they needed and nothing to fear. Indeed, it was this very fact that would ultimately fast-track them to their doom. But these birds had an enviable climate to enjoy in the meantime. This unknown island lay near the twenty-third degree of latitude south of the equator, nudging the Tropic of Capricorn, meaning it would be a land of two, and not four, seasons. Scientific records show that the climate has changed little throughout its 10 million years of existence, with the hot and humid summer months from November to April usually hovering around 30 degrees Celsius during the day, dropping to the low 20s at night. This was also the wet season, sometimes demonstrated by a short, sharp, tropical shower of fat and intense raindrops, and sometimes in the form of the punishing cyclone. For this weather system, then and now, was a cross to bear for tropical areas everywhere and a capricious hazard from which only those places falling within the equatorial zone were spared.

That said, the contrast with the winter months, when daytime temperatures would have hovered in the low-to-mid 20s, was not hugely significant, although rainfall was harder to come by. But the lush forest had enough sustenance over the course of the year to help it grow and indeed thrive. The more constant temperatures were to be found around the coastline, which was usually flat and enticing, whereas the mountains of the interior had formed a central plateau where greater rain and cloud made life more varied for those creatures that chose to reside there.

And where there are forests and mountains, there will inevitably be streams. None were technically rivers, for this was not a giant island—indeed, it could be snugly fitted three times over within the M25 London Orbital—but they more than served

STAR AND KEY

their purpose. These fourth- and fifth-order streams—forty-six in total—slithered their way through the dense forest to the ocean below. They gently shaped the valleys and distributed the nutrients of the waters and soils from high up to low down, ensuring a healthy ecosystem for the burgeoning freshwater life that was also taking hold, including small fish, shrimps and eels. At many of the estuaries could now be found mangroves, forming those briny semi-aquatic forests that provided such limitless goodness for the creatures that resided there permanently, as well as acting as a nursery for the youngsters of the larger fish that would eventually leave and brave the open sea.

The ocean which hemmed in the island was as rich in life as those forests. The suffocating embrace by the coral reef of nearly the entire island—bar a gap to the south—was offset by the litany of fish that soon swarmed there to make it their home. Huge Groupers and Giant Trevallies patrolled the outer rim of the reef, feeding on the less circumspect smaller fish nestled within the coral—and in the latter's case, possibly the occasional seabird too. Parrotfish, Butterflyfish and Moorish Idols added a kaleidoscope of colour to the lagoon. Just beyond, in deeper waters but still within sight of the coast, rays and Dolphinfish skimmed through the tropical waters, often feeding on an embarrassment of calories when the oxygen-rich cooler swells from the south brought with them a wealth of food sources.

Just beyond the horizon were the huge deepwater fish that invariably triggered fear in the others. Huge congregations of Yellowfin Tuna and Bonitos would regularly pass the young island, forever hungry and built by evolution into the most perfect of killer torpedoes. An array of sharks, resident and itinerant, was never far away, including the Mako, Tiger and Hammerhead Shark. Another arrival from nearby seas was the Lionfish, or Laffe, an almost motionless brown hoverer in medium-depth water, with unpleasant eyes seemingly always fixed upwards, as

THE NAMELESS ISLAND

though in a perma-threat. Sometimes they conducted their stately swim alone and sometimes in pairs, but they were almost always lethal to anything that had the misfortune to touch one of their leafy tendrils or spines.

Most impressive of all was the empress herself: the Marlin. Three different types of this magnificent, mysterious and extraordinary fish would have been found off all shores of the island: the Black, the Blue and the Striped. Huge specimens, 1,500 pounds in weight, would not have been uncommon, and a flash of their sabre would likely have been the last thing many unlucky fish would see. Perhaps they should have stayed in the green haven of the mangroves after all.

After countless years of aggression, the volcanoes eventually passed puberty and grew up. The last eruption was no later than 100,000 years ago, or thereabouts, allowing the encroaching trees to finally pounce and encase all the craters in yet more verdant forest. Beforehand, though, one volcano had a last and unique trick to pull. In the southwest of the island, as the basalt decomposed and reacted with existing compounds in the soil at a variety of different temperatures, the iron and aluminium in the soil reacted—somehow—to form a volcanic sand rainbow of seven colours: yellow, purple, blue, green, violet, brown and red. As though suspicious of each other, the volcanic sands wouldn't mix: even if the ancient rains lashed them into a mud, they would soon separate themselves out again. To the best of our knowledge, such a geological formation didn't happen anywhere else on earth, and we don't fully know why it happened here.

This new, more docile period of the volcanoes meant that the coastline, too, was given a break, and beaches started expanding, eventually extending to over 100 miles. It didn't take long for the currents to start inevitably washing up the hardy coconuts from distant palm trees, and these took hold to frame the beaches as they do in so many tropical islands.

STAR AND KEY

By now, our island was no longer alone. On a smaller scale, 350 miles to its northeast, another geological roll of the dice had occurred. This burgeoning landmass had had an equally violent upbringing, shorter but sharper, leaving a mere 42 square miles above the ocean, with sometimes as much as 1,500 feet above it. All the clues to its volcanic origin had been smothered by time; even then, any search for hot springs—the last relic of any volcanic activity—would have been in vain. Like its bigger cousin to the southwest, it too was embraced by a heartbreakingly beautiful coral reef and a comparatively huge lagoon. It would play an intimate part in our island's future.

In turn, a mere 125 miles to the west—and almost yesterday, in the freakishly long time frames of geological time—another new neighbour sprang to life. It was slightly larger, and being younger meant that it continued (and continues to this day) to squirm and pulse. Its larger, angrier volcanoes maintain a semblance of shape for now. But back then, the vibrant orange of fresh lava flowed with abandon, meaning that a coral reef probably and instinctively tried to form, but repeatedly failed. Its beaches could not help but capture the blackness of all things volcanic, giving the island's rim a sombre look to contrast with its spectacular interior forest and mountains, also replete with its own wildlife. This place, too, will play its part in this story.

Squatting in the middle—both in terms of location and size— was the oldest of the three, and the one that would have the most fascinating story to tell. This island—hardly ancient in geological terms—had been magicked from the ocean by the underground forces of tectonics, and after a stuttering start had not looked back. It had nurtured a plethora of species for so long that—like on so many isolated islands elsewhere—many were unwittingly found there and there alone. Thus, an enviably Arcadian life continued for both flora and fauna for untold generations. They were oblivious to the world beyond, as indeed that world was to them.

THE NAMELESS ISLAND

But the island had bided its time long enough. It was ready to show itself.

It was ready for a name.

2

EXPLORERS IN THE SEA OF ZANJ

Between the ninth and fourteenth centuries CE, no single people or 'nation' ruled the Indian Ocean, but one culture certainly dominated it.

Two centuries earlier, a new religion had exploded like a supernova on the Arabian Peninsula and rapidly spread its indefatigable tentacles to many shores beyond: a fresh take on 'truth' that was carried on horseback within the minds of so many men who were adamant that they had a new—and ultimate—revelation to share with all. To some, it would initially prove to be a message laced with aggressive conquest, but it was not just the sword that overwhelmed vast swathes of the Middle East: the pure drive of logic, scientific thought and discovery that accompanied Islam would also have equally powerful repercussions.

This flowering of enlightened thought and experimentation was light years ahead of such activities in Europe at the time, and it transcended many disciplines. In mathematics, Arab scholars built on the great works of their Greek and Egyptian predecessors, developing algebra and geometry in new directions, whilst shaping a new set of numerals that, with little change, would be

STAR AND KEY

used even to this day throughout most of the world. Medical progress was also made, with an understanding of the treatment of contagious diseases such as smallpox and measles centuries ahead of the archaic classical methods employed throughout Europe. And in physics, the twelfth-century thinker Ibn Bajjah made the claim that for every force there is a reactive force. If he had just included the word 'equal' before 'reactive', he would have beaten Isaac Newton to the third law of motion by nearly 500 years.

A thirst for knowledge often travels hand in hand with a thirst for exploration, and the Arabs of the medieval world were no different. Their navigation was outstanding, and the shores of India and Eastern Africa were becoming their extended backyard. Again, in terms of scale, they dwarfed the vision and capabilities of their European counterparts of the time. The driver, predictably, was trade. Forever keen to strike the next deal and make a tasty profit, and harnessing the trade winds—a secret they had long cracked—they pushed back the boundaries of their known world and were not afraid to set up trading posts as they sailed in their *dhows*, drawing comfort from the comparative accuracy of their trusty astrolabes, the precursor to the mariner's sextant.

Exploring the eastern seaboard of Africa, they soon gave this unexplored ocean a name that would remain theirs and theirs alone for centuries: Bahr-el-Zanj—'The Sea of Blacks'. It is a raw name that reverberates starkly and somewhat unpleasantly on the modern ear. But it should be placed in context: the Arab traders were spreading in many directions around this little-known ocean and encountering strikingly different peoples as they did so. To that end, it might have been nothing more than an easy reference point as they devised their plethora of beautiful maps. Conversely, some were unequivocally slave traders, and the appellation could very well have been pejorative. We'll likely never know.

EXPLORERS IN THE SEA OF ZANJ

In our current age of instantaneous map-making to almost frightening levels of accuracy, it is easy to forget just what a monumental—and undisciplined—undertaking cartography was until the Age of Enlightenment. Every snippet of knowledge gained at first or second hand from any traveller was greedily but arbitrarily drawn onto parchment by the map-maker, cobbled together like Frankenstein's monster and often leaving a contradictory and wildly inaccurate tool. Consider this 'insight' shared by none other than Marco Polo, describing the island of Madagascar—a place he had personally never been anywhere near:

> It is four thousand miles in extent ... its inhabitants are Muslim and all live by trade. In this island ... there are more elephants than anywhere in the world, and there are found there also leopard, lions, giraffes and wild asses. In the 'countries' [islands] which be yet further off is found the 'Griffin' or 'Roc', which is not, as related, half bird and half lion, but is rather a gigantic eagle which ... carries off elephants in its talons. These it drops down from a height and then feeds on the crushed flesh.

Any European or Middle Eastern cartographer, keen to assist in the opening up of potential new trade routes, would have lapped this up, peppering their drawings of this massive Madagascar with pictures of monsters, oblivious to the fact that literally all of it was utter nonsense. It would have been all the harder to counter such brazen fabrications given that the recounter assertively 'corrects' previous inaccuracies, as the great exaggerator Polo was wont to do. In this case, his 'Roc' sounds like a garbled mash-up between the Elephant Bird—a 10-foot ground-dwelling creature, indeed found at the time in Madagascar, and the heaviest avian in history—and the Lammergeier, a huge vulture still found in numbers in Eastern Africa, which drops sheep's bones from a height onto rocks in order to break them up and swallow them in manageable chunks.

13

STAR AND KEY

One can therefore make the case that possessing a map when on a long voyage could actually be counter-productive if too much faith was placed in it. Nevertheless, these were outstanding sailors, assisted by their deep understanding of the stars for navigation, a knowledge passed down through generations like an intangible sacred heirloom. They also cannily constructed sea-going craft of surprising lightness. With their coconut-fibre ropes holding in place caulked planks and their triangular ('lateen') sails, they were able to sail upwind without great difficulty.

It is clear that the passage of the Arabs through these three mysterious islands left no physical evidence: not one coin, tool, weapon, shipwreck or anything else has yet been found. Nevertheless, they certainly knew about them, as the Cantino Planisphere map, dating to 1502, confirms. This stunning map, later smuggled into Italy, where it still resides, accompanied the Portuguese on their first voyages to the Indian Ocean and unequivocally places three islands roughly where they should be, each being assigned an Arabic-sounding name. The largest, youngest one is named 'Dina Margabin'; the smallest, most easterly one 'Dina Moraze'; and the middle island—our island—'Dina Arobi'.

Certain other contemporaneous Arab maps give variations on the same names to the three islands ('Dina Robin' being the most common for the middle island), even if their locations vary markedly. The three together are even given a collective name on another ancient Arab map: the 'Tirakka Archipelago'. A half legend suggests that this name was assigned by an explorer-tradesman named Sulhiman al-Madri in 1489. It is therefore clear that these sailors knew very well that the islands were there and had known for a long time.

But despite the striking beauty of the islands the Arab tradesmen didn't stay, for the simple reason that they found no one there to trade with. With their trading posts dotted all along the Indian Ocean coastline, it made far more sense—from their per-

14

EXPLORERS IN THE SEA OF ZANJ

spective—to develop routes closer to their shores, rather than to hit out into a vast and unknown ocean. The accepted story is therefore that nothing more was seen or heard of these islands for several hundred years until the arrival of the Portuguese in the early 1500s. And yet ...

Eighty years before those Europeans first gazed upon the islands, the entire Indian Ocean was to witness a succession of fleets like none that had ever been seen before. These were the Chinese 'treasure fleets', the brainchild of the Yongle Emperor Zhu Di, third of the Ming Dynasty emperors. They were consigned to a footnote of history for many years, partly due to a later emperor's inward-looking focus and desire to burn most information related to these expeditions, and perhaps also thanks to Eurocentric historians' rather sniffy appraisal of anything medieval that did not originate in Europe. Regardless, these Chinese fleets—seven in total, dating from 1405 to 1433—were monumental in scope and ambition.

Once they set sail, the mastermind on the water was Fleet Admiral Zheng He, truly one of the most fascinating characters in medieval history. A Muslim court eunuch born in Kunming, he played the role not just of military leader, but also of diplomat, explorer and international tradesman. For the aim of these huge fleets was both to seek representatives from around the entire Indian Ocean to bring back to China, and to extract tribute from the peoples and tribes that they encountered. When they 'discovered' each new location, the Chinese would solemnly declare—with some chutzpah—that the town or province now owed tribute to the Chinese emperor, who was 'the superior to each and every one of them'. That so many of these disparate communities so readily agreed to do so, giving these mysterious, newly arrived Chinese mariners and bureaucrats a chunk of their most valuable assets, can only mean that they were truly awestruck by the size and capability of the fleet they encountered.

STAR AND KEY

And they had reason to be. As a comparison, when Christopher Columbus, at the end of that very century, struck out across the Atlantic Ocean to his date with destiny, he commanded three ships; the largest, the *Santa Maria*, was 62 feet in length and had a crew of forty. By contrast, Zheng He, on his first expedition, led a fleet of 317 ships—sixty-two of which were the famed 'treasure ships'. Each of these ocean-going beasts could be up to 492 feet long, and certainly no fewer than 246 feet. His full complement of mariners was over 27,000. This was exploration by shock and awe on an epic scale.

It is maddening that so much information on these Chinese voyages has been lost, including exactly where they went and how they navigated. But we do know that by the seventh and final expedition in 1433, much of the fleet had reached Malindi on the east coast of Africa. We also know that the ships thought nothing of spending a month at sea without seeing land, as they frequently did between Southeast Asia and Ceylon (Sri Lanka). With the overarching aim of the fleet apparently being to project naval power across the whole of the 'Western Ocean' (as they called it), and bearing in mind the jaw-dropping resources available to them, it would seem strange for them *not* to have at least struck out east and southeast from the shores of Africa to ensure that no interlopers or challengers were to be found elsewhere in the ocean.

To be clear: there is no direct evidence that the Chinese fleets found our archipelago in the Sea of Zanj in 1433—at this stage it must be pigeonholed as supposition. And if they *had* visited, they would rapidly have realised—like the Arab sailors centuries before them—that there was no one there to claim tribute from and no one to trade with. But it is conceivable that they *did* make it there, and perhaps one day some digging in the Chinese archives will unearth some exciting new information; or, more prosaically, a diver might drift across a tell-tale stone anchor in

EXPLORERS IN THE SEA OF ZANJ

that part of the ocean, whose provenance could only be from these treasure fleets. Until then, we can only speculate.

What can be claimed unequivocally is that the Portuguese arrived in the early sixteenth century. Once again, however, historical sources have often been confused about who the first European was to set eyes upon the island and exactly when this was. The ultimate trigger for their arrival had been Vasco da Gama's opening up of the maritime spice route between India and western Europe. A choice of sea routes was needed, and the notoriously stormy Mozambique Channel—the 'inner passage' bisecting that country on the mainland from Madagascar—may have been the quickest route as the fish swims but was also hazardous. A route to the east of Madagascar—the 'outer passage'—was also needed, but only if there was somewhere along that route that could provide a stopping-off point for supplies and repairs.

It was the wartime historian Georges de Visdelou-Guimbeau, in his profoundly thorough 1948 book *La Découverte des Îles Mascareignes*, who, having posed the question of which Portuguese sailor actually 'discovered' the island, settled the answer most persuasively: the honour most likely went to Domingos Fernandez in 1511. Suggested earlier dates, including the oft-quoted 1507, are most likely due to the similarity in names between different Portuguese explorers of the time, and Domingos Fernandez' case is strengthened by a simple yet powerful piece of evidence. A prestigious Portuguese map of 1519, as well as several subsequent ones over the next twenty years, all follow the established convention of calling a newly located island after its discoverer. Dina Robin/Dina Arobi was now consigned to history, and the island now tested out the new name of 'Domingos Fernandez'.

Domingos Fernandez (the island) therefore became an option—but no more than that—for the Portuguese spice route

17

STAR AND KEY

to India. It did indeed provide sailors with an abundance of fresh fruit to (unwittingly) stave off scurvy, as well as plentiful timber for vessel maintenance. Yet it would be wrong to suggest that the Portuguese properly 'settled' here. It was a means to an end, but the focus of their burgeoning empire was on resources, trade, land, gold and people, and Domingos Fernandez—idyllic as it was—offered none of these. No Portuguese stayed or lived there.

Nevertheless, they used it as a depot throughout the century, during which time the newer maps had started giving the island yet another name. It was now increasing referred to as 'Cirne' or 'Sirne'. Although not immediately obvious, the most likely explanation for this change—as the sailor Domingos Fernandez faded from history—was that 'Cirne' (meaning 'Swan') was the name of the ship of *another* explorer with a similar name—Diogo Fernandes Pereira—who had actually discovered the larger, more westerly island in the archipelago, which he named Santa Apollonia. Like a virus, the name of Cirne seems to have jumped from one host to another.

That such confusion reigned should in fact come as little surprise. Maps were drawn and copied by skilled draughtsmen who had nevertheless likely never left their home district. The information they received for their magnificent works often only arrived months or years after any 'discovery' had taken place—plenty of time for word of mouth and the rumour mill to get up to their old tricks.

There was a notorious example of this at the time. João de Lisboa, who made several voyages to India traversing the Indian Ocean, mentioned that he had passed an 'unknown' island several times on these journeys between 1510 and 1520. Cartographers in Portugal added the island in, dutifully named after the sailor himself. Some placed it on the inner-passage route to the west of Madagascar, others on the outer-passage route to the east; they simply weren't sure. Many sailors and glory hunters over the

EXPLORERS IN THE SEA OF ZANJ

ensuing three centuries would search in vain for this mysterious island, until, in the nineteenth century, it was finally agreed and indeed proven that it simply didn't exist. João de Lisboa had either been telling tall tales or had genuinely mistaken it for something already established.

But one other mariner of the sixteenth century would have a longer lasting impact, if in name only. Dom Pedro de Mascarenhas was a well-connected explorer and diplomat, who would also be, towards the end of his life, Viceroy of Goa in India. Despite conflicting reports, he may not have visited this archipelago until 1528, and then may only have stepped foot on the largest island. Nevertheless, the short-lived name of Tirakka, used to collectively describe the three islands, would be usurped, as around this time a brown-nosing colleague of the rich and influential Mascarenhas suggested that the archipelago as a whole be renamed the 'Ilhas Mascarenhas' (Mascarene Islands) in his honour. In a land of ever-shifting names, it was the exception that proved the rule, for it is a name that survives to this day.

But after nearly ninety years in the region, the Portuguese had had enough. Their monopoly on the maritime spice trade had long since eroded, their relationship with the island was uneasy and their focus was straying elsewhere, mainly to the African mainland which offered—to their eyes at least—a greater opportunity for permanent settlement. And thus, in the dying years of the sixteenth century they abandoned the island for the last time, leaving no human trace but having begun to introduce exotic animals, including the dog and the cow, to an island that had no evolutionary idea how to cope with them.

Yet as one door closed, another door opened; for the men from Lisbon had barely left before, in the same decade, another burgeoning European power arrived and aggressively staked its claim to the island. Its influence would be significantly more profound, driven by the all-consuming ambition of the largest

19

STAR AND KEY

company to have ever existed, which in turn paid lip service to the fragile ecology of the island.

Cirne was about to be irrevocably turned upside down.

3

THE DUTCH CENTURY

The Netherlands' legacy on the island that had been known as Cirne is complicated.

In truth, the island's inhabitants of today feel very little—if any—cultural link to the Dutch. The little that has been taught, or which is still remembered from generational pass-down, tends not to be overly positive, and is inevitably superseded or overshadowed by the heavy influence of the two European superpowers who would take the place of the Dutch as masters of the Sea of Zanj. Yet, whether acknowledged or not, the Dutch influence can still be seen from almost every single vista that the island has to offer in the shape of a crop that would become an essential cornerstone of the economy and come to define the island like no other. And, by extension, their influence can be felt equally deeply by what is no longer there to be seen.

It seemed auspicious at first. In 1595, with the Portuguese barely over the horizon, Dutch captain Cornelis de Houtman travelled around Madagascar and took the outer passage to skim past the Mascarenes on his way to open up the Indian spice route for his nation. His successful return two years later prompted excitement and, more tangibly, the first Dutch expedition to truly attempt something more specifically geared towards establishing a developed victualling point amongst those islands. With the other two islands offering no natural harbours, and the middle one offering several within the cosiness of its ample lagoon, they understandably homed in on Cirne.

Yet they nearly didn't make it. In 1598, Admiral Cornelis van Neck headed up an eight-ship expedition assisted by his deputy, Vice-Admiral Wybrandt van Warwyck. The latter had command of the ship *Amsterdam*; the admiral himself took charge of a ship which had the Latinised name of Maurice of Nassau, second son of William of Nassau, the founder of the Dutch Republic: the ship was called *Mauritius*.

Upon rounding the Cape of Good Hope, the fates dictated that a huge unseasonal storm—not a cyclone, as it was not the season—crashed upon them, splitting the fleet but fortunately sinking no ships. Van Neck nursed his ailing ship and two others to Île Sainte Marie off Madagascar. Van Warwyck now had effective command of the other five ships—the *Amsterdam* being joined by the *Vriesland*, *Utrecht*, *Gelderland* and *Zeeland*—until such time as Van Neck arrived. The ships crawled east, badly damaged, until the island hove into view on 17 September. They soon found a natural harbour in the southeast corner, anchoring their battered ships just outside the coral reef.

Van Warwyck lost no time in naming this charming harbour after himself—Warwyck Haven—and his journal would claim that the sailors 'wept for joy at the sight of this spellbinding island'. After their terrifying few weeks at sea they had much repairing to do, but only after their accompanying priest led prayers to thank God for their (very) good fortune. Within three days, Van Warwyck had seen enough to convince himself that this was indeed a good island to claim for the Dutch Crown, which he did on 20 September.

THE DUTCH CENTURY

He also needed to give it a new name to distance it from its earlier Portuguese links. That he chose Mauritius has often been assumed as a direct, rather than indirect, homage to Maurice of Nassau, but it is just as likely that he was naming it more prosaically after Admiral Van Neck's still-absent ship, which was a well-known convention. Either way, Maurice of Nassau had found his name immortalised on subsequent maps—although the island wouldn't fully accept it for a while yet.

Building makeshift shacks under the palm trees in true Robinson Crusoe fashion, the Dutch noticed something else. Many of their sailors who had previously visited Madagascar had rapidly fallen sick there of what they called 'fever', but which evidence suggests could only have been malaria. They and so many others had found that large and beautiful island to be a haunted place. Conversely, the opposite was true on Mauritius: any sick mariners rapidly got better. Indeed, the accounts from those early journals evoke images of excitable schoolboys exploring forests, climbing hills, fishing in the lagoon, all without any threat from other men or beasts. Paradise doesn't exist, but to these Dutch sailors in 1598, there was a feeling that they had found somewhere pretty close to it.

They were overjoyed to be joined within a couple of months by Van Neck, who had by now repaired his ships in Madagascar and found his way to the same harbour. A quick comparing of notes between the two admirals soon made it obvious whether Mauritius or Madagascar should be the stopping-off point for Dutch ships on their way to the East Indies. The fleet left again on 8 January 1599, making its way without any problems to the fledgling East Indies colony at Bantam.

It wasn't long—in the time frame of those days—before the next Dutch ships arrived, with Commander Hermansen's fleet dropping anchor in September 1601. Mariners need feeding like everyone else, and the Dutch approach was captured in the jour-

23

STAR AND KEY

nal of the sailor Willem Ysbrandts, and would be echoed by others that followed: 'We found a quantity of geese ... and other sorts of birds; tortoises, of which there were sometimes twenty-five under the shade of a tree. We took as many of these animals as we wanted for they did not run away.'

Word spread that there was something special being uncovered, but it was not just the Dutch back home who heard it; both France and England were likewise scouring the Indian Ocean for somewhere similar. A new approach was needed to secure both the European trade with the East and the places along the way that made the long trips feasible. To contain the potential threat posed by the French and the English, a decision was made by the Dutch government on 20 March 1602 that would change the face of global business forever. They directed a large number of small Dutch trading companies to join into one organisation, giving them a twenty-one-year monopoly over the spice trade in India and the East Indies, and encouraging them to diversify as they saw fit. Hot on the tails of the English, they had established one of the world's first multinational corporations and conglomerate in one, and they named it the *Vereenigde Oostindische Compagnie*— the VOC, or Dutch East India Company.

Within a couple of years, bonds and shares in the Company were being offered to the public—another world first, as this essentially kick-started the process of having a public listed company and, indeed, a stock market. This forward-sighted and seismic shift in the way global trade was conducted was looked upon by envious eyes elsewhere, even as England and France set up their own versions at roughly the same time. But they were playing catch-up, as this vast, state-sponsored Dutch behemoth grew in both size and power.

In the 2020s, we are staggered at the size of the tech companies that have ballooned in value. Apple and Amazon hover in market capitalisation value between the US$2 trillion and US$3

THE DUTCH CENTURY

trillion mark. Yet by 1637, adjusted for inflation, the VOC would have a worth of over US$8 trillion, making it the richest company at any point in history and worth more than the modern-day GDP of the UK, France and Germany combined. With devolved powers to act as a legal entity in its trading bases—imprisoning whoever it saw fit, and indeed whoever it saw as a threat—and with even a remit to wage war if necessary, it broke the shackles of being a mere company: it was, in all but name, an empire.

For all its power, however, the VOC was no more in control of the unpredictability of the weather than anyone else. This was seen tragically in 1615, off the island's west coast. Pieter Both, a canny trader with a rare streak of diplomacy, had been set up as the first governor-general of the Dutch East Indies in 1610, a post he would hold for four years. Based in Batavia (present day Jakarta), he lost no time in developing links with the Moluccans and Timorese to enrich both himself and the Company.

In late 1614 he therefore left for Amsterdam with four ships overflowing with spice-based bounty, planning a stop-off in Mauritius on the way. As they dropped anchor in a newly discovered port in the northwest in February 1615, the island welcomed them with a monumental cyclone, lifting the ships like autumn leaves and dragging them fully 20 miles down the west coast until they crumpled on the reef, drowning all on board. Pieter Both's name remained on the island though, where the second highest peak, at 2,685 feet, was named after him. It is a truly bizarre mountain, with a huge circular boulder seemingly perched precariously on the summit's shoulders, with legends soon growing that if ever this boulder fell, it would spell doom for the island.

Despite this setback, Mauritius at this stage remained very much part of the VOC's plans for domination. Their efforts initially focused on the Far East, where many spices were to be found. But with the prowling of other European powers in the

Indian Ocean, with some even brazenly sneaking onto Mauritius to help themselves to the plentiful ebony trees, a more formal arrangement was needed. Finally, on 7 May 1638, the VOC officially claimed Mauritius for itself by introducing two key elements: Mauritius' first actual settlement of people and an appointed governor to oversee it.

'Settlement' was something of a misnomer: initially it consisted of a garrison of merely twenty-five men under the first governor, Cornelius Gooyer, all housed in a rather perfunctory wooden building, optimistically named Fort Frederik Hendrik, located near Warwyck Haven. It was perhaps the tiniest of all the VOC's global outposts, and since Gooyer did precisely nothing to develop it into the ebony and ambergris trading centre it could have been, he was summarily replaced the following year by Adriaan van der Stel.

Although at six years his stay was longer, and included his wife Maria producing a son called Simon—probably the first child ever born on the island, and certainly the first registered there—Van der Stel again failed to make a positive imprint on the island, and soon after departing for the East he was decapitated in a fight with the local Sinhalese in Ceylon. Simon had a more prosperous future, going on to become one of the most successful governors of South Africa and giving his name to Simonstown, at the base of Table Mountain. Conversely, in almost his last act before departing in 1645, Van der Stel Senior introduced something abhorrent: slavery. It was the fate of ninety-five inhabitants of Madagascar to be deported to Mauritius to assist in the felling of ebony trees, whilst the Dutch themselves focused on trying to find enough to eat in the forests and lagoon. These initial slaves were soon joined by a further 108 from the same island, courtesy of the new governor, Jacob van der Meersch.

The horrors of slavery are well documented elsewhere and usually accompanied by tragic stories. The initial circumstances

THE DUTCH CENTURY

for these 203 slaves seem to have been no different, but for once some were able to do something about it. Incredibly, a few of them managed in the first two years to secretly construct ocean-going craft that they were then able, astonishingly, to sail back to Madagascar. To have displayed such ingenuity, such knowledge of construction and such a profound understanding of navigation demonstrated nakedly that they were significantly more resourceful than their Dutch masters. Others chose to try their luck instead by disappearing into the thick forest, where they hunted some of the wild animals introduced by the Dutch—goats, boar, rabbits and hare—and where they occasionally, in turn, became the prey of the Dutch settlers who chose to hunt *them*.

This negative pattern seemed to shadow all the first seven governors during that initial attempt at settlement. The price of ebony was dropping, few ships actually seemed to pass by on their way to Batavia and, despite the garrison being ostensibly a defensive arrangement, very little actually happened, as the external threat had temporarily subsided. In a rare moment of foresight, sugar-cane cuttings were brought over from the East Indies, and thanks to the insight of the token doctor of the camp, Jan Bockelberg, who grew and experimented with the crop, it was demonstrated that the climate was ideally suited to growing it. Little did Bockelberg realise that sugar cane would eventually become an economic mainstay of the island, covering fully two thirds of its land. For now, his companions used it only to produce arrack and to get blind drunk. This was a colony going precisely nowhere.

In 1658, Governor Abraham Evertsz took the inevitable decision to abandon the island to the two remaining runaway slaves who had defied recapture, as well as a nameless cabin boy who chose to stay there on his own. Yet a mere six years later saw the French finally get their act together in Paris, bringing various commercial arms together to form their own consolidated East

India Company. Neither they nor the English did anything to hide the fact that controlling the Mascarene Islands as a whole—and not just one of them—would be of great benefit to them in fulfilling their own ambitions.

This was the spark of intent that compelled the Dutch, now under Jacobus van Nieuwlandt, to return to Mauritius from their base on the Cape of Good Hope, this time with something resembling a sense of purpose. New forts were quickly built in the southwest at Zwarte River (Black River), Noortwyk Vlakte in the east (a name which would morph into 'Flacq') and Noordwester Haven (Northwest Port), which, the Dutch had eventually realised, was actually superior in size, strategic location and prevailing winds to their initial home of Warwyck Haven at the opposite end of the island. The French, meanwhile, were beefing up their resources on the neighbouring island to the west, which they had now called Île Bourbon after their royal family.

Settlement 2.0 wasn't perfect either, though. The small camps were eventually supplemented by further colonists arriving from the Cape, almost all being ex-convicts who thought nothing of plundering their neighbours' stores. Indeed, as one observer pointedly observed, 'The parent authority at the Cape of Good Hope now regarded Mauritius as a convenient penal settlement.' This wasn't helped by Van Nieuwlandt himself discovering the joys of arrack and, in a stunning achievement, managing to drink himself to death within a year.

With occasional French and English ships visiting and being allowed to fell trees for a significant toll imposed by the Dutch, a new, uneasy, peace was achieved. But by the 1680s, the drudgery of life had returned, punctuated only by bouts of sickness. In 1682, a mysterious and debilitating stomach illness affected every single islander, but medicine—and indeed medical expertise—was essentially non-existent, leading to sixteen nasty deaths—more than 5 per cent of the colony's total population. Ten governors

THE DUTCH CENTURY

succeeded Van Nieuwlandt over the ensuing four decades, none distinguishing themselves and all realising too late that by taking on this seemingly dream post, they had been sold a pup. Many died unhappy and early, and weren't lamented. Only Governor Isaac Lamotius' fifteen-year stint, lasting until 1692, amounted to anything; yet even that ended ignominiously when he was deported for the attempted rape of a neighbour's wife. The VOC was now a global superpower, and the complexity of its tentacles meant that it had to prioritise its bigger and more prosperous ventures. Mauritius no longer fell into that category.

The only diversion that these Dutch colonists allowed themselves was hunting. Often this was for the various species of wild game that the first colony had released, which were now running amok and destabilising the island's natural balance. But there were endemic species, too, that these initial colonists sought out. Indeed, from their very first arrival in 1598 they had frequently encountered a ground-dwelling bird that Warwyck in his journal called 'Walghvogel' ('Tasteless bird'). We universally know it now as the Dodo.

That we use the phrase 'Dead as a Dodo' and not, say, 'Dead as a Thylacine' or 'Dead as a Passenger Pigeon' is only one insight hinting at the transcendental impact that this ultimately inconsequential bird has had on us. Of course, Lewis Carroll's *Alice's Adventures in Wonderland* helped raise the Dodo's profile further during Victorian times, but the greatest contradiction of all is that everyone *thinks* they know this unique avian, and yet in truth so much about it is utterly shrouded in mystery.

What can we say with confidence? The Dodo shared an ancestor with the Nicobar Pigeon of Southeast Asia, and via the oft-noted evolutionary trait of island gigantism in certain species, it grew to a size larger that a turkey, weighing up to 88 pounds. It had a large beak, could no longer fly, fed largely off ground-lying fruit, nuts, seeds and possibly crabs, and was, thanks to isolated

STAR AND KEY

evolution, ecologically naive. Incredibly, for something so apparently 'recognised', everything else is uncertain.

Where did that name come from? Some suggest that it is from the Dutch 'Dodaars', meaning 'Fat Arse', for self-explanatory reasons. Other go back further to old Portuguese, where the word 'Doudo' meant 'Stupid fool'. Yet there is no mention of the Dodo in those limited Portuguese records, hinting that it may have been more localised than initially thought. Neither did it necessarily have a 'fat arse', as some third-hand descriptions implied that it did. That it gained its name from the onomatopoeic 'doo-doo' call, so common in the pigeon and dove family, is also just a theory, but a better one than most.

It is in fact the Dodo's very appearance that has caused so much confusion. The most likely reason for this uncertainty was the act of shipping some specimens abroad, the ignorant taxidermy that would have ensued upon death, and the subsequent exaggerated European paintings that had nothing natural to draw upon.

When the Dutch sailors, intrigued by this odd-looking creature, thought that it would make an impression in the courts of Europe—for a good fee, of course—they would have kept them in the holds of their ships for many months, being fed inappropriate food and with no opportunity for exercise. On arrival, therefore, the few that made it, in the period up to and including the 1620s, would have been decidedly plump and bulbous compared to their free-roaming friends. There is no accurate record of how long they lasted in captivity, but it doesn't seem to have been for very long. They were, unsurprisingly, an obvious target for taxidermists to prepare for royalty, but these animal stuffers would never have seen a live wild specimen, and did their best based on a dead, oversized, captive specimen. This was a recipe for inaccuracy.

It seems that these few poorly stuffed beasts—many long lost to time—were the individuals that 'posed' for the painters of the

THE DUTCH CENTURY

period who tried to capture for posterity this unique bird that, it turns out, very few people would ever see alive again. One such portrait, Dutch painter Roelant Savery's celebrated 1626 effort, became the template for all subsequent visualisations.

Yet a glance at the sketches of the few Dutch settlers in the early 1600s who took the time to amateurishly draw these birds in the wild shows a very different picture. No one could ever accuse them of being skinny, but these wild Dodos are leaner, more upright and decidedly more athletic-looking than the images in our mind. This casts some doubt on the retrofitted theory of their name deriving from 'Dodaars'. Warwyck's 1598 diary entry gives us a few further hints:

> Blue parrots are very numerous there, as well as other birds; among which are a kind, conspicuous for their size, larger than our swans, with huge heads only half covered with skin as if clothed with a hood. These birds lack wings, in the place of which 3 or 4 blackish feathers protrude. The tail consists of a few soft incurved feathers, which are ash coloured. These we used to call 'Walghvogel', for the reason that the longer and oftener they were cooked, the less soft and more insipid eating they became. Nevertheless their belly and breast were of a pleasant flavour and easily masticated.

Intriguingly, tail aside, there is no clear indication here, or in any other account, of what colour they were—grey, blue-brown, white and other colours have all been suggested—which might just indicate that there was some variety.

Tender underside it may have had, but the Dodo clearly wasn't a gourmet feast for a Dutch settler. It had no instinctive fear of humans; it had not evolved next to any land-based mammal so had no initial reason to be cautious. Only when sailors tried to capture them did they apparently use their outsized beaks for defence. So it seems unlikely that it was humans who directly wiped them out. Indirectly, however, it was unquestionably their responsibility. First, they were demolishing the endemic forests

STAR AND KEY

that the Dodo had made its home, leaving them increasingly short of habitat. Perhaps more tellingly, the Portuguese and Dutch had introduced monkeys, pigs, dogs and rats to these pristine islands, either by choice or accident. All were running rampant through the island, and the one thing they all had in common was a well-known love of eating birds' eggs. The Dodo's clutch, eyewitness reports confirmed, consisted of no more than one egg lying in a rough nest on the forest floor, suggesting that until humans arrived, and with no predators to harm them, the chances of young birds surviving was very high.

But by the first departure of the Dutch in 1658 it was already evident that Dodo numbers were minuscule. There was simply no way out of their conundrum: the rats, pigs and monkeys were going nowhere, and there was no other territory to escape to. They were an extinction waiting to happen. It just remains to try to work out exactly when the inevitable occurred. The last definitive sighting was in 1662—during the brief interlude between the two Dutch settlements on the island. It came, ironically, from the shipwrecked Volkert Evertsz, who found himself washed up on an offshore islet on the east coast of Mauritius. He had been on a return journey from the Dutch East Indies, having never been part of the Mauritian settlement, so what he saw was new to him:

> These birds are unable to fly, and instead of wings, they merely have a few small pins, yet they can run very swiftly. We drove them together into one place in such a manner that we could catch them with our hands, and when we held one of them by its leg, and that upon this it made a great noise, the others all on a sudden came running as fast as they could to its assistance, and by which they were caught and made prisoners also.

It is likely that he was on what was later known as Île d'Ambre, off the northeast coast of Mauritius, but there is a chance too from his descriptions that this could have been Île aux Aigrettes

THE DUTCH CENTURY

in the southeast. No matter. These Dodos (for that is surely what they were) still had a few individuals living together on a small islet to which the introduced animals—amongst which we could include humans and rats—had yet to find their way.

Four more sightings were claimed. An escaped but recaptured slave called Simon, in 1674, claimed to have seen them twice—and only twice—during his eleven years hiding in the forest. The fact that he was a slave meant that the Dutch didn't take his claim seriously, even though he had no reason to make it up. Next, the Englishman Benjamin Harris had stopped briefly on the island in 1681 on his ship the *Berkley Castle*, on his journey back from India to England. His journal entry of 11 July of that year makes mention of a bird that sounds very much like a Dodo, but the context is unclear as to whether he actually saw one—as was initially thought—or whether he was merely recounting tales of it from others. It would certainly have been fortuitous to have merely passed by the island and spotted a bird that had not been seen there definitively for over forty years, by any settlers. We therefore have to take this account with a considerable dose of salt.

Finally, Governor Isaac Lamotius himself claimed to have seen one on a hunting trip to the interior in 1688. This latter witness account may seem like an outlier, considering it had been fifty years since a Dodo had been seen by a Dutchman on the mainland, but later research suggests it just might have been possible: journeys into the thickly forested interior were hard work, except for the purpose of seeking refuge from slave masters. In a November 2003 article in *Nature* magazine by conservation biologists David L. Roberts and Andrew R. Solow, mathematical modelling and statistical analysis based on other extinction data gathered in the interim was used to give an estimated extinction date of 1693. Worth highlighting too is that by this stage, *all* the large invertebrates on the island—including the vast tortoises—had disappeared, a mere century after Warwyck's arrival.

STAR AND KEY

Yet it was this flightless bird, of all the animals that once roamed on this island and everywhere beyond, that found its way into our modern psyche to be the unwitting poster child for all doomed species. There were flutters of excitement, therefore, in early 2022, when University of California geneticist Beth Shapiro announced that she and her team had succeeded in sequencing the Dodo's genome, thanks to well-preserved scraps of DNA taken from Dodo remnants housed in the Natural History Museum in Copenhagen. Immediately, the Jurassic Park question was asked: could they be resurrected? She quickly stifled that possibility, explaining how near impossible this would be, based on the DNA that they had. But also highlighted by others was the fact that the endemic forests that had once covered the island, and which evolved in unison with the Dodo and other species, had all but been logged to oblivion. Even if science fiction could bring back the Dodo, there would be no natural habitat in which they could live.

The disappearance of a species is heart-breaking and evocative to modern sensibilities. On the one hand, it would be misguided to superimpose the judgements of our modern culture onto the mindset of seventeenth-century Europeans: ill-educated, often illiterate, with dockside upbringings distanced from nature and with mouths to feed being their chief preoccupation, 'preserving a species' would have been very far down their list of priorities. On the other hand, even by the standards of their day the Dutch in Mauritius—largely ex-criminals—were a pretty ruthless bunch, and sustaining a viable population of wild animals for future consumption seems to have been beyond their strategic comprehension.

Extinction is never pretty, and the last emotion for many doomed species, including the Dodo, could well be one of loneliness. Consider these hypothetical yet haunting words from celebrated US science writer David Quammen's 1996 opus, *The Song*

THE DUTCH CENTURY

of the Dodo, his exquisite exploration of island biogeography in an age of extinctions:

> For the last half dozen years of her life, she has not set eyes on another member of her own species. In the dark of an early morning ... during a rainstorm, she took cover beneath a cold stone ledge at the base of one of the Black River Cliffs. She drew her head down against her body, fluffed her feathers for warmth, squinted in patient misery. She waited. She didn't know it, nor did anyone else, but she was the only dodo on Earth. When the storm passed, she never opened her eyes. This is extinction.

The short-sightedness of wilful, unending slaughter to a point of no return was just one of the reasons why the Dutch eventually abandoned the island that they had once seen as an archetypal paradise. Just a few decades after the re-establishment of their fledgling colony, and having casually destroyed swathes of pristine ebony forests and driven large, unique birds and reptiles to become mere memories, the ship *Beverwaart*, laden with a final cargo of precious ebony as well as the last of the unsavoury island settlers, lifted her anchor from the northwest harbour on 17 February 1710. This was a port that would eventually become the bustling capital of this still mysterious place, but that future was of no concern to the mariners or their slaves on the *Beverwaart*, as they made their way to the mothership Dutch colony on the Cape of Good Hope. The island was again, briefly, empty of humans and had won its latest battle not to be tamed. But what else was driving the Dutch away from an apparent sanctuary that had once promised so much?

The reasons were threefold. Firstly, they went hungry far too often—almost unforgivable in such a bounteous location—and they never seem to have adapted to the relentless regularity of the cyclone. The fact that it would occur every summer season, on either a mild or catastrophic scale, was a climatic truth that

STAR AND KEY

seemed intolerable to them, and their efforts to plan for this—to literally ride out the storm—by adapting construction methods and materials were essentially non-existent. Thus, their precious crops failed too often. It was the Dutch, too, who had deliberately introduced macaques to their new home, presumably for hunting; yet they complained bitterly when those same monkeys proliferated in number and boldly went about helping themselves to the sailors' supplies.

Secondly, we can now acknowledge with the benefit of hindsight that occupying an uninhabited island doesn't automatically bring about a new and prosperous society. The Dutch population in fact never rose above 300, and the quality of men sent there—for they were almost all men—was lamentable. The Dutch in seventeenth-century Europe had a reputation for courage and drive, but also for impatience and for not being instinctive team players. A settlement made up exclusively of self-preserving Dutch convicts and fortune seekers, and largely void of women and children, was ultimately never going to work, especially if there was never a truly skilled administrator overseeing it all, and even more so when the VOC turned its strategic focus elsewhere.

But above and beyond these rational explanations stood the third reason, and this one they were less open to admitting: fear.

For a foul westerly wind was blowing from far away, arriving here from the other side of the world from where it had finally been expelled. It carried with it a force that was pernicious, without a moral compass, remorseless and uncompromising; even the Dutch ex-convicts were scared. It was a force that didn't recognise national flags and cackled menacingly in the face of law and order. It would threaten the very existence of all that was good and decent in the Sea of Zanj.

The pirates were coming.

4

TERROR ON THE OPEN SEAS

Close your eyes, focus hard and try to picture a pirate.

Whilst there's a chance that you may have in mind the twenty-first-century Somali versions who are known for hounding the Horn of Africa, it is far more likely that the image in your head is of something resembling an intimidating and pungent cross between Long John Silver in *Treasure Island*, Captain Hook in *Peter Pan* and Johnny Depp in *Pirates of the Caribbean*. We can't help ourselves. Yet there are no photos and very few realistic portraits of these seventeenth- and eighteenth-century scallywags for us to use as a steer. So where did all the clothes, the attitude, the speech and the sheer camp villainy that we now so intimately associate with the Golden Age of Piracy originate from? The question is asked with a shrug, as though the answer is lost in time like a cough in a hurricane. Yet in fact we most certainly *do* know. It all came from a book published in London in 1724 called *A General History of the Robberies and Murders of the Most Notorious Pyrates*, written by 'Captain Charles Johnson'.

With a no-nonsense, mouth-watering title such as that, you would hope that it would be a juicy read, and it more than delivers. This was the book, claiming 'first-hand evidence' throughout, that first introduced to the masses the idea that pirates actually buried some of their treasure; that some pirates had wooden legs and wore eye patches as marks of distinction from a life hard-lived; that all pirates proudly raised the Jolly Roger flag in the run-up to boarding and seizing a ship; and that Blackbeard, Calico Jack, Anne Bonny, Black Bart and other famous pirates of the era led an edgy but glamorous existence on the high seas. All of these motifs are now irrevocably woven into the fabric of what we deem a pirate to be, and Captain Charles Johnson had breathlessly, generously, let us into that adventurous world. So, who was he? Could he be, as first thought, an ex-pirate who had simply settled down to count his loot and write his memoirs? In fact, no he wasn't, because Charles Johnson didn't exist.

It rapidly became clear that this was a *nom de plume* used by a local London wit to entertain the masses, as there was absolutely no mention of a Charles Johnson in any record or archive concerning pirates kept in the New World or the Old. To this day, the jury is still out as to who definitively the mysterious face behind the quill was, but the overwhelming favourite is a man who remains world famous for *another* book that he definitely did write: Daniel Defoe. He admitted nothing at the time, but this genius novelist, trader and part-time spy ticks all the boxes, and while other names have been bandied about, he is as good a guess as any. If we thought *Robinson Crusoe* was influential in shaping the very essence of the early English novel, then *A General History of the Pyrates* has been equally monumental in shaping an entire subculture, likely all springing from his prodigious imagination.

Which is all to say that when we explore the world of the pirates between 1685 and 1730 in what we now know as the Indian Ocean, we should bear in mind that a lot of what we

TERROR ON THE OPEN SEAS

believe might in fact be very misguided. First, however, we need to understand why this menace of the seas was making its way to Mauritius and its neighbouring islands in the first place.

Piracy had been a mainstay of the Caribbean almost since the first conquistadors set sail in the early sixteenth century. The rich pickings, limited legal infrastructures and pleasant environment ensured that as many as 2,400 pirates were plying their 'trade' by the mid-seventeenth century. With European land wars taking up all the energy of the major players throughout that century, there was little capacity to counter the piracy threat across the Atlantic. Only when huge amounts of cargo and wealth were being systematically removed from European coffers and directly affecting national economies did each power eventually send an increasing number of navy vessels to guard merchant shipping. England's Royal Navy alone managed to grow its presence to 124 ships by 1718, aided by sending Commodore Woodes Rogers—a former privateer himself—to be governor of the Bahamas to finally rid the West Indies of the evil scourge. The pirates realised that they would have to move their bases elsewhere in the world to stand a fighting chance of obtaining regular booty, which was in any case drying up in the Caribbean. Eyes initially turned to the west coast of Africa, and much success was had there. However, the greatest prize by the late seventeenth century was the immense amount of merchandise being carried back from the newly opened up Orient to Europe, and that meant travelling across the Indian Ocean. Piracy would now have a new headquarters.

Pirate terminology from this period is ripe for confusion, and there remains disagreement over certain technicalities about what constituted piracy. In essence, 'pirate' was a catch-all phrase used for anyone doing what we picture pirates as doing: plundering, pillaging and stealing. But there were different kinds who saw themselves as more or less legitimate. A 'privateer' was one who

39

STAR AND KEY

had officially obtained a *'lettre de marque'* (letter of marque) from a sovereign or other head of state that gave them free rein to harass enemy naval ships during wartime. In practice, most went way further and used it as a pretext to plunder anything they could get their hands on. This was hardly new; Francis Drake had been doing just that a century earlier. 'Hero' he may be to the English, but to the Spaniards he remains categorically a pirate. The French word for a privateer—*corsair*—has gradually found its way into the English language too, sometimes with its original meaning, and occasionally with overtones of something a touch more glamorous. The separate era of the French corsairs in Mauritius is covered later.

Privateers in turn had subcategories. 'Buccaneers' were specific to the Caribbean, invariably of European descent and at the budget end of privateering, although they could make quite a stir—Henry Morgan and his raids on Panama being a good example. Then there were 'Freebooters', who were initially unpaid privateers, but to all intents and purposes pirates, plain and simple. Their name derived from the Dutch word *vribuit*, meaning plunder. What all these groups had in common, regardless of how they saw themselves, was that they were usually rotters of the first order.

Pirates had occasionally been active in some form around Mauritius since the very first arrival of the Portuguese in the early 1500s. This, however, was on a whole different order of magnitude. And much as in the Caribbean, where the pirates needed a base from which to launch attacks, feel relatively safe and help plan next steps without bother, so it was in the Indian Ocean. In the West Indies there were several such places, although the best known was probably Tortuga. However, even that evocative island was nothing compared to where they set up off the northeast coast of Madagascar in the late seventeenth century: Île Sainte Marie was the greatest pirate lair the world has ever known.

TERROR ON THE OPEN SEAS

It was first established in 1690 by Adam Baldridge, a freebooter making himself scarce after being chased out of Jamaica. When he first laid eyes upon the island—known now as Nosy Boraha ('Island of Little Abraham')—he knew it would be perfect, not just for him but for others of his ilk. It was, and remains, a beautiful but deceptive place. Drenched in heavenly deep blue water and shimmering with a preponderance of fish, the 86-square-mile island—shaped like a crocodile floating menacingly on the surface water—is serendipitously protected by a coral reef to the south, meaning that the channel between the island and the mainland is almost permanently calm. Equally importantly, on the landward side can be found an almost perfect natural harbour, capable of anchoring twenty large ships. Surrounded at the time by tropical forest, sparsely inhabited and away from the prying eyes of navies, it would be the perfect stronghold for hundreds of pirates over the ensuing thirty years. And Mauritius would become one of their prime targets.

Word rapidly spread, and Baldridge essentially started a bartering system with the pirates who either passed through on their way to Mauritius or the Red Sea, or who stayed and loitered. Initially he supplied cattle in return for weaponry. His early accounts of visitors and those who chose to stay longer still exist, and offer a Who's Who of the dark pirate names of the 1690s: the horrid Edward Coates; the especially odious Thomas Tew; the mysterious Phillips Brothers. It was not uncommon for some of these ne'er-do-wells to settle down there, take a local wife (or more than one) and give up on pirating in any consistent sense. Some unquestionably died there too, and a haunting cemetery exists to this day that must contain many pirate bodies, although we simply can't be sure who was ultimately interred there. That said, the rumour spread in Johnson's riveting book that these heavy-drinking, fornicating chancers had in turn set up an independent state called 'Libertalia'—including their own laws and even their own language—but that was another fun exaggeration; there was too much marauding to be done to overly concern oneself with setting up a parallel legal system. It did not take long for the pirates of this ocean to start trading in the same lucrative 'business' that had been such a mainstay in the Atlantic for privateers and landlubbers alike. It was the most horrific trade of them all: human slavery. The Dutch had not hesitated in bringing Malagasy slaves to Mauritius throughout the seventeenth century, and even as they considered their departure, there were still plenty of ships passing to and from the East, stopping by to continue this odious tradition.

At one stage it was thought that as many as 5,000 pirates were active in the ocean around this time, and it became the exception rather than the rule that ships returning from the Orient would stumble across this pernicious menace at some stage or another, often not far from the shores of Mauritius. Authorities kept lists of those who had started their alternative livelihoods here, as well as those who had made it over from the Caribbean—indeed, some were still doing both, marauding on the east coast of the US then crossing the Atlantic diagonally, rounding the Cape and going all the way up to the Red Sea to do the same, a route known infamously as the 'Pirate Round'. There is only space here to focus on a few of these individuals, each with their own special flavour.

John Bowen's origins were as nebulous as those of many seafarers of the time. It is most likely that he was originally John Ap Owen, of Welsh parentage, and first saw the light of day in Bermuda around 1660. Like many pirates he started off with good intentions, sailing on a ship in the West Indies—some say as captain, others merely as a petty officer—until it was overrun in 1698 by French pirates, who took on board most of the crew and then sailed it to Madagascar, stopping *en route* for a campaign off West Africa. Approaching southern Madagascar they

TERROR ON THE OPEN SEAS

were shipwrecked, whereby the resourceful Bowen, together with two other captives called White and Boreman, grabbed 'their' ship's longboat and hot-footed it to the nearby Saint-Augustin Bay. The problem was, he had evidently been seduced by the lifestyle and easy pickings that his erstwhile captors had been enjoying. Therefore, conscious that he had no immediate ship to take him back to the West Indies, Bowen decided to stay and become a pirate himself.

Soon enough, he offered his services to a passing ship under Captain Read, which in turn joined forces with another ship, captained by the notorious George Booth, and off they went north for some marauding. In April 1700, harbouring at an Arab outpost off Madagascar, they came across a gem: an immense 450-ton English slave ship called the *Speaker*. It was imposing, possessing fifty cannon, thanks to it being a refitted French man-o'-war (we can only speculate as to how it got into English hands). But Captain Eastlake of the *Speaker* was unconcerned by the presence of the two pirate ships. Although his crew of forty was only a fifth of the number of pirates mingling nonchalantly in the port, he was confident that his sleek, fast and armed ship would best them if needed. What he did not reckon with was either how much the pirates yearned to possess that magnificent specimen, or that one of his crew, Hugh Man, would be bought to betray him for £100.

Whilst Man quietly drenched his own ship's gunpowder, the pirates invited the *Speaker*'s off-duty crew for a drink and predictably got them completely curtained on punch. Eastlake had been caught out, and quietly surrendered to avoid further bloodshed. But it was a risky life being a pirate, and no sooner had the marauders, in their wonderful new ship, sailed to Unguja Island off Zanzibar to restock their supplies, than the local Arabs pounced on Booth and murdered him, as well as nineteen others. The *Speaker* left quickly, but it needed a new captain, and in the

STAR AND KEY

bastardised form of democracy that was practised on such ships, it was Bowen who was elected by his international crew of raiders to take over the role. There was some success over the ensuing two years, with the capture of the English merchant ship *Borneo* as well as two Arab ships (from an initial flotilla of thirteen), all of which allowed each member of the crew to get a £600 share of the bounty.

But their luck ran out in December 1701, as the notorious cyclone season hit them and drew them further south. On 7 January 1702, after days at sea in a horrific storm, an island came into view to the northwest, but before they could identify it, the *Speaker* smashed into a reef, later called St Thomas' Reef, and was completely lost. The exhausted pirates, who numbered nearly 250 including various prisoners, nevertheless scrambled ashore, no doubt cursing as their ill-gotten plunder sank irretrievably to the sea floor. As they took stock, slaughtering three oxen for dinner as they did so, they realised from their maps that the river they found themselves by was the one now known as Grande Rivière Sud-Est, and that the island was Mauritius. Furthermore, the Dutch had spotted them.

Not that there was much that the Dutch could easily do at first. With only a measly fifty-three people manning that outpost at the time, they saw that they were outnumbered, and pirates were hardly renowned for keeping their word. The governor at the time, Roelof Diodati, had a call to make about how best to approach these stranded, desperate but ultimately dangerous men. In a rare victory for clever diplomacy at the time, he reached out to care for the sick and injured whilst also allowing trade between the two camps, fully realising that the arrivals were likely making plans to take over the island for themselves. The pirates continued to salvage what they could from their shipwreck, and in turn were able to politely trade. But this situation carried on for three months and was not sustainable.

TERROR ON THE OPEN SEAS

Diodati's master stroke was to sell them his own small three-masted slaving ship, the *Vlieigente Hart*, which he used for trips to Madagascar to perpetuate his foul trade. For £170 and some modifications, Bowen agreed, and sailed off on 24 March in the far-too-small schooner, leaving his erstwhile Arab and English prisoners to the Dutch, or more likely to their own devices.

It had been a tense stand-off, and hammered home to the Dutch that the situation could easily have turned out very differently; it cemented their view that they wanted out of Mauritius. This was only compounded when, after a few more months of capturing gradually larger ships around Madagascar and Île Bourbon (now Réunion), Bowen sailed back east and was spotted cruising off Noordwester Haven (now the capital Port Louis), as though pondering whether or not to make a proper go of taking the whole island. He decided against it at the time, choosing instead to join forces with fellow bad guy Thomas Howard and to capture US$120,000-worth of loot further north. But he had a taste for Mauritius and couldn't keep away. Once more, in February 1704, he returned, this time to the opposite end of the harbour at Frederik Haven (now Vieux Grand Port), sporting on this occasion his latest capture, a large schooner which he had aptly renamed *Defiant*. This time, however, there was no offshore loitering, and the pirates dropped anchor and went ashore.

The pitiful Dutch colony had a new governor, Abraham Momber van de Velde, who was even more deeply wary of the pirates than Diodati had been. There was no shipwreck this time, so why were the pirates there? The answer never really materialised, for Bowen's men—surprising everyone, probably including themselves—remained polite, asked to trade, always paid up promptly in full for everything they obtained and never threatened anyone on the island. They stayed for two months, made no discernible repairs to their ship and then, on 5 April, quietly weighed anchor and set off for the neighbouring island of

STAR AND KEY

Bourbon. There, Bowen and his men negotiated with the island's governor and settled down to a peaceful post-pirate life. Bowen died a year later.

It may be fanciful and speculative but a nagging question remains as to why Bowen made that final trip to Mauritius. He could have taken the island if he wanted, but he chose not to. He could at a minimum have dispossessed the Dutch of their worldly goods, but again, it never seems to have been on his agenda. Just maybe, having spent three months there previously during harder times, he had seen beyond the basic and badly managed Dutch camp there and instead saw an island that he found beautiful, an island which, more than any other during his adult life on the seas, he saw as a home.

Bowen was that rare thing: a pirate who retired peacefully from this life of plundering. Conversely, Edward England's experiences of Mauritius were not so relaxed. He was born Edward Seegar, in Ireland, and we can only speculate that this was likely in the late 1680s. England had been a naval officer on a single-masted trading sloop when, in 1717, the pirate Christopher Winter took his ship in the West Indies and forced England and some of the crew into piracy. As it transpired, England, like Bowen, took very little convincing to swap sides and on reflection it's not that surprising. Conditions on many merchant and naval vessels at the time were awful—in other words, no better than on a pirate ship, but without the possibility of getting filthy rich. The infamous and brutal press-ganging of unwilling sailors into such a degrading life ultimately did nothing but encourage more trained sailors to become gamekeepers-turned-poachers.

England was so popular that he was voted to become commander of the next ship seized by this motley crew. One reason for this was that England—unlike almost all his ilk—was not inherently cruel. He didn't inflict punishment, he hated torture and may just have had the kernel of a moral compass hiding

46

TERROR ON THE OPEN SEAS

within him. But this was now 1718, the year that the poacher-turned-gamekeeper Commodore Woodes Rogers was issuing his famous edict from Nassau: 'Go now, or I will hunt you down and destroy you.' England chose the former option, heading off first to West Africa where he quickly captured a succession of larger ships, only to realise on trying to plunder the town of Ouida in present-day Benin that there was nothing left to steal. Someone had got there first, and that someone was legendary French pirate Olivier Levasseur. Their paths would soon cross.

In 1720, England, now in a larger ship named *Victory*, was accompanied by his first mate John Taylor to Madagascar for some shore leave before they made their way towards India, ransacking and purloining a considerable quantity of trade ships including an impressive 44-gun Dutch ship, which he whimsically renamed *Fancy*, before returning to Île Sainte Marie. Their time there was predictably debauched, and only after they had whored, drunk and gambled away all their booty were they forced to set sail again, with England now self-proclaimed commodore overseeing both the *Victory* and the *Fancy*. Confidence was high, and when they stumbled across a ship of the English East India Company called *Cassandra* under Captain James Macrae, they expected a quick victory. Macrae had other ideas.

Macrae would later write to his bosses in London about what happened in extreme detail, but in essence a full-blown battle raged for an entire day, with Macrae's courageous men not giving an inch. Thirteen of his men died, while incredibly they in turn took out ninety of the pirates. Eventually the overwhelming pirate numbers told and Macrae was forced to surrender, giving up his US$120,000-worth of goods. *Fancy*, however, was left barely seaworthy, leaving England to take the *Cassandra*. Macrae took a chance and accepted England's invitation onto his ship, where England's first mate, now Captain Taylor, furious at the deaths of his men, demanded that Macrae be executed in petty

47

STAR AND KEY

vengeance. England, though, as usual preferred the merciful route, and after taking all he could, left Macrae and his remaining crew on the ruins of the *Fancy*. It was a rare act of compassion in the pirate world. And it would cost England dearly.

As they approached the island of Mayotte, the party stumbled across a shipwreck with some angry men ashore. They had to find out more. It was the party of none other than Olivier Levasseur, who had beaten England to the pillaging of the West African coast. Urgently needing more men, England and Taylor happily took on Levasseur's company, which would make them formidable indeed. Sure enough, they did some further pillaging before returning to Île Sainte Marie to celebrate Christmas 1720. They proceeded to drink non-stop for three days, and even washed the decks of their ships with rum. The revelry, however, did not last long. Word got to them that Captain Macrae had not only been rescued, but had rapidly been given command of a flotilla of the East India Company's ships to exterminate the pirates. Île Sainte Marie would not be safe, so they agreed to head out east to Mauritius where the Dutch had been known to turn a blind eye to visiting pirates. They arrived there in mid-February 1721, hoping to lie low, restock on provisions and plan next steps.

In fact, they arrived at Fredrik Haven to a near-deserted island; they had not kept up with the news that the Dutch had left the island for good ten years earlier. In fact, another nation had claimed Mauritius for itself, although had yet to do much about it. The pirates came across virtually no one save, further inland in the forest, a group of runaway slaves. For nearly two months they loitered, although Taylor and Levasseur took the opportunity to talk. Taylor was still livid at England's presumed 'weakness' in the face of Macrae. Levasseur—a particularly treacherous individual even in those circles, as we shall find out—did nothing conciliatory, instead using his silver tongue to drive a further

TERROR ON THE OPEN SEAS

wedge between the two former friends. By April 1721, they had decided to leave for Île Bourbon (Réunion). And they weren't taking England with them.

England's protests were in vain. Three of his fanatical supporters refused to leave his side. The two ships left, each with a clear commander, and England was stranded on the essentially deserted island of Mauritius with no way off. The four men spent the next few months gathering scraps of wood and fashioning a small, barely seaworthy, craft in which, incredibly, they set sail and eventually reached Madagascar. It was an astonishing feat of survival, but it had taken its toll. England had absolutely nothing to his name and could only beg on the streets of Saint-Augustin Bay, where he died in abject misery late that year.

It had been a harsh lesson: there was no space for mercy or humanity on these missions, only torture and death. One pirate who was never likely to be found guilty of being a soft touch was Olivier Levasseur. If any single pirate in the Indian or Atlantic oceans was the major source of the clichés that now abound about the pirates of those times, it was surely Levasseur. He actually did have a scar across one eye and eventually took to wearing an eye-patch; he did indeed fly a version of the Jolly Roger; and he was as trustworthy as a room full of bankers. Born sometime in the 1680s, he came from money, had an expensive education in architecture in his native France, and obtained the 'letter of marque' from Louis XIV to become a privateer in the West Indies, as his father Paul had been. The difference was that when called back home in 1716, he instead stayed where he was and became a full-on pirate, having a marvellous time for a year or two and teaming up with such infamous legends as Benjamin Hornigold, Black Sam Bellamy and even Blackbeard himself, Edward Teach.

As with Edward England, the 1718 Woodes Rogers proclamation sent Levasseur sailing quickly east, and it was the *Indian*

49

STAR AND KEY

Queen that he had shipwrecked when rescued by Taylor and England. Taylor, after deserting his erstwhile comrade, scoured the northern part of the ocean near India with Levasseur with considerable success. Levasseur had by this stage accumulated two nicknames that sent shivers down the spine of anyone who heard them. First was 'La Buse' ('the Buzzard'), due to his extreme navigational proficiency that allowed him to home in on a ship and attack it with great speed. The second was a bastardisation of the first, 'La Bouche' (literally 'the Mouth'). Levasseur had a sharp wit about him which he expressed in several languages, and this invective was often the last thing that many sailors heard before being put out of their misery.

A year after leaving, Levasseur and Taylor returned to Mauritius. This was emphatically not because Taylor had had a change of heart and was there to rescue his former ally, England (who by then was dead). Rather, it was because they had intercepted a letter from a Commodore Matthews of the East India Company—tasked to root out all pirates in the area—in which he requested a rendezvous with his ships in Mauritius. And Levasseur was keen to have any of those ships for himself. Yet after two months of loitering, none of the ships arrived, causing the bored pirates to leave Mauritius and hunt elsewhere. In classic pirate fashion, Levasseur carved a message on a tree and left a note in charcoal on the wall of the tomb where many passing ships left letters, which read: 'We were here in the *Cassandra* and *Victory*, expecting your coming. We left this place on 4 April and are heading to Madagascar.' Such brazen chutzpah was clearly Levasseur's thing.

In fact, they went to Île Bourbon instead. And there, in the harbour of Saint-Paul, lay one of the most magnificent ships they had ever seen: the 72-gun *Virgem do Cabo* of the Portuguese East India Company, in port for repairs after a cyclone. Levasseur did not hesitate, and after a brief battle secured the ship. Even

50

TERROR ON THE OPEN SEAS

these seen-it-all pirates were blown away by their booty: count-less gems, row upon row of gold ingots, pearls, ebony furniture and, above all, a colossal ruby-encrusted golden cross that needed three men to carry it. In total, it is thought by modern standards to have been worth up to half a billion dollars, and was likely to have been the largest trove of treasure ever obtained by a pirate in the Indian Ocean and possibly beyond. Levasseur and Taylor carried on to Île Sainte Marie, renamed the Portuguese ship *Victorieux* and distributed a vast sum to each very happy crew member. The Levasseur/Taylor relationship became strained with all their wealth, however, and they split angrily during their next marauding session.

By 1724, the pirate numbers were dwindling due to more effective countermeasures, and the governor of Îsle Bourbon was offering an amnesty to the remaining pirates. Many accepted, but Levasseur's negotiator came back from the island to announce that the amnesty came with a catch: they had to return all their stolen treasure. That wasn't going to happen, thought Levasseur, who went off to hide in the Seychelles. After six years, with piracy almost eliminated, he snuck out to Île Sainte Marie, thinking that he could quietly go about his business again. He was wrong. The French authorities had not forgotten him and ordered Captain Sieur L'Hermitte of the *Méduse* to capture him alive. L'Hermitte succeeded in taking the escaping Levasseur off the coast of Fort Dauphin, further south in Madagascar, and the inimitable French pirate was taken to Saint-Paul on Îsle Bourbon. There he was imprisoned, interrogated many times and eventu-ally found guilty. On 7 July 1730 he was taken out to be hanged. It marked a perfect grisly coda to the end of the Golden Age of Piracy. Yet even then, Levasseur—ever the showman—may have provided a last glorious tease.

As he advanced to the gallows at approaching 5pm, he threw out a piece of paper. On it was a fiendishly complex cryptogram.

51

STAR AND KEY

As he did so, he shouted: '*Trouvez mon trésor, vous qui pouvez le comprendre!*' ('Find my treasure, those who may understand it!'). Olivier Levasseur was hanged within minutes and buried in Saint-Paul, where his grave can still be found. Although some still believe the whole tale to be twentieth-century fiction, a coded parchment later turned up in the Seychelles that seemed to fit the bill, and the spectacle of buried treasure offers yet another perfect hook for the modern pirate lover. Over the last three centuries, Levasseur's final flourish has remained absolute catnip for treasure seekers. Pushing aside the fact that the majority of pirates simply didn't bury their treasure in secret locations, preferring instead to immediately spend their ill-gotten gains on gambling, drinking industrial quantities of rum and debauchery, gold-diggers have persisted in looking both for La Buse's treasure chests and for any other hoard of doubloons that may be stashed in some unassuming corner of Mauritius, Réunion, Madagascar or the Seychelles. Large and organised expeditions were set up in 1902, 1912, 1925, 1932, 1940 and 1950—to name but a few. And ultimately that enormous golden cross must be somewhere. Unsurprisingly, though, virtually nothing of any real note has turned up. This is not to say definitively that there is nothing there, only that the motive—or lack of it—for any pirate to actually bury his or her treasure and then walk away is never properly considered by the modern gold seeker.

Regardless, before La Buse's grand final gesture, times had already long changed in the Indian Ocean around Mauritius. With the East India Companies of each nation now providing better protection for their ships, and with governmental carte blanche to treat any pirate with extreme prejudice, the era of the Golden Age of Piracy had died with the hanging of one its most colourful protagonists. That said, towards the end of the same century a different breed of pirate—the French corsairs—would be making their mark on Mauritian history, including perhaps

TERROR ON THE OPEN SEAS

the most famous and successful of them all in Mauritian folklore. But since 1715, the island of Mauritius had been claimed by another great European power, France. This marked a big shift, as the French-led colony would eventually transform the island— soon to be renamed again—into something sustainable, unique, special ... and, to those powers who coveted it with envious eyes, extremely desirable.

5

ÎSLE DE FRANCE

European history has often been defined by unrelenting turmoil, and the early eighteenth century was no different. At the time, it was usually best to assume that you were at war with your neighbour unless you explicitly knew otherwise. Even then, the rivalries that were made more immediate after the opening up of the East and West were intense, both for economic dominance and for political advantage. One most obvious way of noting this was the setting up of the various East India Companies over the seventeenth century.

Although England had been first out of the block in 1600, the size, scale and ambition of the Dutch equivalent—the VOC—just two years later, was a shot across the bows of the English. The Danes were next in 1616, followed not long after by the Portuguese, whose equivalent only lasted a paltry five years, from 1628 to 1633. Sweden and Austria would wait until the eighteenth century to kick-start theirs. Of the great powers, only Spain resisted, both due to its enormous commitments in the Americas and to its grudging acceptance of Pope Alexander VI's jurisdiction, in the 1494 Treaty of Tordesillas, that Spain could

STAR AND KEY

'have' the western hemisphere, and its great rival Portugal could turn its attentions east of an imaginary line 1,363 miles west of the Cape Verde Islands.

France had done things differently, although not exactly by following a grand master plan. A 1604 edict signed by King Henry IV gave a certain group of merchants a chance to do something similar, but there was neither planning nor funds. Only when taken over by two Rouen-based merchants in 1614 did it gain any legs, as well as a proper name: the *Compagnie des Moluques*. Even then, its focus was lacklustre. It took the canny intervention of legendary French statesman Cardinal Richelieu in 1642, just before his death, to essentially set up a rival called the *Compagnie de l'Orient*. These two companies carried on in parallel but with precious little strategy, until in 1664, with a new king Louis XIV installed, a long-overdue decision was taken to amalgamate the two into the *Compagnie des Indes*—the French East India Company.

The Company's initial focus in the Indian Ocean had been away from Mauritius out of necessity. On 20 July 1665, as one of the first acts of the newly merged company and on concession from the king, twenty rugged settlers arrived on Mauritius' sister island, Île Bourbon. This number had grown to around 1,200 by 1720. Something similar was also happening in Madagascar. Meanwhile, in 1674 the Company also obtained Pondicherry on the Indian coast. With the subcontinent being the ultimate focus of so much trade, it made sense to make Pondicherry the administrative hub from which all France's (limited) interests around the ocean could be directed, and the settlement would grow rapidly to around 80,000 people within a century.

With the Dutch quietly departing Mauritius in 1710, France knew that there was a conundrum. The Hollanders were leaving because it had proved—to them at least—a relentlessly unforgiving place to settle and grow, and it would likely be the same for

ÎSLE DE FRANCE

anyone else who tried. Conversely, they were loath to let any other great power—least of all the dastardly English—gain a foothold there, in case they could make a bloody-minded success of the place in a way that the Dutch had not. For all its superficial horrors—massive cyclones, voracious rats, aggressive monkeys, impenetrable forest and more—Mauritius was an outstanding strategic location in the ocean for ships passing either way. It also had a huge advantage which Îsle Bourbon lacked: excellent natural harbours.

The English dithered; the French did not. Orders were passed by the French King Louis XIV on 31 October 1714 to the French East India Company to formally annex Mauritius. The message passed slowly via various channels until the most pragmatic choice amongst their men to make the official claim was made: Guillaume Dufresne d'Arsel, who captained a slightly worn-down ship called the *Chasseur*. In May 1715 he was in fact in Yemen collecting coffee plants to take to Îsle Bourbon, where the climate for growing that particular crop had been deemed ideal. He was quietly asked to drop off his cargo and then go to Mauritius with a flag and a brave face. He arrived off the shore on 27 August 1715, but he was initially hesitant. Neither he—nor anyone—genuinely knew if anyone else was already there.

On the one hand, he was right to be wary. Since the Dutch had sailed away over the horizon five years before, Mauritius had been the lair of two types of folk, neither of whom were exactly welcoming. First, there were still many pirates stopping there to make repairs and using the island as a base from which to do more plundering; second, it was suspected that the Dutch may have simply left slaves there to fend for themselves, or that runaway slaves had carried on living a haunted, clandestine existence in the thick forest.

Dufresne d'Arsel did two things that would have a profound impact on Mauritius. First, as instructed, he claimed the territory

STAR AND KEY

for France, planting the royal fleur-de-lys flag in a symbolic gesture at an exact location now lost to time, but certainly very close to the sea and likely in a harbour. Second, again on instruction, he left a note there saying in very clear language that this island was now, like it or not, French territory and was to be referred to not as Mauritius, but as Île de France—about as unsubtle a name as one could imagine in the realpolitik of the time. (I have chosen to keep the original form of 'Isle' that was used in the name at the time, rather than the later convention of 'Île'.) Thus, Mauritius would get itself, for another century, yet another name, although it would eventually revert to the earlier Dutch one.

But claiming the island was not the same, of course, as colonising it. The focus was still on Île Bourbon, Madagascar and Pondicherry, along with the greater strategic aim of trying to contain the growing English might. That, however, was proving to be a losing battle, as England had come out of various European conflicts as the pre-eminent local superpower, notably due to its awesome naval power. As English ships started to sniff around the Mascarenes, France realised that it needed to act. In 1719, the *Compagnie des Indes* grew further by joining forces with the *Compagnie de Chine* and the *Compagnie d'Occident* to mutate into its final guise: the *Compagnie des Indes Orientales*. They now needed to act fast, and in February 1720 they agreed to colonise Île de France before they were outmanoeuvred. The most obvious way to kick-start a settlement was simply to shift some settlers from Île Bourbon to Île de France, just 90 miles away.

First, an official governor needed to be chosen, and in picking Denis de Nyon—a structural engineer based in Pondicherry, as well as a colonel and Knight of the Royal and Military Order of St Louis—they were making a statement: Nyon was an expert in building forts, demonstrating that France was still clearly conscious and fearful of attack from day one. The man himself, however, was not able to make it to the island until April 1722,

58

ÎSLE DE FRANCE

needing first to return to France to collect his instructions as well as a boatload of extra settlers. Yet after several years of rumination, the French were now firmly of the opinion that there wasn't a moment to lose. The Company therefore instructed Major Duronguet Le Toullec to lead sixteen settlers from Île Bourbon to Île de France, to ensure that there was at least a tiny French footprint somewhere on the island. They made landfall on 1 December 1721, automatically setting up where the Dutch had based their colony around the southeast harbour. These few men—including a chaplain as well as a surgeon who moonlighted as the group's barber—were the first official settlers of the island whose descendants remain there today.

Unofficially, however, they weren't alone. Runaway slaves—to be dubbed, somewhat pejoratively, *les Marrons*—lurked in the forest in unknown numbers, but which later algorithms suggest could have been in three figures. Having had the island to themselves for over a decade, barring the odd pirate, they resented the new presence. They would make themselves heard soon enough. Even more mysteriously, Le Toullec himself stumbled across a European man living in blissful solitude, by the name of Wilhelm Leichnig. Hailing from Cologne in Germany, records do not show how on earth he found himself there or when, although his existence was very much attested when he moved to Île Bourbon soon after and married. Solitude seeker or not, the name of this enigmatic Robinson Crusoe of Mauritius lives on in Plaine Wilhems, one of modern Mauritius' nine administrative districts.

Nyon and his party arrived on Sunday, 5 April 1722, in two ships, the *Diane* and the *Atalante*. Unlike the Dutch attempts, this was a more rounded mini-society, including thirty children, twenty women and over 200 soldiers. The Company had tempted these settlers with promises of 'liberal assistance' (i.e. cash) as well as grants of land, in exchange for an obligation to grow spices, coffee and other plants as a rival to the Dutch-controlled East

59

STAR AND KEY

Indies. The vast majority of the settlers, both then and in subsequent influxes from France, hailed from Brittany and Normandy, both of which were suffering from extensive poverty and under-investment at the time; many were glad to try anywhere else, and had a firm reputation for farming.

But unquestionably, these Europeans did not come alone. Amongst their party—and soon to be augmented regularly during trips out west—were Malagasy slaves. It is likely, though hard to be sure, that many of the fugitives hiding in the forest were also of Malagasy descent. Some of the newly acquired slaves also found a way to escape inland. Indeed, by December 1726, the Company sent orders that all slaves coming to Mauritius should only be of mainland African or Indian descent, as it was supposed that there was something in the Malagasy culture that made them prone to escaping. For the Company to have thought along such lines again hammers home how little they began to comprehend the horrors of life as a slave, regardless of their origins.

Yet it wasn't just the slaves who were running away; some of the workers were too. Whilst Wilhelm Leichnig appeared to have found a peaceful equilibrium for a colony of one, it was infinitely more challenging for a colony numbering several hundred people, and some weren't prepared to tolerate it for long. Many soldiers and leaders soon resorted to the demon drink, leaving little time for actual work. Further, just as they had with the Dutch, the island's booming and unchecked rat population was causing carnage to both stores of food and crops growing in the fields, with one missionary dubbing the island 'the Kingdom of the Rats'. The settlers were soon starving, and the dark side of Mother Nature continued unabated too, with the annual cyclone season often destroying the wooden buildings that the settlers had made—the monster of 23 December 1723 being particularly destructive. Even without the pirates, it was abun-

ÎSLE DE FRANCE

dantly clear why the Dutch had left, and history was agonisingly repeating itself. By 1724, many, including the governor himself, were desperate to return to the motherland—a feeling compounded when they were told that they would now fall under Îsle Bourbon orders rather than Pondicherry.

Aside from fort-building and farming, those who preferred an active life distracted themselves with three main tasks. The first was to chart the island properly, a task achieved in 1722. It is here for the first time that the second settlement of the island, in the Noordwester harbour area, is documented as Port Louis, named after the reigning Louis XV. The second challenge was a thankless attempt to market Îsle de France as a desirable place to live, both to those on Îsle Bourbon and in France. It was driven by sheer desperation, of course. Nyon and his immediate successors must have felt like Erik the Red, seven centuries earlier, trying to persuade the Icelanders and other mainland Norse to come and settle in his newly discovered 'Greenland'. Finally, a set of basic laws needed to be written up. Needless to say these laws were far from universal. The European lay people were subject to one set and the clergy to a second, thanks to agreements between the Company and the Catholic Church. Unsurprisingly, the slaves—to compound their misery—were subject to a third set of laws (the *Code Noir*), which ensured that they had no right to own property, had to convert to Catholicism, and would be subject to barbaric cruelty and corporal punishment if they stepped out of line—a line which itself remained opaque.

In late 1725, after three years, Nyon departed, leaving a colony that still numbered only a paltry 213 people, half of whom were soldiers. The island then stagnated under the incoming governor Pierre Benoît Dumas, not least because he was put in charge of both the sister islands and based himself on Îsle Bourbon, leaving the Company and the colony spread even more thinly. He more than had his work cut out on Îsle Bourbon when a ship coming

STAR AND KEY

from India brought smallpox with it, wiping out a swathe of that island's population. Further, the *Marrons* were gaining in determination and confidence. By now, any journey into the interior had to involve an escort. Hardly ever seen, yet deadly when they chose to be, the *Marrons* laid booby-traps everywhere, and even gathered together to chase away the soldiers at an outpost at Savanne, in the south of the island, presumably to steal their food and other provisions. Ironically, they also fought amongst themselves, for stories later percolated through of fights to the death over who had access to the better hiding places across the island.

Evidently Île de France needed its own governor after all, and in October 1728 the next governor, Nicolas de Maupin, was appointed, this time uniquely for Île de France. This coincided with a further marketing surge (read: desperate plea) to France to send over more married workers and sailors as well as, if possible, some unmarried women. Indeed, when a group of a dozen unmarried maids from Brittany arrived, things seemed to perk up a little, as they soon found themselves partners and for the first time in a long while there were parties being held to celebrate the new unions—assisted no doubt by these couples rapidly being given new land concessions. More groups of young Breton women, keen to try their luck at the other end of the world, would arrive in dribs and drabs over the ensuing years.

Once again, however, it was something of a false dawn of hope, but this time the only entity to blame was the governor himself. From the moment he arrived on 20 April 1729, Maupin was a violent bully, pure and simple. Beatings were commonplace, as he thought himself above the law—and the distance from France and the Company certainly provided some protection for him. At one stage there was even a soldier rebellion, which could nearly have spelled curtains for the entire establishment. Eventually, via various petitions, word got through to Company seniors regarding Maupin's behaviour and he was warned to tone it down—which

62

ÎSLE DE FRANCE

he did, barely. Astonishingly arrogant, he repeated to anyone who would listen that the job was utterly beneath him. He undermined the colonists' confidence repeatedly by insisting that such a 'forbidding' island would only ever be good enough to be a stop-off point for ships and would never grow to be a stand-alone, self-sufficient inhabited island.

Maupin spent six years on the island, and whilst Îsle de France's fledgling colony was only too keen to see the back of him, he did introduce two major initiatives that would have a long-lasting impact on the island to this day. The first was to finalise plans to build a road between the two settlements of Port Louis in the northwest and the original settlement, still confusingly named Port Bourbon (latterly Grand Port). Sent from France to assist him was an infuriating genius of an engineer named Joseph de Cossigny, who developed the plans further but had an uncanny knack of arguing with almost everyone he came across on the island, finally flouncing off once his blueprints were nearly ready, but not hanging around to oversee any actual construction. But at least the template was there.

Secondly, and more pertinently, Maupin made a profound decision: the capital would no longer be in the southeast, where it had been since the Dutch arrival, but instead in the newer village of Port Louis. In retrospect, it was a no-brainer and long overdue: the northwest harbour of Port Louis had always been safer, as the Moka range of mountains protected it from the prevailing southeast trade winds—the same winds that made dropping anchor at Port Bourbon a nightmare, as they seemed to endlessly want to shove every ship onto land. Only 156 ships would call at the island between 1721 and the end of Maupin's governorship in 1735—not even one a month—and that number urgently needed to grow.

But these, in the scheme of things at the time, were small developments for a colony that was only growing slowly and

STAR AND KEY

which often found itself living a hand-to-mouth existence. A further massive cyclone in 1731 followed by a wave of them in 1734 hammered home how precarious life could be on the coast of an island that was so far from a big land mass. Much of the hope and optimism that one usually associates with the pioneer spirit had long dissipated into something approaching despair. Maupin's unhappy tenure had only exacerbated that. The Company urgently needed someone to take over who would not just steady the ship but begin to fundamentally transform the colony from a lurching, perilous base into a permanent and desirable establishment.

But they struck lucky. The incredible man they chose more than excelled in his brief.

6

THE MAN WHO CHANGED EVERYTHING

An energetic man paces up and down the deck of a French sailing ship as it approaches Port Louis. He is of medium build, possessing a heavy brow and a long straight nose. His dark, wide-set eyes are kind and welcoming. He sports an enigmatic grin, betraying the wisdom and vision that he brings to the island. He sees the idiosyncratic coastline for the first time since twelve years ago, when, as a more junior officer, he came here bravely in a small dinghy on a rescue mission from Îsle Bourbon to save an ailing East India ship. He is still strong yet quite youthful looking, despite only sleeping three hours a night. Beside him, his wife Anne-Marie Lebrun de La Franquerie looks wistfully at the place that, little does she know it, will be her home for the rest of her short life. She is by now immune to her husband's boundless energy, but can see that even he is excited by what lies ahead. It is 5 June 1735, and Bertrand-François Mahé de La Bourdonnais is about to change the island forever.

Mauritius unquestionably would have its more recent heroes, yet even they admitted that nothing would have been possible without the initial input and drive of La Bourdonnais. Put simply—and existentially—without him, there would be a Mauritius so radically different that it would not be remotely recognisable as the island or people of today. He was not a perfect man, but he did have the most perfect of plans.

La Bourdonnais was another son of Brittany, baptised as an infant in Saint-Malo on 11 February 1699. His upbringing was in relatively poor but loving conditions, yet a harsh blow was dealt when his father died while an English prisoner of war. Such news was only ever going to galvanise him to seek quiet revenge. He was a mere 10 years old, but clearly precocious, joining the navy as a deckhand, a position usually reserved for 16-year-olds. He toured the South Seas before becoming an ensign aged 14 in the Philippines, moving to the Levant three years later. By the time he was 20 he was a lieutenant in the French East India Company, and it was as a mere 24-year-old that he first saw these Mascarene shores, albeit under the pressure of a rescue mission. Clearly, though, he liked what he had seen. His formal education may have been slight but his brain was a natural sponge, and by now he had taught himself—and mastered—navigation, astronomy, shipbuilding and maths. He moved then to Pondicherry, covering himself in glory first by using his strategic nous to defeat the Indians in the siege of Mahé—gaining himself that soubriquet in the process—before being recruited by the Portuguese in the region to ward off the pirates along the coast of Goa in southwestern India. Such was his success that his employers awarded him the Cross of the Knight of Christ—almost unheard of for a foreign national.

Returning to France in 1733, he found time to marry La Franquerie in his hometown, before he caught wind in the Company corridors of the ongoing disaster that was Maupin's governorship in the Mascarenes. He was not alone in coveting the role for himself—it was considered as prestigious as Pondicherry—but he had two things on his side. The first was

THE MAN WHO CHANGED EVERYTHING

that he knew the right people, and in Philibert Orry, the Comptroller General of the French East India Company, he was friends with the man who had both decision-making power and held the purse strings. Yet that alone was not enough, as brown-nosing in the corridors of power was a regular activity for all employees with ambition. La Bourdonnais, however, supplemented his pitch with something else that the others did not have, and which the Company needed in order to run the island meaningfully: a strategic vision.

La Bourdonnais proposed to Orry that Île de France, not Île Bourbon, should become the Mascarene hub for France, despite being less developed. Its harbours were superior, and its natural resources had greater potential. Further, its main port should be transformed into a storehouse where other ships, not just French ones, could aim to dock when returning from or going to India and China. Finally, he suggested nothing less than that the island should be shaped into a major French naval base to embed France's claim further. Orry was swayed and La Bourdonnais got the job, but he was under no illusions that it wouldn't need a towering effort to even begin to turn his ideas into reality. He also had to overcome his natural naval tendency towards strict and harsh ordering of his men; only some of the colonists were soldiers and it was clear that they had not responded positively to Maupin's brutalist approach.

To that end he played a master stroke on arrival, gathering many of the colonists, disarming them with his (slightly limited) charm and offering them a contract that essentially went like this: 'We can only do this as a team; there is no other way. I will work hard for you if you promise to work hard for me.' Further, to persuade them—contrary to Maupin's rantings—that they did indeed have a future, he stuck to his word and immediately made Île de France, rather than Île Bourbon, his headquarters in the Mascarenes. To the long-suffering pioneers, such drive and optimism was a cool drop of water after an age in the desert. And before waiting to see if they would fulfil their side of the bargain, La Bourdonnais—the consummate leader—immediately and tirelessly set to work himself. It would be wrong to say that the tasks he undertook were sequential. Rather, he would set up countless projects all at the same time and made a point of personally overseeing each one by travelling incessantly across the island to inspire development.

The port itself needed upheaval, so it was dredged and deepened to allow bigger ships in. He ensured too that buoys were placed strategically around the harbour to help ships navigate into the port, and support ships were sent out to help guide them in if needed. The port was backed up on land by a new dockyard that could both repair visiting ships and build new ones of up to 150 tons—unheard of previously on the island. More prosaically, he asked everyone to stop referring to the settlement as 'Le Camp' and to start calling it Port Louis, the name it had been given in the previous decade as part of the mapping exercise. This would both encourage passing traffic as well as instil a greater feeling of permanence amongst the colonists. He also wanted to minimise the risk of continual droughts by developing a wonderful aqueduct from Grande Rivière Nord-Ouest to Port Louis that spanned 6,000 yards and dropped only 6 feet.

Equally, he needed to recalibrate the entire agricultural proposition. First, he reintroduced serious sugar cultivation to the island. This had been dropped since the Dutch had departed—and they had only ever grown it to make arrack and get blindingly drunk, rather than to trade. The sugar would need basic mills to process it, and two were soon established. Then La Bourdonnais encouraged poultry farming, coffee plantations and rice fields, and the colonists responded. He ensured that cotton was grown again, conscious of the potentially huge market for it in Yemen and Persia (Iran). Again, he practised what he preached. Having

THE MAN WHO CHANGED EVERYTHING

moved his home to outside Port Louis in the less steamy Pamplemousses—where he named his splendid new residence 'Mon Plaisir'—he himself was frequently found sowing and digging, or on his knees, trowel in hand. His communications persuaded the island that their ambitions should lie beyond subsistence living, and that by growing more vegetables and fruit, as well as tobacco and other produce, they could start making a better living by trading with the ships that they were encouraging to come. Once more, La Bourdonnais didn't hesitate to offload some of his own produce from the grounds of Mon Plaisir to the storehouses of Port Louis, as well as handing it out to 'his team' as gifts. This was the leadership that they had craved for so long.

La Bourdonnais had barely started though. It was well known that a lot of passing sailors frequently got sick, whether of dysentery, scurvy or other debilitating ailments. To that end, to the north of the town, he oversaw the building of a 300-bed hospital (now the Slavery Museum) to accommodate both sick locals and sick visitors. It was far bigger than it needed to be, but it made a statement of ambition that did not go unnoticed. The key here was introducing stone and brick to build these new establishments, bringing in stonemasons from Brittany and India as needed; the cyclones would struggle to knock these down. To keep the industry circular, he ensured that a small brick-making factory and a limekiln were set up too. In parallel, he got started on making something of the road that would join Port Louis to Port Bourbon. He never managed to make it more than a rough track, but even that was vital; with the *Marrons* having overrun the military posts in both Savanne in the south and Flacq in the east, the smaller settlement was exposed and isolated, ripe for a pincer movement from the fugitives. He knew too that settling down and investing in building a Government House in Port Louis would likewise send the message that he—and by extension France—was here to stay.

STAR AND KEY

All these projects, of course, needed people to deliver them. The colony was growing, with more settlers from the motherland, including increasingly wealthy families who were encouraged by the news about Île de France that was percolating back to France. From a mere 200 European colonists and 600-plus slaves on La Bourdonnais' arrival in 1735, this had grown to over 3,000 within four years, again with the slaves notably outnumbering the white Europeans. The rate of escape unsurprisingly dropped, although this should in no way be seen as condoning the fact that La Bourdonnais, for all his administrative genius, was still a product of his time and had no conceptual problem with the horrors of slavery. Indeed, for all his supportive methods, La Bourdonnais was still a military disciplinarian, and there were strict rules for both French colonists and slaves who broke the rules. He saved his worst excesses for the *Marrons*, however, and was somewhat surprised to find out that they were not just originally Malagasy but also of African, Indian and Indonesian origin, and even included a few French ex-workers who couldn't bear life under the previous administrators—all of whom preferred to live in the forests off their own wits. La Bourdonnais saw them all as a menace, regardless of their heritage, and in a shocking move to display his steely determination, he condoned the burning alive of a runaway slave known locally as 'Sans Souci' in November 1739. It was an uncharacteristically grotesque decision by the governor, but it had the effect he wanted and attacks on the colonists dropped.

Port Louis had changed in merely five years from being a ramshackle encampment of thatched huts to a bustling little town with stone houses, shops, a market and even a theatre. It was protected by well-manned and sturdily built forts, both onshore and on islets offshore. The soldiers now had their own purpose-built barracks. The clergy were happy too, as a small church was built in Port Louis, and later a second near Mon

THE MAN WHO CHANGED EVERYTHING

Plaisir itself, dedicated to Saint François. La Bourdonnais played his hand cunningly with alcohol too, encouraging the colony to grow and sell more goods which he would then reward with gifts of French wine—fiendishly expensive to ship out to the islands, then as now. Modern leadership gurus would no doubt also be impressed by the fact that he placed an emphasis on celebrating success. He held regular parties at Mon Plaisir, where invitees were not limited to any one group but open to all. Neither did he neglect his duties on Île Bourbon, which he also oversaw. Each year of his tenure he would go there from July to October and oversee key bridge-building projects, further embed the coffee plantation industry and build warehouses as an extra risk mitigation for both islands.

Île de France, perhaps for the first time ever, was a happy place. It had a purpose, it had optimism and it now felt as though it had a future. Ultimately, as one missionary recounted at the time, 'it now had a soul'. It had indeed been a team effort, but it would surely all have been impossible without the extraordinary and indefatigable leadership of La Bourdonnais. Yet fate dealt him the first of a number of crushing blows in 1738, when tragedy reared its ugly head at the worst moment. His eldest son, François-Gilles, died on 16 February, leaving the governor grief-stricken. He took small solace in the fact that his wife was again pregnant. In fact, it got worse, as on 9 May, just three months later, his beloved Anne-Marie died from the complications of childbirth. To complete the triptych of misery, the child was stillborn. La Bourdonnais was a tough man, but he had every right to feel utter despair and loneliness at the macabre cards he had been dealt. He requested, and was given, a year's leave in France to recover from this dreadful turn of events, hopping onto the *Prince de Conti* accompanied by his beloved son Philibert-François. As it happened, the timing of this return was prescient.

STAR AND KEY

Then, as now, the machinations of capitalism and mercantile profit were always accompanied by the backchat, the whispers in corridors and the sly insinuations, designed only to shamelessly undermine one rival for another's benefit. La Bourdonnais occupied a plum and sought-after post; he was also making a great success of it. This was a perfect breeding ground for jealousy and intrigue. He would therefore spend part of his time in France recuperating, and part of it defending his honour. The accusations—of debauchery, theft and other ludicrous inventions that had made their way via letter and word of mouth to Paris—were rapidly dispelled, both by La Bourdonnais' explanations as well as plain common sense. Although he offered his resignation, it was wisely ignored.

Nevertheless, in 1740 the Company's interest was piqued when the governor explained that due to the complicated European warfare that was playing out on the home continent, which would likely spill over into a head-to-head between England and France in defence of critical trading positions in India, La Bourdonnais was determined to pre-empt it by hitting the English hard there before they thought to do the same. The Company was wary; they were in the business of making vast pots of cash, not of spending it on military campaigns. However, they saw La Bourdonnais' logic and furnished him, in due course, with a squadron of nine ships holding a mind-boggling 348 cannon, all held together by 3,310 men, ready for conflict in India when needed.

Even on the return to Île de France, La Bourdonnais was focused on what could make life better for his island. Stopping off in Rio de Janeiro—as many ships did then due to the trade winds—he picked up several cassava plants and, after his ship had arrived back in Port Louis on 14 August 1741, immediately instructed for them to be grown and propagated. It was, yet again, an inspired choice, as cassava—or manioc, as it would

THE MAN WHO CHANGED EVERYTHING

soon be known on the island—produces a big starchy tuber that has two tremendous advantages. First, the plant is resistant to all but the biggest cyclones; second, even the fattest rats struggle to gnaw their way into it, making this simple plant a godsend in staving off long-term hunger. Along with the sweet potato, it became a staple for all, including the slaves.

In 1744, however, he faced another huge challenge, this time not brought on by any person but by Îsle de France's treacherous reefs. The sugar industry was developing well, but needed some new machinery and cauldrons to make the processing feasible. Mauritius was short of cash too, and suffering from a lack of food, despite precautions. It was also always open to receiving new colonists. All of these key ingredients were scheduled to arrive that August on one ship, the *St Géran*. This seemed at the time like an efficient answer. With the benefit of tragic hindsight, we now know that it was an outrageous risk.

Under Captain de la Mare, the ship approached the northern coastline on the evening of 16–17 August. Yet having not steered there for nearly twenty years, the captain had forgotten the layout of the reefs and recklessly chose to press on through the night. At 2.30am, the weather suddenly changed to deliver a storm, just at the moment when the *St Géran* was trying to get through a reef by Île d'Ambre, hanging off the northeast of the island. It didn't stand a chance, and quickly and fatally crumpled. Of the 192 souls on board, forty drowned quickly as they panicked in the dark, threw themselves in the water to try to reach the shore and were bashed onto the reef.

A raft was somehow built from the wreckage, with the captain gallantly refusing to jump on at the expense of passengers. What he didn't vouch for was the sheer bloody-mindedness of two of these, Mlle Mallet and Mlle Caillou. Sporting the large and heavy dresses in fashion at the time, they were pleaded with to remove them so that they would not get pulled underwater by

73

STAR AND KEY

their weight. Yet such was their primness that they refused to shed their clothing lest they develop a reputation for immodesty, preferring instead to drown in the name of decorum. As it transpired, it may not have made much difference. In the dawn light the raft set off, only to be thrown back by the waves, tossing everyone into the swell. Most couldn't swim, and when help finally arrived only nine passengers survived to tell the tale. It had been a harrowing experience and one that would not be forgotten by the island, either in the immediate aftermath or, as we shall find out later, by world-famous literature.

It led to a tough spell for the islanders, but their new-found resilience saw them through. La Bourdonnais, meanwhile, was soon prepped for war in India. His military background meant that he had to take the lead in battle as well as in administration. His squadron left Île de France in February 1746, only to be swiped at by a massive cyclone, forcing him to stop to repair the ships in Madagascar until May. Making his way to the Coromandel Coast, the squadron only got as far as the coast of Ceylon, now Sri Lanka, before being challenged by a feisty group of six British ships under Lord Peyton. There was a stand-off all day as they prowled around each other at a distance. Finally, the English—as La Bourdonnais had hoped—fired first. La Bourdonnais then unleashed, with Peyton confessing later that '[I] had never seen one so hot.' Three hours of relentless pounding of cannon ensued, and the English—the masters of the sea, but not the masters of La Bourdonnais—could take no more, skulking off under cover of darkness. La Bourdonnais pursued but couldn't get to them. It had been a typically clever piece of naval manoeuvring by the canny governor, but even this challenge was nothing compared to the one he would ultimately face in Pondicherry after he arrived there on 8 July. Now, though, it wasn't the English who were the problem, but one of his fellow Frenchmen, and the man who would be his nemesis.

THE MAN WHO CHANGED EVERYTHING

General Joseph François Dupleix was governor of Pondicherry and also high up in the Company, but that is where the similarities between these two heavyweights ended. Needless to say, both were imbued with substantial egos, and had last seen each other eighteen years previously. They didn't like each other then, and things had hardly thawed since. Where La Bourdonnais was all navy, Dupleix was an army man, and where La Bourdonnais was keen to follow orders, Dupleix preferred to do his own thing and ask forgiveness after. The friction rekindled as soon as La Bourdonnais arrived, when Dupleix—doubtless playing mind games—deliberately received his fellow governor's arrival with a welcome consisting of fewer honours than Dupleix himself would have insisted upon. There were technically no guidelines as to whether army or navy took precedence, or whether Pondicherry was still a more senior post to the governorship of the Mascarenes. Dupleix knew this full well, and if he thought his games would enrage his visitor he was absolutely correct.

There are seldom 'pure good' and 'pure evil' sides when dealing with colonialist leaders; shades of grey dominate throughout, and it was no different here. What is known is that Dupleix—at 49 years old two years older than La Bourdonnais—was despite his high rank an inordinately petty and jealous man. He had coveted the governorship of the Mascarenes too, and made his anger clear when his rival was given the post. The appointment didn't stop him from sending several undermining letters to his superiors in Paris, including one where he whimsically reflects: 'I do not understand how the Company allowed itself to be deceived by the nonsense of this scatterbrain.' In parallel, he had sent a letter of congratulations to La Bourdonnais, promising his 'devoted support'. La Bourdonnais' judgement not to trust him an inch was right.

As a consequence, what should have been a great victory ended in carnage of the wrong kind. The taking of Madras,

STAR AND KEY

which was controlled by the English and offered a threat to French interests, had received the governor's go-ahead. La Bourdonnais would lead the effort. Sure enough, thanks to great planning, perfect execution and clever leadership, La Bourdonnais, in a matter of days, was able to obtain the British surrender on 21 September 1746. It was another textbook display of military execution, and the fact that the English governor Morse afterwards handed his sword to La Bourdonnais showed a respect both for the latter's prowess and for his magnanimity in not making it a bloodbath. La Bourdonnais believed that he was under instruction from the Company to first take the city and then immediately ransom it back to the English for an enormous sum; again, all the East India Companies were profit-making institutions first and security outfits second.

Dupleix, however, was having none of it, and insisted that Madras be razed to the ground lest it immediately restart as a successful and threatening trading post, this time with unfinished business against the French in his own backyard. What had hitherto been a simmering discontent between the two men now, inevitably, exploded into outright conflict and overt hatred. It was only circumstances that stopped it going further, as La Bourdonnais needed to return to Île de France before the weather turned. However, what even he hadn't realised is that long before the Madras affair, Dupleix had been highly active in discussions with his supporters back in Paris, shamelessly spreading a litany of lies, accusations and insinuations against his rival. If La Bourdonnais was pleased to see the back of India and Dupleix, and looking forward to returning to Île de France, he was in for a nasty shock.

As he arrived back at Port Louis in December 1746, there was a slightly different feeling in the air and La Bourdonnais wasn't sure why. As he walked into Government House to find out more, the answer immediately became apparent. In his office was

76

THE MAN WHO CHANGED EVERYTHING

Barthélemy David, another senior French East India Company official, and he was not there just for a social visit. Such had been Dupleix's deceitful skulduggery over the course of the year—before, during and after La Bourdonnais' trip to India—that not only had they sent out a replacement governor, but they had also opened an inquiry into both La Bourdonnais' administration overall and whether he had pocketed illicit gains during the siege of Madras. It was all complete tosh of course, and merely reflected that the people in power back at the Company's head-quarters had all moved around; out went La Bourdonnais' supporters, and in came Dupleix's champions, and the latter had not let his seething jealousy fester any longer: he wanted La Bourdonnais to suffer. And he would.

On 5 March 1747, La Bourdonnais left Port Louis, accompanied by his second wife, Charlotte de Combault d'Auteuil, and three young children all born in Île de France: Pierette, Louis and Charlotte. It was likely not discussed, but deep down La Bourdonnais must have known that he would never again see the island he had so incredibly transformed. He was angry at the sheer perniciousness of the lies spread about him, and that his superiors had been so easily persuaded by them. Even getting back home posed a problem though. By now he was famous, both for his exploits in Île de France and in Madras, meaning that with his family in tow they would have to travel undercover. Tapping into the strong Portuguese contacts that he had maintained, they travelled on an inconspicuous Portuguese merchant ship that stopped at Angola, Martinique and Lisbon. He took further precautions, but was only able to take a vessel to France that first stopped at Falmouth on the Cornish coast. There, English spies spotted him and he was arrested.

It should have spelled doom, and La Bourdonnais likely assumed that his fate would be similar to that of his father: dying as an English prisoner of war. Yet, incredibly, the English had

STAR AND KEY

not forgotten how he had been keen to spare lives in Madras. He had been referred to by an English admiral as 'our greatest adversary', but this was meant as a mark of respect. To that end they granted him bail, knowing that he wouldn't be back, nor would he be one to attack the English thereafter. As it transpired, he never had the chance. On 2 March 1748, just two days after arriving in Paris and fully a year after leaving Île de France, he was arrested and sent straight to the Bastille prison. His despair was only matched by his sheer anger at the absurdity of it all.

Courageously, La Bourdonnais knew that he would need to defend himself, ably assisted by his lawyer Pierre de Gennes. The accusations ranged from the theft of 100,000 gold *pagodes* coins from Madras, to the maladministration of Île de France. He had no choice but to methodically gather all the information he could to show that both charges were utterly baseless and preposterous. But the slow machinations of the legal system meant that it was fully three years before he was exonerated, and during that entire period he was a prisoner at the Bastille. He was finally released on 5 February 1751, but it was an empty and pyrrhic victory: he had spent all his considerable funds to defend himself and was now penniless; he could not work again for the French East India Company that had treated him so abominably on the shameless word of a jealous rival; and three years in a harsh prison without being able to see his family, compounded with the exhausting life he had led on land and sea, all combined to give him scurvy, dysentery and more. He was a broken man.

We will never know what went through Mahé de La Bourdonnais' mind in his house on Rue d'Enfer in Paris as he approached his end on 10 November 1753. If his thoughts were still dominated by the challenges that had been thrown his way, then no one would have begrudged him. Conversely, we hope that he realised that his efforts in Île de France had made the difference between its success or failure, and that he had helped shape the destiny of a future country like few since. (Indeed, that

THE MAN WHO CHANGED EVERYTHING

Saint-Malo is now one of Port Louis' twin cities is itself another of his indirect personal legacies.) The government thereafter awarded his widow, Charlotte, a huge annual pension of 2,400 *livres*, conscious of the ghastly injustice it had thrown La Bourdonnais' way. It was scant solace.

La Bourdonnais was not perfect. He had a temper; he had an ego; he was known to have several illegitimate children both in Île de France and France itself; and his grand plans were only ever deliverable on the assumption that there were plenty of slaves to bring these schemes to fruition, regardless of their non-existent quality of life. While he was no worse than other slave owners of the time—and slavery was practised on every continent by every creed at this period—it is always hard for the modern ear to hear any story about slavery without, rightly, wincing. Notwithstanding this, La Bourdonnais also had all the classic traits of a hero: vision, courage in the face of adversity, tragedy, redemption and several personal flaws.

It was around this very time that the French East India Company was trying to market its increasingly exciting possession, Île de France, as the 'Star and Key of the Indian Ocean'. It worked, as not only was the island's reputation in the ascendant, but it hangs on to this day on the front of every Mauritian passport, albeit translated into neutral Latin (*'Stella Clavisque Maris Indici'*). What perhaps we could add is that the 'Star and Key' was not just the island but also the man who, during his eleven years there, made it possible. The fact that La Bourdonnais' statue now stands in splendid isolation in Port Louis' Place d'Armes, and so many important buildings around the island still invoke his name, is testament to this. The island presented a replica of the statue to La Bourdonnais' hometown, Saint-Malo, in 1988, funded by public subscription.

Despite the loss of its irreplaceable talisman, Île de France had a regalvanised future. The problem was that others knew this, and openly lusted after it.

79

7

THE CALM BEFORE THE STORM

After La Bourdonnais' departure, Île de France gradually grew over the ensuing four decades into the place that he had always known it would become. However, it was still on a path that was littered with challenges, bad luck and external threats. What even the great ex-governor couldn't have guessed was that the very Company that had managed the island since the 1720s would itself implode, leaving Île de France more exposed than ever. Even so, it was now a place with a sense of direction, resilience and purpose, and the inhabitants weren't going to roll over easily.

Barthélemy David's aim was mainly to embed the fantastic progress made under La Bourdonnais and to keep an eye out for the pesky English. He had barely started when he faced his first test. On 6 July 1748 there hove into view in the northwest a fleet of over twenty-five English ships. Their cannon weren't raised as they approached, yet the governor wisely put his men on alert. The fleet was commanded by Admiral Boscawen, who was on his way to India to lay siege to Pondicherry. Whether he had orders to provoke the French or whether he just felt it would be fun, he

81

STAR AND KEY

dropped anchor in Baie du Tombeau, only a few miles north of Port Louis, to see what would happen. It transpired that he had done exactly the same thing off Îsle Bourbon earlier in the week. The French were undermanned, and merely made vast amounts of noise in the bushes to give the impression of their imminent attack if needed. The English moved on the next day, but it was clear to all that there was something approaching a Cold War between the two nations and mind games were going to be part of that.

For his part, David preoccupied himself thereafter with two main pursuits: building a new official residence and women. Perhaps in the name of efficiency, he found a way to conjoin the two. Identifying a beautiful spot on the plateau behind Port Louis, at the convergence of two ravines and a small waterfall, he named it 'Le Reduit' ('The Redoubt'). Built in 1749, the house was made of the finest stone, had a red roof and was surrounded by an increasingly beautiful garden, all paid for by the island's limited coffers. To refute his critics, he used the somewhat lame excuse that it would be a safe place for the ladies to find refuge when war finally arrived. An open secret around the island, however, was that plenty of women were finding refuge there on his explicit invitation, regardless of the lack of a war, to 'relieve their stress'.

Hunger persisted on the island, however, so it was imperative that the agricultural situation did not become lax. The most positive news was that by 1750, the sugar industry had started to turn a noticeable profit, from which it never really looked back. That said, it remained dependent on slave labour for many years yet. At the time there were also half-hearted attempts to establish a French colony on Madagascar, this time without the attention of pirates; but its mosquito-ridden climate, not to mention the fact that unlike Îsle de France it had its own indigenous population, prevented a similar establishment from taking hold

82

THE CALM BEFORE THE STORM

there in the same way. David left after six years. Progress had been limited, but there had certainly not been an active regression. The same applied to his successor, Frigate Captain Jean-Baptiste Bouvet de Lozier, whose main claim to fame had already happened fifteen years earlier when he discovered an island between the southern tip of Africa and Antarctica and modestly named it after himself. Treating Mauritius like a retirement post, his focus was also the gardens of Le Reduit, where he grew both vegetables and plants of supposed medicinal value, mostly for use by visiting ships' crews. When Bouvet de Lozier himself left, on 9 January 1755, Captain René Magon de La Villebague was next to try his luck as governor for the ensuing four years.

This coincided with the advent of the Seven Years' War in Europe (1756–63), which forced upon almost all European nations an ever-shifting and utterly untrustworthy set of alliances and pacts that were hard enough for the residents to keep track of, let alone colonists over 6,000 miles away. Magon wisely chose to keep minds on the more existential matter in hand: growing food, diversifying the island's crops to include more rice and maize, as well as increasing sugar cultivation. More salt pans were also built around the shores, still in use today, and cattle were imported for meat and to turn the sugar mills. There was a growing concern that European conflict would once more prevent vital goods from being imported.

Magon's role was also an increasingly ceremonial one, as well-known scientists and explorers began to stop off at Île de France—now that it felt more settled—and to be welcomed there. These included the explorers Yves-Joseph de Kerguelen-Trémarec, Louis-Antoine de Bougainville and Comte de Lapérouse, and the astronomer Nicolas Louis de La Caille. This was an extra and prestigious string to Île de France's bow, not least because not all these great minds of the Enlightenment stopped off in either Madagascar or Île Bourbon; it was increasingly accepted that

STAR AND KEY

Île de France was the hub. Nevertheless, Magon became frustrated as the Company—to his mind, increasingly complacent—was giving little support or cash to the island, and he resigned in 1759, to be replaced by former engineer Antoine Desforges-Boucher. Although no one knew it at the time, Desforges-Boucher would be the last French East India Company governor of the Mascarenes.

Part of this was a local issue: Mother Nature continued to batter the island with off-the-scale cyclones, notably in January 1760. The colonists were also quickly losing faith in the local paper currency and began insisting on transactions in gold coins. Printing of money would be a huge problem in Île de France for the rest of the century, exacerbated by the administration quickly descending into overt corruption. But by now, far bigger problems lay back in France. The Company was overstretched and quietly going bankrupt. It had lost most of its Indian possessions, and King Louis XV was unimpressed at how the Company's insatiable thirst for profit, all off the back of a royal charter, never seemed to refill the royal coffers to the extent that he believed they were owed. The inevitable happened in 1764, when the French East India Company—on the point of folding—was ordered to hand over the administration of the island directly to the French government. On the one hand, it had ended rather ignominiously. Conversely, it had only ever been the power, wealth and drive of the Company—driven, of course, by its endless quest for wealth rather than any sort of altruism—that had made the colony permanent and largely thriving.

Even so, the island's population had grown substantially—it now numbered well over 18,500, compared to the 250 settlers who had first arrived in 1722—and industry, landownership and more were growing in complexity. The decision was therefore made to split the top role into two, with the governor taking charge of security matters, while an 'intendant' would be occu-

84

THE CALM BEFORE THE STORM

pied with finance, economy and agriculture. As with so many power-sharing agreements that involve egos and instinctive human intrigue, over time the idea that looked so good on paper did not exactly work out in practice. That said, the very first intendant was both familiar with Île de France, having first visited in the late 1740s, and would be the island's most successful leader since La Bourdonnais.

Commander Jean-Daniel Dumas would be the new governor, and he arrived on 17 July 1767 on the same ship as his intendant. Bearing in mind how the two men were to clash almost from day one on the island itself, one can imagine it must have been a pretty horrendous journey just getting there. The intendant was Pierre Poivre and, in a wonderful twist of nominative determinism (*poivre* meaning 'pepper' in French), he was an expert in botany and spices. With Dumas settling into Le Reduit and Poivre helping himself to Mon Plaisir, all should have been roses. Dumas, however, was essentially an out-of-his-depth loafer and was doing precious little leadership. Petitions were quickly signed, and the men's disagreements over who should do what got so out of hand that Dumas tried to invoke the Conseil Supérieur—there merely to instil Company or royal decrees into law—to throw Poivre out. In the event, Paris got wind of the ruckus and chose to bring Dumas back instead, less than a year after his arrival. The massive lesson learned was that the judiciary urgently needed to be separated from the administration to give the island any sort of integrity, and this was rapidly enacted in 1772.

Serving with two other mediocre governors thereafter—both of whom he also clashed with, albeit to a lesser degree—Poivre was nevertheless one of Île de France's shining lights during his five-year tenure as intendant, and fulfilled the role of governor in all but name. Having previously travelled to China, Southeast Asia, India and beyond, both to act as a missionary and to learn

STAR AND KEY

everything he could, his grounding in botany, agriculture and administrative leadership was unimpeachable. The travel had also cost him more than money, since his ship, the *Dauphin*, was attacked by the English and he had his hand blown off, with his whole gangrenous arm amputated soon after. It never slowed him down. He had first visited Île de France in 1749 as a scientific researcher, when he had persuaded Barthélemy David to allow him to introduce pepper and cinnamon to the island, which he rightly felt offered them the perfect climate to grow in. Asked at the time, but not answered, was how he had managed to procure these seedlings that were so jealously guarded by the Dutch in the Moluccas. Based on a certain episode he organised in 1770, we can have a fairly good idea.

At the time, Dutch wealth was overwhelmingly founded on the VOC's control of the spice market in the East Indies. Many of the plants only grew on small remote islands, and the knowledge and location of these were kept secret, while the islands themselves were protected by soldiers who did not hesitate to shoot-to-kill anyone who dared approach them. Nutmeg and clove were not the only plants that elicited such lust, but they were the ones that Poivre, with his wide knowledge, was now focused on. He sent Captains Etcheverry and Tremignon on a secret voyage to steal some nutmeg and clove plants. Maddeningly, we don't know how they managed it; but on 24 June 1770 they came back with 400 nutmeg plants, as well as thousands of nuts and many seeds. What knowledge Poivre shared with them beforehand is unknown, but it made a huge difference, and there were celebrations six years later, long after Poivre's departure, when the first seeds started producing fruit. With the Dutch stranglehold now broken, this would only be of long-term benefit to the Mascarene economy. Within fifty years, Île de France had grown and traded 200 tons of cloves, bringing in much needed cash.

THE CALM BEFORE THE STORM

Poivre, aided of course by slaves, had in turn transformed La Bourdonnais' garden and vegetable patch at Mon Plaisir into something truly original, bringing in over 600 exotic plants from around the globe to experiment with in a controlled, open-air environment. Some proved to be worthy of wider agricultural benefit to the island. As Poivre reasoned, however, the very worst that could result would be a stunning ornamental garden. Two and a half centuries later, we still marvel at the garden now known as *Le Jardin de Pamplemousses*. Poivre's other legacy was to further develop Port Louis, replacing all the remaining wooden buildings with stone ones, paving the roads and, in his simple words, 'making it a better place to live in'. For Poivre was more than an administrator and scientist; he was also a published philosopher and one of the first colonial leaders to question the ongoing use of slaves. In the scheme of things his hands were tied, but his morality shines out repeatedly, not least in one of his first actions on arrival when he had pleaded with factory owners and other entrepreneurs not to ill-treat their workers, including the slaves.

As for the population itself, it was indeed steadily developing. Apart from Breton farmers, other skilled professionals were gradually making their way from France to the island, including engineers for the numerous building projects and doctors to treat the ever-present tropical diseases—although these were still outnumbered by the sailors, craftsmen and labourers. Positivity seems to have been the norm. We can partly deduce this from the various evocative names that pepper the island's landscape to this day, many dating from this period. Although there is the odd name (e.g. Mon Chagrin, Cap Malheureux) that evokes more sombre feelings, these are reassuringly outnumbered by the happier ones that persist: even aside from Mon Plaisir, we have Esperance, Bel Air, Beau Bassin, Belle Mare, Riche-en-Eau, Bois Cheri, Belle Vue, Mon Choisi and more; these all instil a general feeling of a

STAR AND KEY

people content with their lot. There was a disarming tendency to give names to places around the island based purely on their geography and geology: Roches Noires, Grand Baie, Grande Rivière Nord-Ouest and Forest Side are names still in use dating from this period. The idiosyncratic mountains—technically large hills—that dominate the island's views were also given the names that persist to this day, and all are evocatively descriptive: Le Pouce, Les Trois Mamelles, Le Lion and Le Corps de Garde—to name but a few. The latter name—given because from certain angles the mountain looks like a soldier lying prostrate—is part of a pattern of names chosen to reflect the fact that the armed forces still had a major presence on the island: Quartier Militaire, Camp Diable, Pointe aux Canonniers and Baie de l'Arsenal (also known more prosaically as Baie aux Tortues) are just some from this era that have stood the test of time.

Even so, there appears to be evidence that general contentment amongst most of the colonists was greater on the coast than inland. This, in many ways, isn't a great surprise, with the investment, international interaction and more general activities taking place on the shores, and the interior largely the preserve of farmers, including an increasing number who were raising cattle—commonplace then, but rarer now on the island. At least by this stage, according to the records, more regular and more confident journeys were being made along the inner road, with less threat from the *Marrons*, suggesting that the latter's numbers were diminishing, either from attrition or the encroachment onto their old territory due to the growth in the colonist population, or most likely a blend of the two.

It is from this period also that we can glean the first ideas of what the colonists were doing in their social time; indeed, until then it may simply have been that they didn't have any, for straightforward existential reasons. Nevertheless, by the 1770s we are granted insights into the balls, banquets and card-playing

88

THE CALM BEFORE THE STORM

evenings (amongst the French colonists, at least; details of the activities of other groups remain far more scanty).

We also find out about a rare miss by Pierre Poivre regarding which plants could grow and be made profitable. In December 1780, we are informed that the first harvest of grapes took place, whereby a mere 'four barrels of bad wine were made, and gave rise to much pleasure and amusement'. Whether this means they were amused at how awful the wine was, or—perhaps more likely—that they drank it regardless and got off their faces on it, we cannot be sure. What is certain is that for all its perfect climate for growing so many plantstuffs, locally grown grapes and wine do not feature on a Mauritian menu anymore.

That such card and dance evenings remain a mainstay of the island to this day is indicative of the culture being shaped and embedded during this period, and many families still on the island can trace their ancestry to some of the settlers of this giddy period. Sad to say, the optimism did not persist. Initially, thanks to Poivre's foresightedness in ensuring food security through his diversification of produce, and the general opening up of the island's trade after being passed into governmental hands, things had looked promising. Yet after his departure, confidence in the island's paper money shrank as it was not recognised anywhere else, and there was once again a regression to bartering. To counter the inevitable inflation, in 1781 the administration under the new governor, Viscount François de Souillac, tried to ban paper money for a while; but it didn't help in the long run, ultimately leaving the motherland to foot a large bill. The timing was pretty awful too, as once again war against the British was in the air.

Yet this time there was a difference. England had been preoccupied with the American War of Independence for nearly a decade, and the United States' Declaration of Independence had been a knife wound to the stretched British fleet. When the first

89

STAR AND KEY

US ship, the *Grand Turk*, arrived at Port Louis in April 1786, it marked something of a statement for the islanders and a kick in the teeth for their enemy, and was further helped by the significant support given to the ships stopping off on their way to fight in India to protect France's rapidly dwindling interests there. The fact that the head of the French fleet, Vice-Admiral Pierre de Suffren, chose to base his ships in Île de France, in between various inconclusive forays against the English off the Indian coast, was telling. Indeed, there was a four-fold growth in ships docking and trading on the island from 1769 to 1791, with vessels being spread across Port Louis as well as the two other ports at the time: Grand Port (where the original Dutch and French settlements had been) and Souillac on the southern tip of the island. For the island's suffering economy this was a godsend, with the swathes of sugar cane now not only being reserved to make arrack for consumption by the colony itself, but also to sell to the visiting sailors.

It felt as though Île de France was now fulfilling a greater destiny than it had at first realised, and on 15 August 1785, the authorities in Paris made a huge decision to reflect this. The main seat of French power east of the Cape of Good Hope would be moved from its long-term home of Pondicherry in India to Île de France. This partly reflected France's diminishing foothold in the subcontinent, but it equally reflected that Île de France's maturity and stability had grown to such an extent that it would have been foolish not to act in this way. With a new focus on investment on the island, the horizon was once again looking bright for the colonists. Yet on 14 July 1789, something happened in Paris that would have seismic repercussions, not just on this distant island but throughout the liberal world.

Furthermore, after lying dormant for many decades, piracy was back with a vengeance. The difference this time was that it would be the Mauritians themselves doing the privateering.

8

REVOLUTION AND CORSAIRS

It had all looked so promising for Thomas Conway.

An Irishman by birth, his family had emigrated to France when he was a child, and on reaching his majority he had enlisted in the Irish Brigade of the powerful French Army. Conway's natural abilities were soon spotted, and his star ascended to the rank of colonel at the age of 37 in 1772. Volunteering soon after to help the rebels in the American War of Independence against the dastardly English, he had returned as a major-general and was thereafter made governor-general of Pondicherry in 1797, before arriving in November 1789 in Île de France as its chief administrator. Although not exactly a retirement post, it was precisely the kind of senior role that his experience warranted. He therefore arrived feeling both chipper and hoping for something of an easier life. Within two months, those dreams were dashed very hard.

The harbinger had been the arrival in port of the ship *Paquebot No. 4* under Captain de Coriolis on 31 January 1790. The news he breathlessly brought with him was political dynamite. It transpired that six months earlier the resistance amongst

91

STAR AND KEY

common folk against the naked abuse of power of the absolute monarchy under King Louis XVI had reached a tipping point. Incendiary words had been published against both Crown and Church to no avail, leaving protesters with little choice but to up the ante. This was immortalised on Wednesday, 14 July 1789, when the masses stormed the infamous prison of the Bastille in eastern Paris—a building which had long acted as a metaphor for political tyranny, and of course where La Bourdonnais had been incarcerated. Although in fact only seven prisoners were held there at the time—all released before the building was trashed—the repercussions of that day continue to echo down the centuries, as its ultimate outcome continues to shape the very essence of Western liberal democracy. As the revolutionaries chanted their new slogan of 'Liberté, Égalité, Fraternité', it was soon clear that no one in the royal family, the aristocracy or the clergy was safe.

Conway—a conservative royalist and very much part of the French ruling establishment—was rightly worried, a feeling exacerbated when Coriolis unshipped some boxes of rosettes, known as cockades, in the new red, white and blue colours of the revolutionaries, and handed them out to anyone who wanted them. On the one hand, the slave owners, plantation owners and bureaucrats who made the island tick over were hardly the obvious candidates for upheaval. Equally, they were at their wits' end regarding the corruption and disregard that shaped the Parisian ruling classes. They therefore soon caught the revolutionary bug. Crucially, so did the underpaid soldiers. Wasting no time, a set of islanders formed a Colonial Assembly on 4 February, elected a set of members, as well as an Assembly president named Ange d'Houdetot, and the following day the garrison allowed them to march to Conway's residence and effectively—and bloodlessly—stage a coup. The stand-off continued for several months, augmented by the arrival on 25 May of the French naval squadron

REVOLUTION AND CORSAIRS

posted to India under Admiral Count Henri MacNamara. Like Conway, a Frenchman of Irish birth and a staunch royalist, he had sought safety in Île de France as a similar process had played out in Île Bourbon, which he had just escaped. Little did he realise that he was swapping one revolutionary island for another, until it was too late. He was placed under house arrest in Government House and tried to escape and sail away, but was soon caught up and hauled back, with his own sailors turning republican in the process.

Taken to the Colonial Assembly that was sitting in a Port Louis church, MacNamara was never given a chance to plead his case. The building was stormed by a mob of drunken soldiers who saw MacNamara as an inherent part of the problem. He was jeered and struck with sticks as his escort tried to protect him, and he ran. Approaching Government House and rightly fearing for his life, he sprinted into a nearby shop and ran up a staircase, only to be confronted by a locked door. He only had the chance to dispatch one soldier with a pistol he had nabbed, before being set upon, dragged out to the street and decapitated by the frothing crowd, who then put their grisly trophy on a pole. Horrific it may have been, yet incredibly—while 'La Terreur' gripped France in its revolutionary vice for nearly a decade—MacNamara's proved to be the only death that Île de France suffered during its own revolutionary fervour; even the guillotine eventually set up in Port Louis was left unused. By then, however, Conway had seen the writing on the wall and surrendered in late July 1790, pleading his case successfully to return to France, which he did in September aboard the *Nymphe*.

Despite the upheavals, France still felt obliged to send over a replacement, David Charpentier de Cossigny. A nephew of La Bourdonnais' chief engineer of the same name, he rapidly realised that his role would be wildly different to that of his predecessors: the Assembly soon made it clear that he was not there to hold any politically focused decision-making power, but to deal only with the bureaucracy and security of the island. As a basic survival strategy, he stuck gamely to his task, despite witnessing MacNamara's grisly demise. The Assembly, meanwhile, drafted a constitution and simply mirrored any laws passed in Paris' new National Assembly, as and when the news trickled through about them. Although claiming to be representative of the people, these early attempts at electoral democracy still only gave the vote to 1,800 men (no women) out of the total population of 60,000. One lasting piece of legislation, however, was the splitting of the administration of the island into the nine districts that exist to this day.

As Cossigny left after two stressful years, he was replaced by the canniest operator since La Bourdonnais. Hippolyte de Maurès, Comte de Malartic, arrived on 17 June 1792, very conscious that the times had changed. A previous governor of Guadeloupe, this clever Breton was an experienced administrator and a decorated soldier. What he would now also prove to be, during his successful eight-year tenure as governor of Île de France, was a consummate diplomat. Already aged 62, dome-headed and with a world-weary glint in his eye, his first major intervention in fact concerned a health issue. A cargo of slaves would arrive later that year, bringing with it smallpox. It was a virulent strain, soon killing 4,000 inhabitants, and it took Malartic's calm hand to ensure that panic didn't strike. By 25 February 1793, he was standing alongside members of the newly established National Convention at the Champ de Mars outside Port Nord-Ouest—Port Louis had been renamed for the time being to rid it of its royal links—where he calmly swore allegiance to the Republic.

With Malartic not considered a threat to the new status quo in Île de France, optimism once again reigned, not least as the earlier disbanding of the French East India Company's strangle-

REVOLUTION AND CORSAIRS

hold over trade made the island now tariff-free, hinting that an economic boom was hoped for and even expected. But in late 1794 came news of a decision made by the revolutionaries in France, which—to the plantation owners at least—was as welcome as the smallpox virus had been the previous year. In the name of solidarity with fellow human brothers around the world—at least in the French overseas territories—the practice of slavery was, the revolutionaries claimed, to be 'at once' abolished as a 'disgrace to mankind'. (In fact, Napoleon would have other ideas.) Our modern eyes applaud this humane gesture in the face of the odious horrors of slavery, yet most settlers—who depended completely on the 49,000 slaves for their livelihood—soon realised that no compensation would be offered, and they rapidly lost their revolutionary zeal.

Angry meetings ensued throughout 1795, and in these times of high tension and tinderbox emotions, Malartic had to walk a narrow diplomatic tightrope. As an enlightened man of the age, he agreed with the principle of abolishing slavery, and subtly said as much. Conversely, he was far more aware than the distant legislators in Paris of the immediate impact this would have on both the local economy and, by extension, the island's security. He therefore sought financial compensation from the motherland. They responded in 1796 by sending out two representatives—a lawyer named René Baco and the bureaucrat Étienne Burnel—to help thrash out a deal. Accompanying them was a sizeable battalion of soldiers to help support Paris' edict. For once, however, the settlers—still possessing some royalist sentiment and beginning to be suspicious of the unpredictable nature of revolutionary zeal—were prepared and provided their own show of strength, menacing the visitors from the moment they arrived and making it clear that although they agreed with the concept, they most certainly didn't agree with the execution. On the island for a mere three days, a mob soon hounded the two terrified visitors back onto their ship the *Moineau*.

STAR AND KEY

Îsle de France had now rebelled against the rebels, with most inhabitants quickly dispensing of their cockades and other reminders of their initial revolutionary tendencies, but this left them badly exposed. There were calls for declarations of independence—and in many ways, they were acting like an independent country already—although these were swiftly shot down in the Colonial Assembly as there was simply no back-up plan, and they needed to keep options open. Further, the island's soldiers remained overwhelmingly republican and stayed that way for two years, until on 25 April 1798, many settlers—largely comprising slave owners—surrounded the barracks and gave the 800 remaining soldiers an ultimatum to leave or face the consequences. They chose to leave.

During all this time, Malartic sided with the settlers, understanding their immediate needs but still uncomfortable with the ongoing slavery; as an educated man, he understood that the world was changing and wanted Îsle de France and its people to move with it. He continued his impressive task of trying to make the island work for eight years, gaining the respect of the settlers not just for siding with them but also for his level-headed judgements in the face of the hardships they were experiencing. He could speak truth to power in a way that made the Assembly listen rather than bristle. His instincts were strategic, acting as a solid counterweight to the knee-jerk immediacy of revolutionary zeal. However, his balancing act came to an end in 1800 when he suffered a stroke on his way to church. He passed away two days later, on 28 July, and was mourned in a rare moment of togetherness. Not only was he given a huge funeral, but his memorial—containing his ashes—still stands proud at the Champ de Mars by the modern-day racecourse.

That said, the situation that he had foreseen had come to pass. The mayhem of the 1790s had left the economy shot through, inflation sky-high and with no immediate support from the

REVOLUTION AND CORSAIRS

homeland that had been its lifeline for so long. Indeed, the ongoing revolution in France had left that nation with no bandwidth either to patrol the seas of the Indian Ocean or to continue the fight against the British. Law and order in Île de France was gradually eroding. The situation was therefore ripe for illegal profiteering. And this, inevitably, meant corsairs.

This time, however, the privateers were encouraged by the residents, including Malartic himself. From 1794, a local syndicate of plantation owners had financed the building of an initial batch of corsair ships that they could use to start raiding: there was plenty of local shipbuilding expertise to tap into. Some ships were a mere 50 tons, with a crew of only thirty; others were considerably larger, including the 600-ton *Psyche*, which had no fewer than thirty-four guns and 278 crew. The one thing they all had in common was that they were blindingly nimble and fast. What they needed were captains who possessed the chutzpah to go toe-to-toe with British trading ships on their way to India, and to come out on top. Île de France was now in a position to provide these, as well as to import them.

Although these corsairs leave us with a slightly different feeling compared to the out-and-out pirates of a century earlier, their outlook was hardly different: they were as capricious, greedy and ruthless as their forebears. Many of the names of the corsairs who ruled the Indian Ocean with fear from 1794 to 1810 have been passed down through the ages, although it is worth dwelling in some detail on a few of them.

It is perhaps completely unsurprising that François Le Même—like so many settlers before him—originally hailed from Saint-Malo in Brittany. By the age of 14 he was already sailing the seas on a merchant vessel and was soon captured by the English during the American War of Independence. He split his ensuing years between more merchant ships and the French Navy. It was while in the latter as a navigational expert at the rank of captain that he was entrusted, as a 27-year-old, in January 1790, with taking a three-masted schooner to Île de France. He plied the Indian Ocean without much fanfare between 1791 and 1793, triangulating between Pondicherry, Île de France and the Dutch East Indies, initially in the *Liberté* and later as captain of the *Hirondelle*. So far, so normal.

But with inevitable war declared yet again between Britain and France in 1793, and conscious of the French armed forces' necessary prioritisation of Europe, Le Même didn't hesitate to turn the *Hirondelle* into a corsair ship. Rapidly issued by Malartic with his 'letter of marque', he set off from Port Louis on 10 June and within days had captured two British naval vessels. He had clearly thoroughly enjoyed himself and proceeded to make five more forays to do similar, each time in a newer and better ship than the last. What he struggled to do thereafter was share his immense booty from all these raids with the authorities in Île de France, or indeed with Paris. Such corsairing, once again, was straying mighty close to straight-up piracy.

His luck ran out in 1801, when the English warship *Sybille* finally bested him. The English kept him locked up for a year until a prisoner swap took place on the signing of the Treaty of Amiens in 1802, which had been signed to form a brief cessation of hostilities between the two great powers. On his return, he was able to pick up his waiting share of the loot: a cool 1.4 million francs. Having twice been a British prisoner, and keen not to make it a hat-trick, Le Même tried to go straight for a couple of years in Île de France. However, his prowess as either a trader or a banker was non-existent compared to his swashbuckling captaining of a ship. Further, like many who find themselves with mountains of booty, he seemed to have absolutely no problem spending it almost as soon as he had amassed it. By 1803, with Napoleon's forces now fully in charge of France and the British ramping up their counter-efforts, Le Même didn't need

REVOLUTION AND CORSAIRS

asking twice about returning to the life of a privateer, this time commanding the *Fortune*.

He was again spectacularly successful, on one occasion in May 1804 even managing to capture no fewer than eight British vessels on a single foray, returning to the considerable adulation of the initially disbelieving crowd that lined the harbour of Port Napoleon (the temporary new name of Port Louis). Yet even the greats can't resist one last job. In November of the same year, Le Même was back on the high seas and caught sight of a huge East Indiaman called the *Concorde*, under Captain John Wood, not far from Pondicherry. Massively outgunned, the risk-taker Le Même launched an attack anyway, but despite a valiant and bloody attack and subsequent defence for a gruelling hour, he and his crew were captured on 7 November. He had completed his unwanted hat-trick of British imprisonments. This, however, would be his last. Initially incarcerated in Bombay for three months, he was then sent to England in early 1805 on the *Walterstow*. His health, however, soon deteriorated, and he passed away at sea soon after rounding the Cape on 30 March 1805—still only aged 41.

The corsairing career of Jean-Marie Dutertre was hardly any less impressive. Another Breton, this time from Lorient in the south, he had sailed below the radar until that fateful year of 1793, whereafter this forthright 23-year-old, having travelled to Île de France in a merchant ship, had no issues with immediately offering his services as a lieutenant aboard the *Volcan de Mascarin*, a ship actually built on the next-door island of Bourbon. He very quickly got a taste for risk, danger and loot, and by September 1796 was captaining his own ship, the aptly named *Modeste*, which carried a mere twenty guns but was lightning quick. But six months later, by the coast of India, it was the English ship the *Fox* that got the upper hand, with Dutertre having to be ransomed.

STAR AND KEY

Far from being put off, on his return to Île de France in 1798 he proceeded, like Le Même, to set off on each expedition in a different ship: these included the *Heureux*, the *Passe-Partout*, the *Bonne Cuisine* and ultimately the small but nimble *Malartic*, which became his favourite. Again he was relentlessly successful, picking off four East Indiamen in quick succession and having to split his crew of 120 to a bare minimum so that he could sail them all. But once more greed got the better of him during an 1801 campaign, when the British vessel *Phoenix*, having set out explicitly to capture this growing menace of the seas, succeeded after a long chase and a bloody battle. Like Le Même, Dutertre then came to know the inside of a British prison well, this time in London, before also being released via the Treaty of Amiens two years later.

His most daring act, though, was yet to come. In late 1803, the governor at the time, General Charles Decaen, entrusted the fearless Dutertre with a secret mission: to take the governor's emissary, Courson de La Villeneuve, and to drop him off on the west coast of India. La Villeneuve was almost certainly an intelligence officer, instructed to agitate the English in their Indian territories and generally stir up mayhem. Dutertre chose to undertake the journey in the *Passe-Partout*. Try as he might, though, his journey was not kept quiet, and the British were able to locate and capture him before he made landfall. Despite being badly injured in the attack, Dutertre was given no medical treatment and was instead placed in the next British ship that was returning to England. His situation looked bleak. Ever the resourceful type, however, he waited until the ship made a layover for supplies at the remote island of Saint Helena in the Atlantic Ocean—later, famously, the last home of Napoleon. Despite his injuries, Dutertre evaded his captors, jumped overboard and swam to a safe American ship also in the harbour. Ballsy doesn't begin to describe it.

REVOLUTION AND CORSAIRS

Conscious that he had ridden his luck, albeit with a swashbuckling outlook, Dutertre chose to return to Île de France, but this time played it straight as part of the small but official minimal French naval set-up, where he made a name for himself as an able lieutenant on the Piémontaise, using all his corsairing experience to capture English ships—this time without being able to personally keep any of the booty. He died in battle in 1811.

However, even Dutertre's name must play second fiddle amongst the era's corsairs to that of one other, a man whose legend continues to be discussed, studied and admired to this day: Robert Surcouf. Yet another son of Saint-Malo, born on 12 December 1773, Surcouf's story is one of genius ability, strong self-belief and a consistent problem with authority, all underpinned by non-stop adventure. Although he would eventually grow into an imposing figure with black hair, piercing eyes and a round face, he had chutzpah even as a youngster in Brittany, where he was utterly disobedient at school in Dinan— once even biting his headmaster whilst receiving a thrashing, leaping through the window and walking home 20 miles through the snow, nearly dying from exposure on the way. He never did things by halves.

His parents could not control him even when aged 13, and instead shoved him onto the *Heron*, a small trading ship where he would quickly learn to be a ship's boy. By 1789 he had found work on the *Aurore* which was bound for India. That June it stopped in Île de France for refreshments and Surcouf was enchanted, immediately deciding to stay and make the island his home. The ensuing five years involved trading across the Indian Ocean—sadly including slaves as one of his commodities. Although word had by then reached the Indian Ocean that the new French authorities would no longer tolerate this abhorrent trade, Surcouf was not one to follow the rules, then or ever. Virtually no one recognised the strapping, suntanned 18-year-old

STAR AND KEY

who took six months off back in Saint-Malo. But this was a fleeting visit; his heart was now in Îsle de France. And when the corsairing started in earnest in 1794, he soon decided that he would be part of it to make his fortune. Still only 21 years old, he waited for his 'letter of marque' while passing the time as captain of the *Creole*, once again trading in slaves in Mozambique. By 1795 he was made captain of the 180-ton corvette *Modeste*—formerly captained by Dutertre—which he renamed *Emilie*. Governor Malartic, however, didn't trust Surcouf—with good reason—and continued to refuse to issue him with a 'letter of marque', instead ordering him to collect tortoises for food from the Seychelles. A livid Surcouf complied, his ire further tested when on arrival he was rapidly hounded by British corsair-hunting ships, with only his canny skill as a navigator allowing him and his crew to escape by snaking cleverly through the islets.

As they sailed east, the entire crew agreed with their captain that it was ludicrous that others should profit from the privateering that was again becoming rife, but that they alone should lose out. They therefore promptly turned into out-and-out pirates—and incredibly successful ones. Over the ensuing six months they captured no fewer than six British ships, including the huge and prestigious *Triton* in the Bay of Bengal, as well as the *Penguin*, *Diana* and *Cartier*. The theme throughout was that the British couldn't believe that such a comparatively small ship as the *Emilie* could pose a problem—especially as Surcouf would often false flag and raise the British Standard on approach. The *Emilie*, however, was fast and agile, and few escaped.

As Surcouf and his flotilla of captured ships returned to Port Louis on 10 March 1796, he was convinced that Malartic would relent and give him retroactive permission to carry on his corsairing ways. But Malartic was a stickler for rules and shocked Surcouf twice. First, he continued to refuse the 'letter of marque'. Even more gallingly, he declared Surcouf a pirate and immedi-

REVOLUTION AND CORSAIRS

ately confiscated the captured ships and all their goods, leaving Surcouf with absolutely nothing. The latter was beyond seething, and soon set off for France to plead his case with the Conseil de Cinq Cents in Paris. He struck lucky and was awarded 1.7 million francs, allowing him to buy a new ship, the *Clarisse*, and to return to Île de France, arriving on 5 December 1798 to first gloat in front of Malartic and thereafter to carry on with his profitable activities, accompanied by more French sailors who had already heard of his burgeoning reputation and its accompanying riches.

Surcouf's spectacular run of success continued unabated, first with a British ship off Sumatra, before he helped himself to the Danish ship *Nostra Signora de la Conception* off Java. Denmark was not the biggest threat to France at the time, but the fact that the ship carried over half a million francs in bullion was reason enough to take it. Only when he came up against the equally rapid British frigate *Sybille*—which had recently caught Francois Le Même—was there a fair fight, and even then Surcouf's resourceful instincts kicked in: he got his crew to offload anything of any weight in the ship, including guns, spare masts and even water, so that he could go faster still and escape. By the time he was back in Port Louis/Port Nord-Ouest, he had captured no fewer than eight further ships, proving himself the true master. It had not all been easy: trying their luck back in the Seychelles and dropping anchor, their rowing boat had set off for shore but struck a sleeping shark. Three men were thrown overboard and the sharks helped themselves to a grisly meal.

Surcouf's new-found gains allowed him to upgrade again in 1800, this time buying the beautiful and sleek *Confiance*, fully 490 tons and seventeen guns of corsairing perfection, to be crewed by 204 greedy men. In October of that year in the Bay of Bengal he struck the mother lode. The *Kent* was the (English) East India Company's flagship, coming in at over 1,000 tons and

103

STAR AND KEY

armed with 38 cannon, and each of the 437 soldiers it carried believed it to be invincible. Surcouf—ever laughing at the odds and a firm believer that attack was the best form of defence—quickly approached the baffled ship and his crew jumped aboard, soon killing the captain and seventy others, with sixteen of the corsairs themselves perishing in the process. Yet they had succeeded in the ultimate David-and-Goliath sea battle, with Surcouf's guerrilla instincts outsmarting the much larger ship. Even with his enviable track record it was a massive success, and jaws dropped as he brought it into Port Louis soon after. Valued at just shy of 2 million francs, the ship was the most valuable corsair booty in the Indian Ocean—and probably anywhere in the world—during this period.

Surcouf took it as a badge of honour that the British now placed a colossal 250,000 franc 'dead-or-alive' bounty on his head. He returned to Saint-Malo for a slightly quieter life of shipbuilding for three years with his new father-in-law, having recently married local girl Catherine-Marie Blaize de Maisonneuve. The ships, of course, were all kitted up for corsairing, drawing on Surcouf's incomparable knowledge of what designs would work best. His reputation had by now reached the very top, with Napoleon himself first commending Surcouf for the Chevalier du Légion d'Honneur, before asking him to become a captain of the French Navy. Surcouf—astonishing the little general as few could—said that he would take the role only if he was given a completely free rein to do what he needed (i.e. be able to partake in privateering as and when it suited him) alongside his naval duties. This was not exactly how the armed forces worked, thus the offer came to nothing.

In any case, Surcouf's new expertise in shipbuilding had produced what he believed was the perfect ship for piracy, and he was itching to captain it himself. He named it the *Revenant*, and it hit the sweet spot between size and speed, coming in at just

104

REVOLUTION AND CORSAIRS

under 200 tons, armed with eighteen cannon and crewed by 192. French corsairing out of Île de France since 1794 had already captured an astonishing 2,266 British ships worth over £3 million—a sum almost incalculable today, bearing in mind how crucial shipping was to both trade and power. Surcouf was keen to add to that figure, despite the British trying to blockade the island, which was now governed by Captain-General Charles Decaen. By the time Surcouf had travelled from Brittany to his spiritual home of Île de France in January 1808 and met Decaen, he once again had numerous British ships with him, all captured effortlessly on the way. Surcouf was never one to just sail from A to B; he wanted others to pay for his transit. His reception in the harbour was, as ever, ecstatic. Yet he and Decaen were of a different ilk and did not see eye to eye. This soon came to a head when word spread that a booty-laden Portuguese ship named the *Concecão* would be passing through that part of the ocean and was ripe for attack. Surcouf—taking a break from corsairing—lent the *Revenant* to his cousin Jean-Marie Potier de la Houssaye to do the honours. Decaen caught wind and immediately forbade it, as Potier had not yet received his 'letter of marque', and instead sent two of his own ships to claim the prize. When the letter did arrive, Potier set off, overtook the two more ponderous navy frigates, captured the *Concecão* anyway and towed it back.

Decaen was livid, and in a rare moment of pettiness confiscated the *Revenant*, renaming it the *Iena*. No amount of protesting by Surcouf would change Decaen's mind. Still only aged 35, but with a lifetime of adventures under his belt and forty-seven British ships captured, Surcouf had had enough of his beloved adopted home, so set off back to Saint-Malo, only for Decaen to force him to take the *Concecão*'s captain and officers with him—a potentially dangerous situation at sea. The ever-emotional Surcouf simply dumped them on a pilot boat as he left harbour. Decaen again struck back and confiscated Surcouf's entire prop-

105

STAR AND KEY

erty portfolio on the island. On his arrival back in France, however, Surcouf's presence and reputation ensured that he got these returned. Amazingly, later in life the two men made up and remained firm friends until Surcouf's death of an unknown disease in 1827, aged 54.

Whether branded a privateer, a corsair or a plain old pirate, Surcouf was that rare beast who was never bested in battle and who died on his own terms rather than in a skirmish at sea. His personal undermining of British power—not to mention its economy—between 1794 and 1807 remains unrivalled, and his name continued to evoke fear, awe and respect on both sides of the Anglo-French divide for many years. His reputation as a pirate and a slave trader prior to that seems to have done his overall reputation little harm. No fewer than five ships in the French Navy since 1858 have been named after him, including a destroyer and an ill-fated World War II submarine, the largest ever built until 1944. Most fittingly named is a stealth frigate, commissioned in 1996 and still in action. Surcouf the corsair would have approved.

For his part, despite his hot-and-cold relationship with the irrepressible Surcouf, Decaen in fact maintained some semblance of normality regarding life in Îsle de France during his 1803–10 governorship. This was far from easy, bearing in mind the Napoleonic Wars raging across Europe and the knowledge that it was a matter of when, not if, that violence would spread by proxy to the Indian Ocean. A native of Normandy and four years Surcouf's senior, Decaen had fought with distinction under Napoleon's generals and was a military man through and through. Jumping off his ship the *Belle Poule* on his arrival, wearing full military regalia, this overt show of power initially sat uneasily with the Colonial Assembly on Îsle de France.

Nevertheless, a calm of sorts descended upon the island, with Decaen displaying his strengths (his energy, organisational skill and respect for the rule of law) and his weaknesses (particularly

106

REVOLUTION AND CORSAIRS

his very short temper) in roughly equal measure. Yet a spectre loomed larger during his seven-year rule than that of any other governor. The British had been kept at bay by fair means and foul throughout the previous eighty years of French occupation. But it was time to face facts: despite Napoleon's victories on European soil, the French territories around the rest of the world were showing an unquestionable decline. Nowhere was this brought into sharper focus than in the Indian Ocean. What Decaen did not realise until it was too late—something which somewhat unfairly tarnishes his reputation to this day—was that he would be the last French governor of the island.

And although no one understood its implications at the time, the beginning of the end all started with the capture of a famous English scientific explorer.

9

THE BATTLE OF GRAND PORT

Matthew Flinders was the perfect mash-up of scientist and explorer.

Born in 1774 in Lincolnshire, the surgeon's son was a mere 17 years old when he first set out to the newly discovered southern continent, recently named *Terra Australis*. Serving first as a midshipman under Captain Bligh (of the *Bounty* fame) he rapidly realised that military and naval life was not for him; science and exploration seemed far more rewarding. From 1798, and now in command of the 334-ton *Investigator*, he began exploring and mapping first Tasmania (which he named Van Diemen's Land) and later circumnavigating the whole of *Terra Australis*, which he chose to assign the pithier name of Australia. These maps would ultimately prove of great value to future settlers.

In April 1802, he spotted and approached a French ship led by Nicolas Baudin, a similarly minded explorer on a comparable mission for his own government. The two countries were at war, as both men knew. But they were not soldiers; they were scientists. Neither hesitated to greet the other as a fellow truth-seeker and they were both very open in sharing the findings of their

STAR AND KEY

respective voyages. By 1803, the *Investigator* was on its last legs, and Flinders was ready to return home after many years away from England. The only ship going that way was the tiny 29-ton *Cumberland*, which Flinders was given command of. It, too, was in poor condition, and Flinders was obliged to make port in Île de France to make repairs in December 1803. But he was sanguine. The two countries may have been enemies, but Flinders was by now a renowned scientist with no military links, and therefore posed no threat. In any case, he knew that Baudin himself had planned to stop there, so was keen to catch up with his new friend.

Flinders was spectacularly mistaken, as he had not accounted for two things. First, Baudin had indeed arrived in Île de France earlier that year, but had sadly passed away in September. He would therefore not be there to vouch for Flinders. Second, Decaen was of a naturally suspicious disposition, and couldn't trust *any* Englishman. All he wanted to see in Flinders was a naval spy, and he rapidly put him under house arrest. Flinders was understandably livid, whilst Decaen—displaying an astounding lack of awareness—was baffled that Flinders refused to join him and his wife for a dinner invitation.

It was a situation that should have been rectified within a few months. Yet delays in seeking guidance from Paris, coupled with Decaen's overall weakness, meant that Flinders would be stuck on the island for fully *six and a half years*. During this frustrating period, the poised Englishman tried to make do with what he had. He eventually persuaded his captors that his notebooks contained nothing of military intrigue, only purely scientific research. Decaen eventually—and grudgingly—caved in, giving Flinders a freer rein to both write up his discoveries of Australia and explore the island with a chaperone, all from his base in the midland town of Vacoas where he stayed with a family who taught him French and how to play the flute. But when word

THE BATTLE OF GRAND PORT

returned from Paris in 1806 that Flinders would be released, Decaen's paranoia kicked in again, as by now he believed that Flinders' extensive exposure to the island's naval defences would immediately be relayed back to Britain and taken advantage of. So, in Île de France he stayed. Later historians have been keen to point out that any scientific research at the time could not have been undertaken or sponsored by a state without the *quid pro quo* of a certain amount of espionage on the side, as and when the opportunity arose. Although this was undoubtedly the case with some scientists and explorers of the period, there remains little evidence that Flinders was either tasked with a spying remit before leaving England or had chosen to do so if he wasn't. He was certainly obliged to debrief naval officers on his subsequent return home, but it is unlikely that he had any unique information that had not already been garnered by more official methods.

Flinders' ongoing imprisonment was not the sole reason for Britain deciding on a new and more forceful approach towards Île de France, but it acted as the touchpaper. Enough, thought London, was enough. With corsairing having punctured the British economy and power projection, as well as the East India Company's profits and prestige—and with the European Napoleonic land battles proving bloody and unfruitful—extra efforts were now made to rupture France's Star and Key of the Indian Ocean once and for all. The British had tried blockades during the start of the privateering period but with little success; more ships were therefore deployed, coinciding with the corsairing activity tapering off.

In 1809, Britain would do a trial run for the capture of Île de France by first attacking the two neighbouring Mascarene islands now known as Rodrigues and Réunion—the latter had been known since August 1806 as 'Ile Bonaparte' by the French, in a further rejection of the Royal House of Bourbon that had ruled

STAR AND KEY

France up until 1789. This, the British figured, would leave Île de France even more exposed. When a British squadron therefore arrived in July 1809 on the island of Rodrigues, 350 miles east of Mauritius, it was 200 strong and supplemented by 200 more Indian reservist Sepoys, all under Lieutenant-Colonel Keating. It was far too easy, with absolutely no resistance provided by the limited French settlers and no hope of any support from Île de France itself. Quickly galvanised, plans were immediately made to do something similar on Île Bonaparte—which the British were still calling Île Bourbon, partly to irritate the French. With this, the largest of the Mascarene Islands, just over 100 miles south-west of Île de France, the pincer movement would be set.

In August and September 1809, repeated lightning raids were made on Île Bourbon led by Major-General John Abercromby, successfully destroying whole neighbourhoods and capturing a French garrison of 604 men at Saint-Paul, as well as three warships, all before its sister island of Île de France knew anything about it. By 7 October the British withdrew, leaving the island devastated. The French governor of Île Bourbon, Nicolas Ernault des Bruslys, recognising that the French forces were stretched globally thanks to their Caribbean and North American ventures, that his own forces would not be replenished and that he would be at the repeated mercy of these terror raids, quickly gave up all hope, taking his own life soon after.

Although the cyclone season from November to March provided temporary relief from the British ships, if not from the elements, all now recognised that 1810 would be a pivotal year regarding the long-term fate of the Mascarenes. Sure enough, on 7 July the British landed 16,000 men under Commodore Rowley at the Île Bourbon capital of Saint-Denis, taking it after just two days of resistance from the paltry 450 French soldiers on the island, before the inevitable surrender on 9 July. From there on they would be governed by the British administrator Robert

112

THE BATTLE OF GRAND PORT

Farquhar, who would later help shape the destiny of these islands like few others.

Îsle de France was effectively surrounded; nor had the British been ignoring it as they helped themselves to the two neighbouring islands. Being the strategic gem which controlled the whole of this part of the ocean, they knew it would be by far the hardest to take, as its defences were in a different league compared to those of its neighbours. What the British needed to do first was use mind games to dispirit the French, and in Captain Nesbit Willoughby they had just the man. The 33-year-old had already led a colourful life in the British Navy, having been court-martialled for insolence towards a commanding officer and later demoted for unnecessary cruelty. He was not exactly one of the good guys, but he absolutely knew how to probe an island for weaknesses. From March 1810 onwards, Willoughby had been sailing repeatedly around Îsle de France on his ship *Nereide*, occasionally spotting chances to make a raid and unsettle the inhabitants. He was remotely supported by Farquhar, who had prepared propaganda leaflets for Willoughby to drop on land which encouraged the settlers to turn against their French administrators. The skirmishes in the southwest by Black River were particularly violent and prompted the British to focus their strategic aims on another coast. By July, they had decided where.

On 28 July, Willoughby set sail from Îsle Bourbon captaining the *Nereide*. He was probably canny enough to know that his next intended move would kick-start a full-out conflict that remains to this day the biggest battle ever fought in the Southern Indian Ocean. His and Britain's objective was to sail to the southeast of Îsle de France to the bay that had formed the backdrop to the first home of the Dutch settlers over two centuries earlier: the Bay of Grand Port. Still an important settlement, but at the opposite end of the island from Port Napoleon (another new short-lived name for Port Louis), Willoughby had concluded that its strategic

113

STAR AND KEY

importance was still evident and that it was comparatively under-protected. Further, the entrance to the bay was guarded by four small islands. One of these, Île de la Passe, was of critical military importance. A rocky islet barely 820 feet across, it was home to a garrison of eighty-three French soldiers under Captain Escussot. It did not take an expert military strategist to work out that who-ever controlled the islet controlled the whole bay, and by exten-sion the whole southern half of Îsle de France. And taking that islet was precisely Willoughby's aim.

Willoughby was known to be a sneaky sailor and almost always pounced under cover of darkness. He made no exception on the night of 13 August, as the 140 sailors under his command kept deathly silent until landfall, leaving the eighty-three guards totally unprepared. Although managing to take out seven British sailors, the guards were soon overwhelmed and surrendered themselves and their eighteen cannon to Willoughby very soon after. The settlers on the mainland were horrified the next morning to see the Union flag fluttering in the distance above Île de la Passe. Willoughby spent the next five days carrying out further niggling sorties, taking out French cannon and capturing a French defence post at Pointe du Diable. Panic was spreading on the island, just as he had hoped it would.

A week after the initial capture came the crunch. A glance at the horizon saw a row of ships slowly approaching. Willoughby guessed rightly that they were French: it was Captain Duperré in the *Bellone* returning from a raid on British ships east of Africa, and indeed two of the ships were British prizes, the *Wyndham* and the *Ceylon*, while two others were captured American mer-chant ships. Unknown to Willoughby, another in this mini-flotilla was the *Victor*, formerly the mighty *Revenant* which had previously been such a success for Robert Surcouf and such a scourge of the British. But Willoughby was in the mood for more dastardliness. Quickly running down the Union flag, he

114

THE BATTLE OF GRAND PORT

ran up the Tricolore on both Île de la Passe and the *Nereide*, just in time for Duperré to make it out.

Duperré was wary, but his doubts were assuaged by a light signal sent from the islet to the ships that read: 'The enemy is off Coin de Mire' (Gunner's Quoin, another small islet to the north of Îsle de France). This was Willoughby being brazen again, as he had secured the French codes from Escussot's men. Duperré finally committed to entering the bay. Once close enough and bound to enter the bay due to the layout of the reefs, Duperré looked on in horror as Willoughby re-raised the Union flag and fired. The die was cast. The *Victor* was hit broadside, but neither it nor most of the following ships could escape anywhere other than further into the bay, and pressed on at full tilt, only just avoiding further hits. Only the *Wyndham* fired off a shot of its own before securing a passage out, almost by accident. It tried to escape to the southwest of the island to Black River, only to be intercepted by the British ship *Sirius*, carrying reinforcements for Willoughby. Succeeding in taking it back, the *Sirius* then got wind that Willoughby had not waited before making his move and had sailed off for the Bay of Grand Port.

The British were committed. The French equally knew what lay ahead, but their numbers were at the time evenly matched. With a safe anchoring point found as close to the shore as possible and just out of reach of the *Nereide*, with the reefs offering further temporary protection, a brief pause was inevitable as each side weighed up its next move. Duperré quickly dispatched one of his men to Port Napoleon to inform Governor Decaen that the British attack they had feared for so long was finally upon them.

On 22 August both sides were replenished. The *Sirius* arrived in the bay to support the *Nereide*, not long after Decaen and a battalion had finally arrived on exhausted horses after a long ride. It looked quite even once more until, to the delight of the British, two further Royal Navy frigates, the *Iphigenia* and the

115

STAR AND KEY

Magicienne, hove into view from the south. A dispirited Duperré saw no way out other than to scuttle his ships and burn them to prevent them falling to the British, allowing his sailors to reinforce the soldiers on land. His vocal second-in-command, Captain Bouvet, disagreed and thought taking the fight to the British at sea would not be what the enemy expected.

Decaen sided with Bouvet, although not without reservations. Up until then, Napoleon had taken all before him in Europe as head of the French Army, carving up the continent with one spectacular victory after another, consistently displaying a tactical genius that eluded his opposite numbers. But even that great general knew that when they left land and it came to naval issues the British were far superior in terms of resources and ability. However, the French had one advantage which the British did not fully appreciate. Having been resident on Île de France for nearly a century, they knew the layout of the treacherous reefs far better than the British. They therefore wasted no time, under cover of darkness, in removing the marker buoys that directed ships in and out of the bay safely. They were not going to give up easily.

Willoughby—never one to be dictated to by his patience—saw no reason not to attack on 23 August, and together with Captain Samuel Pym of the *Sirius* launched an assault mid-afternoon. To do so within touching distance of dusk suggested that they were extremely confident of victory, although they were also conscious that French relief ships were on their way from Port Napoleon under Commodore Hamelin. The squadron of four French ships—the *Bellone*, *Minerve*, *Victor* and *Ceylon*—had 146 cannon between them. The four British ships—*Sirius*, *Nereide*, *Iphigenia* and *Magicienne*—numbered slightly more, at 165. Yet with Bouvet directing the French guns admirably, the French were no pushover. First the *Sirius* and then the *Magicienne* got hooked onto the reefs, partly disabling their superior firepower. Regardless, the other ships pressed on, and the noise of 200 cannon unleash-

THE BATTLE OF GRAND PORT

ing simultaneously in both directions was likely the loudest sound ever to have been heard on Île de France. Several accurate shots pounded the rigging of the *Minerve* and the *Ceylon*, driving these directionless ships into the current and jamming them hard up against the *Bellone*, which now exposed its port side dangerously. With *Iphigenia* taking on *Ceylon* and *Minerve*, and the still-grounded *Magicienne* taking long-range potshots at *Victor*, it was left to the two command ships, *Nereide* and *Bellone*, to go for each other. The French ships were pushed further towards the shore over the next two hours, although this didn't prevent *Bellone* from firing repeatedly on *Nereide*. One of these shots smashed into and destroyed *Nereide*'s stern anchor cable, immediately making the ship swing round broadside in the lethal shallow currents. A desperate Willoughby threw caution to the wind and went parallel as the two unleashed hell at each other.

Long after dark, at 8pm, Duperré's front-line courage was undermined by grapeshot shrapnel lacerating his cheek and leaving him unconscious. Keen not to make the British aware of this, his men placed him under a flag and took him below for treatment. Bouvet immediately took command and cleverly introduced a bridge system to gather all the available cannonballs and shot together onto the *Bellone* to uniquely target the *Nereide*. Decaen offered support by directing an 18-pound cannon from the shore towards the same target. What the French had not appreciated in the darkness was that the *Nereide* was already all but destroyed, and that at 10pm Willoughby had lowered his flag in surrender. Only a French prisoner aboard the British command ship, managing to escape and swim in the dark to his fellow countrymen, was able to pass this message on to his dubious colleagues. There were rumours too that Willoughby himself had suffered a serious injury to his left eye due to a flying splinter.

An eerie silence pervaded the entire night of 23/24 August, as the sleepless sailors on both sides assessed their damage. Pym

STAR AND KEY

spent the night trying fruitlessly to free *Sirius* from the reef, and likewise Captain Curtis of the *Magicienne*. The only punctuation was a small rowing boat at 11pm making its way to the *Bellone* from the *Nereide*. Bouvet remembered Willoughby's false flag ruse from the previous week and decided to err on the side of caution and sink it. It was, in fact, Willoughby's men offering their surrender, as their situation was now hopeless.

Even so, the sight that greeted all at dawn was horrendous, whichever side you were on. The French ships were heaped by the shore, albeit still relatively intact. The *Nereide* was barely recognisable as a ship. The *Sirius* would suffer a big explosion at 11am. The *Iphigenia* was drifting helplessly. Yet still the British attempted to fire their way to an impossible victory, despite the *Nereide*'s state. At 3pm the *Victor*'s second-in-command, Lieutenant Roussin, was instructed to board a party of men onto the *Nereide* to assess the situation. What greeted him was a hellscape. Dozens of bodies were strewn on the dilapidated deck, drenched in blood, with some ripped to shreds by splinters and bullets. In the corner of the deck, half underneath a broken mast and sail, he saw a twitching body under a Union flag. Whipping it back, he saw the bloodstained face of Willoughby, near death, his left eye gouged out. Going down into what remained of the battery, one of Roussin's men later recounted the scene:

> More men, dead and dying ... arms thrown all over the place. Further off, some forty men, the most senior of whom was a midshipman, were sitting huddled together. They said that since the previous day they had called out that their ship had surrendered, that all the officers, including their commander, were killed or wounded, that they had attempted again and again to place a signal on their taffrail, but that each time the men making the attempt had been killed by our gunfire.

Enemies they may have been, but the rules of engagement instinctively kicked in. Having thrown the dead bodies into the

THE BATTLE OF GRAND PORT

ocean, Roussin immediately transferred Willoughby to the *Bellone* where he would be treated for his injuries. In a great irony, he was placed in a cot next to the equally injured Duperré, one brave commander next to another. Willoughby was also provided with an eyepatch that he would sport for the rest of his life. Bouvet, meanwhile, now aimed squarely at the *Magicienne*. That evening, sensing doom and keen for their ships not to fall into enemy hands, the British set the *Magicienne* alight, with a huge explosion witnessed at 11pm as the fire caught the gunpowder stores. Yet by 25 August, technically the British surrender had still not been received—it was almost as though losing a naval battle was so anathema to them that they didn't know how. Pym took a last look at his ship and likewise set *Sirius* alight, before all the men were transferred to the ailing *Iphigenia* in a last-ditch attempt to make a pitiful escape. Even this they weren't able to do, as the squadron of ships under Hamelin was finally spotted, and these frigates quickly sealed the entrance and exit to the bay, sealing the British fate. The two opposing commanders were meanwhile taken ashore for further treatment, in a house in what is now Mahébourg, and which latterly has become a naval museum. It was left to Captain Lambert of the *Iphigenia* to disembark at 5pm on 27 August at Île de la Passe—such a seemingly innocuous islet that had caused so much carnage—to offer Britain's surrender. Decaen quickly ordered the Tricolore be flown from the sole surviving enemy ship.

French losses had not been insignificant: 36 killed and 112 wounded. But their enemy's casualties had been much worse: 105 killed (92 on the *Nereide* alone) and 169 wounded. A total of 1,700 British sailors, officers and soldiers were taken prisoner. A poetically minded French officer of the *Minerve* paraphrased an ancient Greek rhyme as the prisoners were led ashore, much to the mirth of his men:

STAR AND KEY

The Magicienne has gone to Hades,
The Sirius is up in Heaven,
The Nereide has remained in water,
and Iphigenia is off to Aulis!

And well they might cheer, for this was the biggest—indeed, the only significant—defeat of the mighty British Navy during the Napoleonic Wars. To that end, it rapidly found itself immortalised as the only naval battle to be celebrated on the Arc de Triomphe in Paris. Conversely, despite the bravery of their sailors in the face of difficult odds and slightly reckless commanders, knowledge of this huge battle remains virtually unknown in Britain, which was perhaps licking its wounds at the ignominious defeat of its once all-conquering navy; indeed, those experts that did hear of it dramatically minimised its scope and referred to it as a mere 'skirmish'. Perhaps, however, the British were looking at things more strategically. They may have lost the battle, but they were far from done in terms of losing the war. And before 1810 was over, the Star and Key of the Indian Ocean would indeed finally be theirs.

10

MAURITIUS ONCE MORE

The Battle of Grand Port—also referred to as the Battle of Île de la Passe—was a famous French victory. It had also been utterly exhausting for them.

Notwithstanding Napoleonic successes on the European mainland, the simple truth was that the ultimate fate of a small island over 6,000 miles away was extremely low down on the list of priorities in Paris. In certain ways, their brave August victory in the hellish conditions of that battle had only solidified British leadership minds in the view that this island was an asset worth fighting for—if only to get it out of French control. It was Lord Minto, the governor-general of India, who had made the strongest case for taking it, not least as a British Mauritius would reduce corsairing, increase British merchant and naval shipping security in the Indian Ocean—Britain had lost six times as many ships as France in the previous fifteen years of conflict there—and thereby strengthen his own position.

The prior decade had indeed seen an inexorable power shift from France to Britain in the Indian Ocean region—in contrast to the situation in Europe. Îsle Bourbon and Rodrigues had remained

121

STAR AND KEY

in British hands, now bulwarked by regiments of Indian Sepoys. Britain had tried blockading Île de France on and off since the start of the privateering free-for-all in the mid-1790s, but efforts had been disjointed or half-hearted. It was now believed that a coordinated strategic effort, matched by overwhelming superiority of numbers, was likely to make the French authorities on the island buckle, and quickly. But even assuming this panned out as they hoped, it would need extremely wily leadership on the island thereafter to keep it both safe and prosperous. Fortunately for Britain, they had just the man at their disposal.

The 34-year-old Sir Robert Townsend Farquhar had already experienced enough adventures to last several ordinary lifetimes. Yet he craved more. A well-bred and well-connected merchant, as an employee of the East India Company he had made his way to Southeast Asia, learned Dutch and acted both as an interpreter and likely spy amongst the VOC presence in Amboyna (now Ambon, Indonesia) and Batavia. Often overstepping his remit, he still found ways to impress senior decision makers, resulting in his being made lieutenant-governor of Prince of Wales Island—now Penang in Malaysia—in 1804. There he threw himself into both money-saving and money-making schemes, again showing a wealth of ideas regarding the upgrading of infrastructure—although his corresponding book-keeping and accounting were challenging at best, and utterly unrealistic at worst. Eighteen months later he went home to the UK frustrated, and not for the last time tried to make it as a Member of Parliament for Canterbury. He lost, although not embarrassingly so.

During the ensuing year, however, he became increasingly interested in the challenge of how Britain's colonies could reconcile the need to continue making a profit whilst acknowledging that the bedrock of their success up until then—the simple evil of slavery—was becoming a very hot topic in Parliament. More

122

MAURITIUS ONCE MORE

specifically, there was a groundswell of support in London for finally banishing this stain on humanity, once and for all, led in Britain by the persuasive abolitionist William Wilberforce. To that end, Farquhar wrote a paper snappily entitled: 'Suggestions for counteracting any injurious effects upon the population of the West India colonies from the abolition of the slave trade'. Although it did not attract much immediate support and was naturally focused on the challenge faced in Britain's existing colonies in the Caribbean, its concept was transferable elsewhere. And it was this issue—together with his knowledge of it—that both helped him secure the role of governor of Îsle Bourbon when Britain took it in July 1810, and which would shape much of Îsle de France's discourse over the ensuing two decades.

First, though, Britain had to succeed in taking that pesky island, and to do so in such a way as to ensure that no expensive power struggles between the rival powers would drag on thereafter. A force was therefore assembled that was unprecedented in the Mascarenes up until that point. It was left to 66-year-old Vice-Admiral Albemarle Bertie, who was approaching retirement, to muster sufficient soldiers to ensure that victory would be an absolute certainty. Arriving at Îsle Bourbon from India in September 1810, he pressured Farquhar into preparing six ships for some skirmishing and reconnaissance. The ships scoured the waters around Îsle de France, managing at one stage to capture two French frigates, although this had not been their primary aim; ultimately, they needed to find a suitable location for a full-on landing on the island that would minimise casualties and act as a bridgehead. Eventually they found what they were looking for: the depressingly named—but actually strikingly pretty—Cap Malheureux, effectively the very northern tip of the island and 18 miles northeast of Port Louis.

Together with Major-General Abercromby and an already significant number of troops from England, India and Îsle

STAR AND KEY

Bourbon, in November they hastened to Rodrigues to join up with the soldiers already stationed there. By now they had a veritable armada at their disposal: twenty-eight warships and over fifty transport vessels carried nearly 15,000 men across waters that were still infested with corsairs. Whether any of these lingering privateers saw the British as they sailed in a lazy arc from Îsle Bourbon to Rodrigues is unknown (although they would have been very hard to miss), but even the most daring corsair would have realised that it meant certain defeat. Including the 8,000 Sepoys stationed on Rodrigues, the British now had over 23,000 men at their disposal. By comparison, Îsle de France had only a sixth as many, with over half of their 4,000 troops stationed in the capital and a mere 1,500 scattered thinly across the rest of the island.

For their part, the French knew only too well—via intelligence and general political awareness—that the end was in sight, and that their victory at Grand Port would ultimately be a pyrrhic one. Almost in anticipation, in October 1810 they finally released Matthew Flinders from his interminable house arrest and allowed him to return to England. He would eventually get home, but not without an interrogation in South Africa first, where Royal Navy officers predictably pumped him for any knowledge he might have about suitable landing spots on the island for an invasion. Flinders reluctantly told them what he could, but more important to him—and prescient, as it turned out—was his advice that it would be the diplomacy and leniency of the administrators thereafter that would win them the hearts of the islanders, not brute force. Upon touching British shores for the first time in nearly two decades, he threw himself into writing up and publishing his now decade-old findings in *A Voyage to Terra Australis*. He sadly died just before the book's publication, aged only 40, in 1814.

Back in Îsle de France, Decaen's main preoccupation had been working out where the British would eventually land. He knew

MAURITIUS ONCE MORE

any resistance would very likely be doomed, but he still wanted to put up something of a fight. Cap Malheureux had long been discounted as a possibility since there was hardly any infrastructure there, few roads leading to Port Louis, thick scrub to traverse and very little in the way of fresh water to slake the soldiers' thirst. Yet at 10am on a sunny 29 November 1810, despite being delayed by adverse currents, that is exactly where this vast flotilla arrived from Rodrigues, and by nightfall fully 10,000 men had made land via the vast armada of small transport ships navigating the well-reconnoitred reefs.

Barely had the men set off southwest under Major-General Bertie towards Grand Baie than they stumbled across their first small French garrison. The latter were in no mood to resist such an overwhelming force, however, quickly choosing instead to start a minor slash-and-burn policy by blowing up the nearby Malartic gunpowder store. The British force soon pressed on and split into two, with some continuing along the coast and others turning inland towards the scrub. There, they stumbled across their first pocket of firing French soldiers. Despite incurring minor casualties, it was clear that the British numbers were frightening the comparatively minuscule number of French resisters, who were essentially resorting to half-hearted guerrilla techniques, to little avail. After 7 miles progress since landfall, Bertie called a halt at Moulin à Poudre. As Decaen had assumed, lack of fresh water was posing something of a challenge to the invasion force, but it had barely slowed them down.

By early the next morning, though, even that hindrance was overcome as they came across Rivière des Citrons beside an old disused mill. Refreshing themselves at leisure, they sent word to their comrades on the beach to join them. Before they arrived, however, more pockets of token French resistance materialised, including 100 soldiers led by Decaen himself to try their luck against the British. It was rather desperate, with Decaen igno-

125

STAR AND KEY

miniously getting wounded in the heel of his foot, and his hat taking a near-miss bullet, too.

By mid-afternoon, a significant section of the British troops had peeled off to take the succession of fortification batteries lined along the northwest coast, and they made spectacular progress. Starting with Pointe aux Canonniers, they then annexed Trou aux Biches, Pointe aux Roches, Pointe aux Piments and finally Baie du Tombeau; there, the French had again wisely deserted and destroyed the bridge across Rivière du Tombeau leading to Port Louis. It being the end of the dry season, however, the low water levels of Rivière du Tombeau made it straightforward for the troops to ford, notwithstanding a few casualties sustained from sniper fire. Yet even this petered out on 1 December as the British numbers kept swelling.

The French forces were now under General Vandermaesen, who already sensed that it was time for a last stand. He pitched his remaining 2,500 troops on the southern bank of the aptly named Rivière Sèche, counting on the natural barriers of Montagne Longue on his right and the ocean to his left as blockers to more British progress. It made perfect sense, but even he had underestimated the huge numerical advantage of the British forces. First, this allowed Abercromby to try a bayonet charge. The French put up a tough test, with their artillery taking out over fifty British soldiers and wounding nearly 100 more, including two well-regarded British officers, Lieutenant-Colonel Campbell and Major O'Keefe, although the French too lost seventy-two soldiers in a fierce and merciless encounter. But the numbers told, and eventually the British made it through as French forces scattered back to the capital. Second, Abercromby was able to earmark another battalion—initially held back on deck—to make a landing south of Port Louis. Only then did Vandermaesen realise that his brave efforts had been futile, as the British had by now completely surrounded Port Louis in a pincer movement.

126

MAURITIUS ONCE MORE

It was a comfortable and confident night that the British spent bivouacking on the outskirts of the city. Sure enough, the next morning Decaen saw sense, not least as the French munition stores were now virtually empty. His men slowly approached the British camp holding a clear white flag of surrender as well as a piece of parchment. Whilst many of the British spent most of that Sunday, 2 December, getting drunk, the senior leaders also had this mysterious document to peruse. Decaen had a legal background and had already prepared suggested terms of surrender. It was a canny piece of forethought by the French administrator, who knew that presenting something fast and early to the victors—still flush and positive with their success—was likely to mean that they would be in the mood to accept many of its terms. Naturally the British were not expected to accept everything, but Decaen's initially ambitious pitch was worth trying.

The two chief British negotiators, Major Warde and Commodore Rowley, invited Decaen to their camp and he arrived, solemn but calm, at 10pm that Sunday evening. For three hours there were predictably toings and froings over some of the clauses, with the British clear that they would not accept some of them. But by 1am, with both parties exhausted, everyone was ready to sign. Abercromby ratified it, and so, in the early hours of 3 December 1810, Britain's thorn-in-the-side nemesis of Île de France was now finally a threat neutralised; they took the capital bloodlessly that Monday morning, promptly raising the Union flag on all government buildings.

So, what were the details of these terms of surrender? In fact, one would be hard-pressed in the midst of any conflict of the nineteenth century, anywhere in the world, to find anything so staggeringly generous to the losers. Partly this was down to Decaen's professionalism in negotiating, but equally it sprang from a rare moment of strategic non-violent sense by British leaders—influenced, no doubt, by the sage words of such respected

STAR AND KEY

folk as Matthew Flinders. It was their aim to do anything to prevent prolonging the conflict if they could possibly avoid it, conscious that they were themselves stretched to breaking point by the Napoleonic Wars in Europe. Perhaps a sense of modern enlightenment had finally infected the European conscience? And overseeing this would be Robert Farquhar, hitherto the administrator of Île Bourbon but now to have oversight of all three Mascarene Islands from the central and most important one—known for its final few days as Île de France.

There were to be no prisoners. All soldiers and sailors were not only allowed to wander freely but also to keep their arms. They would then eventually be returned to France—courtesy of the British taxpayer—on their own ships (which the British would keep thereafter). Their wounded would be treated in hospitals alongside their British counterparts. All current laws would remain in place. There would be no change of religion: the overwhelmingly Catholic island could stay that way if it desired, with no pressure to take on Anglican sensibilities. No property was to be confiscated and handed out to British officers as spoils of war. Those civilians who felt they couldn't handle the change and wanted instead to live in France had fully two years, until January 1813, to plan and execute their travels. Those whose property had been damaged during the invasion were to be promptly reimbursed by the British.

Although the British made English the new official language, there was absolutely no attempt to immediately enforce this, either at a cultural or scholastic level. The only condition Britain insisted upon was to rename the island: 'Île de France' was now a howling misnomer. With their focus elsewhere and with no clever new ideas, the British decided to revert the island to its original Dutch name: Mauritius. This was used for the first time in nearly a century on 10 December 1810. It is feasible that this was meant to be a stop-gap name until something more powerful

128

MAURITIUS ONCE MORE

and suitably colonial could be dreamed up, but it soon became fixed and has remained the name of the island ever since.

These were astonishingly lenient terms for the time, with British officer Colonel Beaver likely speaking for a few when he petulantly wrote in a letter home, soon after, that 'The terms were rather demanded than supplicated and were far too advantageous for such an undeserving garrison.' Yet in fact it had been a strategic and diplomatic master stroke. The French forces on the island were not foolish enough to raise arms against the new administrators, and indeed some unlikely friendships were forged. Further, with France having been through two decades of upheaval, as well as violently split affinities between a monarchy and a republic, the British laissez-faire approach had cleverly found a third way of pleasing almost everyone. No longer would the plantation owners see their profits harmed by British blockades and neither would there be interference in their business practices—at least, not at first.

Technically it wasn't until the 1814 Treaty of Paris that all this was made official, although it had been formalised and agreed almost from day one. Mauritius' status as a Crown colony would be augmented by it having its own dependencies. Solidifying further its status as the first amongst equals across the islands of the Indian Ocean, it would also administer Rodrigues, the Seychelles and the Chagos Archipelago (fully 1,200 miles away, but populated by Mauritian Creole settlers), with Îsle Bourbon—chronically lacking a natural harbour, and therefore posing no military threat—being thereafter returned to France as an expensive and perhaps unwanted gift. Farquhar would therefore have considerable power, and was allowed a surprisingly long leash from London. Local checks and balances would in turn be provided by a robust legislative Council of Government, to ensure that Farquhar did not get ideas above his station.

Only once was there even a small attempt at retaliation. The year 1815 saw Napoleon's escape from Elba, his march up the

129

STAR AND KEY

length of France back to power and the possibility of a new dawn—ultimately thwarted at Waterloo on 18 June 1815. But news always took a while to get to Mauritius, and in September—with the more Napoleonically minded French settlers believing him still to be in power—a weak attempt was made by 400 men to take over the British fortification at Mahébourg in the southeast. The British caught early wind of this march from the nearby town of Plaine Magnien and, in keeping with their newfound leniency, allowed the men to disperse and only captured two ringleaders, both of whom were deported. There was egg on the faces of the latter when they soon realised they had been acting under the inspiration of a man who was no longer in power in France.

Was all this positivity the result of a sudden British foresightedness in the game of war and diplomacy? Unlikely. The main driver, of all things, had been ambivalence. For a simple yet strange and contradictory truth underpinned the British capture of Mauritius: they didn't really want it. Their rationale had always been that France owning Mauritius/Îsle de France and turning Britain's crucial shipping lanes to the Indies into corners of French power and piracy had been, for decades, an enormous albatross around Britain's neck, both in terms of power projection and the economy. The British already had plenty of strategic bases to choose from in the Indian Ocean, a stretched colonial footprint that needed constant care—notably in the West Indies—and a tropical produce-based economy (sugar, coffee and more) that needed no new competitors. Ultimately, it was simply less hassle *not having France there* than actively progressing a new British colony instead; hence the lack of drive to undermine an island system that, whilst far from perfect, would probably benefit from some hands-off stability.

Unsurprisingly, the first place to blossom was the capital Port Louis itself. Quickly ridding itself of its temporary 'Port

MAURITIUS ONCE MORE

Napoleon' moniker (but again, not being burdened with a new, specifically English name), the trade ships soon came flooding in, happy no doubt that the scourge of corsairing was once more confined to the dustbin of history. The capital's cosmopolitan feel, coupled with its rollicking theatre, enormous market and new sense of purpose, quickly made it a much sought after place to visit, even whilst the conquered French troops remained on the island. Also growing exponentially at the time was the practice of Freemasonry, the slightly mysterious and often misunderstood fraternal organisation based around a lodge system. Although many French settlers had been Masons since the first lodge was set up on the island in 1778, the arrival of a few new settlers from different lodges—not least Farquhar himself—ensured that the social life would be plentiful too, as the lodges had the best organisational infrastructure for arranging balls, ceremonial functions and smaller parties.

Farquhar impressed the locals—farmers, plantation owners and others alike—with his hearts-and-minds campaign. A keen listener (a rarity amongst the ruling elite of the day), he displayed a usually kind character and was in turn treated with respect by those who realised they could have had it much, much worse. A possibly biased account of the day stresses that 'the Governor found the inhabitants extremely alive to kindness and disposed to accept any equitable measures rendered necessary ... and every effort was made to keep the form most in harmony with the colonists' temperament'. Self-serving it may be, but it highlights that this was an approach that was bearing fruit and was worth continuing. Farquhar's approach was met with a population keen to ditch privateering, and equally happy to kick-start many new enterprises to reflect the optimism of the new-feel island, as well as take advantage of the flourishing international shipping trade.

Even when a smallpox epidemic threatened the island in August 1812, the great fortune of timing was on the British side.

STAR AND KEY

Just sixteen years before, Dr Edward Jenner, from his home in Gloucestershire in western England, had essentially invented the whole concept of vaccination using his observations of and experiments around cowpox as a test. As this was quickly adapted to its human equivalent of smallpox, vaccines were sent around the colonies for the express purpose of countering the effects of harsh diseases on fragile island populations. Deaths were therefore kept to a minimum, and social order maintained.

In amongst this seeming transitional bliss there did lie one dark cloud. During the epic battle at Grand Port, the French had captured an attachment of 300 Irish soldiers and sailors fighting on the British side. Although initially put in prison, as the scale of the British invasion became apparent and the French became desperate, the prisoners were co-opted to fight on the French side against their former masters. This, through sufferance, they appear to have done. Although first-hand accounts remain scant and occasionally contradictory (some claim there may have been as many as 500, whilst others state that the entire episode was fictitious propaganda), this contingent of Irish fighters were not presented with the same leniency as their French counterparts. Far from it, it appears that they were summarily shot as 'renegades'. Regardless of the scale of this apparent mass execution and whether it was indeed as large as some claim, it appears to have been the sole stain on the otherwise smooth transition to British rule. Britain has not admitted to this episode, with authorities questioning its authenticity, but either way, it added an extra dimension to the highly complex relationship between Britain and Ireland.

What also struck Farquhar though—and which seemingly none of the later French administrators had noticed—was something more subtle and yet ultimately more profound. Having witnessed at first hand the British colonies in the Far East as well as the West Indies, Farquhar was alert to how the population

MAURITIUS ONCE MORE

make-up of such lands, often from haphazard situations that needed quick fixes, frequently led to either a lack of central control, a breakdown of law and order, or both. Yet Farquhar gradually noticed that Mauritius felt a little different. Naturally there were still pockets of resistance to change who clung—and would continue to cling—mindlessly to 'the old ways', whether they were of French origin or not. By the same token, he was impressed that many colonists—and their slaves—were no longer 'settlers', 'ex-French colonists' or something else intangible. The inhabitants of Mauritius—shaped partly by the century of French attention they had received—were evolving their own separate identity, manifested in many telling ways.

They were becoming, unequivocally, Mauritians.

11

THE SEEDS OF IDENTITY

By 1810, the confusing landscape of colonial life and its political underbelly had become something of an invisible chain around the ankles of many settlers in Île de France—and, needless to say, this was an emotion felt much more strongly by those having to endure the horrors of slavery, for whom the chains were at times very real. The cumulative effect of this, coupled with the existential reality of a distant motherland whom the vast majority of settlers would never see again, ensured that life on the island over the preceding decades had become progressively less 'French', in the truest sense of the word, and was evolving into something else.

As with other colonised islands, nowhere was this more apparent than in language. Since the initial French arrival in the 1720s, slaves had been brought over from various corners of Africa—many from the nearer shores of Mozambique and Madagascar, but also from other parts of that vast and varied continent. With these slaves came their mother tongues, which overwhelmingly were not mutually intelligible, despite some of the mainland languages sharing distant Bantu kinship. It is in

STAR AND KEY

human nature to communicate, and the urge grows further when that communication can centre on the focus of mutual likes and dislikes—in this case, the slave owners. Those slaves consigned to such squalid living nevertheless had the brains, desire and need to at least pick up bits of French from their masters. To that end, a bastardised, pidgin form of French became the first way that these disparate men and women were able to share their hopes, fears and stories. But the language evolution certainly didn't end there.

The main languages brought over from the mainland during the eighteenth century were Malagasy (in fact an Austronesian language), Wolof, Mandinka and several East African languages of the Bantu family. Many words from these tongues were incorporated into the new speech of the workers, and this in turn was picked up by the plantation owners themselves as a *lingua franca*. As with other French-based languages developing elsewhere in the world—including on the neighbouring island of Bourbon— it kept evolving over the decades.

This new Mauritian language had two main phonetic developments. First, it dispensed with the palatalisation of sounds, so that 'Sh' and 'Zh' sounds were simplified to 's' and 'z' respectively; for example *'chaque'* (each) became *'sak'*, and *'aujourd'hui'* (today) became *'zordi'*—this was more in keeping with the consonant sounds of many of the native languages that the slaves had brought with them. Second, it unrounded the front vowels: *'du'* became *'di'*, for example. Whilst neither shift on its own was unique to Mauritius, the two together were. Another way it increasingly diverged from other French Creoles that had continued to evolve in France's Atlantic territories (e.g. in Guadeloupe or Louisiana) was its use of *'ban'* as the nominal plural—thought to be a contraction of the French *'bande'* (group or pack). Therefore, *'ban mézon'* would mean 'those houses', in contrast to the Caribbean Creoles using *'yo'* (from the French *'eux'*, meaning they or them), and,

THE SEEDS OF IDENTITY

moreover, in the Caribbean they used it after the noun rather than before, as had become the convention in Mauritius.

By the time the British arrived, what was once a pidgin had developed its own grammatical structures; there was increasingly an instinctively 'right' or 'wrong' way to phrase things, as understood by the majority of the population. This was the sign that it had stopped being a dialect and was now its own distinct language. It had already long been called Mauritian Creole ('*Kreol Morisyen*'), with some sources claiming to have read documents written in Creole from as early as 1735, likely the formalising of agreements between plantation owners and free workers. Whilst this has not been substantiated, it brings into focus the simple fact that the vast majority of those who spoke it couldn't read or write in *any* language, meaning that Creole's official spelling would not be standardised until well into the twentieth century—and even then it was open to wide interpretation, as its phonetic nature makes it a forgiving language to spell in. The earliest orthographic adoption that stuck, however, was the change from the French '*qu*' to merely '*k*'; so, for example, '*Qui*' (who) had quickly become '*ki*'.

Fundamentally, however, the true litmus test for its endurance was not the first intake of slaves to arrive but the second, third and fourth generations thereafter. By the late eighteenth century, the majority of slaves were speaking Mauritian Creole as their first language and knowledge of the native tongues of their ancestors had been all but lost, driven by nothing but the necessities of their harsh existence. Further, although it maintained similarities with the Creole languages developing on Îsle Bourbon and the Seychelles, by the time of the British arrivals there were sufficient differences for them to be no longer 100 per cent mutually intelligible. Mauritius unquestionably had its own language, and with the huge upheavals in population that would occur from the 1830s onwards, and new arrivals from

STAR AND KEY

a different continent bringing with them more language influences (as discussed later), it would continue to evolve and stay in rude health.

A distinct language therefore helped shape the tender culture that was showing its first green shoots. But it was not just linguistic influences that the various East African, West African and Malagasy slaves had brought with them; they also brought their stories. The folklore of sub-Saharan Africa—then as now—was hugely rich with bounteous tales, both amusing and magical, with each group represented in Mauritius clinging strongly to its folklore heritage—a heritage that mashed up and blended in new ways as these different stories clashed and merged to form new legends, often around the evening campfires. Whilst some tried to keep a few of the old motifs that defined their original stories, they were also increasingly grounded in the Mauritian topography that had become their unwanted new home.

Nowhere was this more evident than in the shaping of tales around one of Mauritius' most recognisable mountains, the Pieter Both. At nearly 2,700 feet the second-highest peak on the island, its idiosyncratic 'head' perched precariously upon the peak had initially been seen by the Dutch as representing the head of the VOC administrator who gave the mountain its name after his death in 1615 (see Chapter 3). But these later inhabitants conjured up a new story, still told vividly to this day. According to this story, a milkman from Crève Coeur, a village situated at the eastern foot of the mountain, would sell his produce in all the neighbouring settlements. Feeling lazy one day, he chose to walk up the hill rather than round it, assuming it would be quicker. Not being the sharpest, he soon felt tired and took a nap. On waking, he found himself surrounded by kindly dancing fairies, who had not spotted him until he stirred. They begged him not to mention what he had seen to others lest he be turned to stone. He promised them he would not, but very quickly broke

THE SEEDS OF IDENTITY

that promise and blurted it out to everyone on his deliveries. He returned via the same route, but the fairies had been made aware of his actions and delivered on their promise. As a result, the 'head' of the mountain represents the head of a milkman whose name has been lost in time.

Whether there were indeed milkmen of any kind in those days is a moot point, as the tale itself has likely taken on several iterations between its inception and now. More immediately recognisable is the profound belief to this day in werewolves, known in Mauritius as 'Lougarou' (close to the French '*loup-garou*'). The Mauritian version finds its roots not only in the familiar European take on the myth, but unquestionably in a variety of African folk tales too, for not only is Lougarou thought to appear at full moon to cause whatever carnage he wants, but like certain of his African progenitors he is designed specifically to scare children; furthermore, protection can be sought from a witch doctor—not exactly common in Mauritius these days, but a well-known motif for those early enslaved folk.

The depth of feeling towards Lougarou, thanks no doubt to the evocative language of those early tales, should not be under-estimated. In 1994, following Cyclone Hollanda's destructive path of collapsed houses and electricity going offline, a new form of Lougarou allegedly emerged in the aftermath. Known as *Touni Minwi* ('Naked at Midnight'), whatever 'he' was supposedly started visiting and scaring women at night. Rumour has it that he first started his visitations in the eastern village of Lallmatie, although very rapidly there were countless second-hand stories of *Touni Minwi* and the original Lougarou all over the island. The hysteria was such that the armed forces were mobilised and the nation's president went on TV to calm the populace and reassure them that these were nothing more than legends that had got completely out of hand and were being taken at face value. We may chuckle in bafflement that such events could occur in the late

STAR AND KEY

twentieth century, but it speaks volumes about the power of the original myths conjured up by those very early Mauritians, based on the timeless folklore that they had brought with them across the ocean. Sadly, neither Lougarou nor *Touni Minwi* were caught on camera.

Yet France, Africa and Madagascar were not the only source of labourers on the island. Since 1745, the first ethnic Chinese immigrants had started arriving. As with their African counterparts, it was not a voluntary journey, as the Chinese had been tricked by the French authorities into moving from their homes in Sumatra on the promise of work, only to find out quickly that conditions were nothing like they had expected. Although these first arrivals soon found a way to be deported back again, it nevertheless started first a trickle and then a steady stream of immigrants from the Chinese mainland, with numbers reaching the thousands in the mid-1780s. As in so many cities before and since, the new arrivals set up a home-from-home in a corner of Port Louis, known in English—here and everywhere else—as 'Chinatown' (or '*Camp des Chinois*' under French rule). This added yet another dimension to Mauritius' burgeoning identity, with these late eighteenth-century arrivals and their families— largely coming from Fujian province, especially the sub-province of Xiamen, and bringing a multitude of dialects with them— quickly settling down to fill the niches of cobblers, tailors, blacksmiths and carpenters, the latter being particularly valuable to shipbuilding, although more often than not they specialised in smaller projects. Again, within two generations, many of their offspring were far more comfortable learning Mauritian Creole than their mother tongue.

The French themselves had of course added considerably to the shaping of this emerging Mauritian culture. To that end, the first and most conspicuous thing a visitor would notice on stepping off their ship in Port Louis or Grand Port would be the

140

THE SEEDS OF IDENTITY

prevalence of a distinct architecture. French colonial architectural design had slowly developed its own local feel as a reaction to the climatic and other challenges that Mauritius presented. Many of the island's most iconic buildings—such as Le Reduit for its leaders, or the various governmental buildings scattered around Port Louis for official use—date from the French period, and even many of those that were built later were clearly inspired by it. Their chief characteristics were the use of brick and stucco, shuttered windows and elaborate, all-encompassing verandas. There were also hints of Baroque and Neoclassical designs, each with something of an island twist. Although wood was used profusely too, the sheer force of the annual cyclones coupled with the tropical humidity meant that compromises were needed for substance over style, without undermining the overall beauty and aesthetic of many of the buildings. The metal fretwork on the wrought-iron balustrades alone was often as beautiful as anything to be found in France.

The British would add to this during the nineteenth century by introducing Victorian and Georgian-style buildings that, when sat side by side with the French edifices, together formed a unique feel to both Port Louis and the wider island, alongside the introduction of the stately veranda columns inspired by the plantations in the US Deep South. Again, there was a new Mauritian identity poking through those magnificent shutters, for this was a unique hybrid architecture, informed by its Indian Ocean setting, emulated nowhere else and renowned to this day as historically significant. Nowhere is this special blend more evident today than in the 1830 plantation house known as 'Eureka', in the village of Moka. With 109 doors and windows to open and shut daily, it is both enormous and evocative of a time past, when the plantation owners vied with each other over size of family, home and garden.

The French had of course brought with them their mastery of letters, and many of the motherland's writers had come to visit

STAR AND KEY

Îsle de France and share with their audiences back home what they had witnessed and equally what they had felt. Yet it is the 1788 novel of one author in particular that has penetrated the centuries to this day as the quintessential book exploring a seemingly idyllic life in eighteenth-century Îsle de France, at the time when a distinct Mauritian culture was first developing. It seems sad, in some ways, that the awful shipwreck of the *St Géran* (see Chapter 6) should form such a tragic backdrop to the story of *Paul et Virginie*, which seems to promise so much optimism. Yet it was part of the author Jacques-Henri Bernardin de St Pierre's consummate skill that he could evoke the naive yet fragile beauty of privileged life on an isolated island that was in the process of developing ideas of its own. He spent considerable time on Îsle de France in the late 1760s, but chose to set his novel even earlier.

In essence, it captures the story of two women—one a widow, the other abandoned by her lover—each with a child, living in Mauritius when the colony of Îsle de France was still in its infancy. The friends choose to live very near to each other for mutual support on this remote and mysterious island—as it was then. They are each accompanied by a slave. The two kids are called Paul and Virginie. Brought up almost as siblings, they are the personification of innocent charm, seductively in tune with their wild, forested surroundings, creatures of the outdoors, yet polite and uncorrupted; there is more than a hint of the angelic about them. As they grow up—and perhaps void of any other options in what was then only a sparsely inhabited island—they slowly fall in love. The two mothers are thrilled with the idea of a union. Yet Virginie's mother, reflecting on her own misfortunes, is concerned about early unwanted pregnancies and the lack of funds that either of them will have at their disposal. When a rich aunt in Paris offers to make Virginie her heir if her mother sends her back to France, the tearful girl is put on a boat to France. And when she returns on a certain well-known ship in 1744, things take a turn for the worse.

142

THE SEEDS OF IDENTITY

Paul et Virginie was apparently Napoleon's favourite book. Famed explorer Alexander von Humboldt loved it so much that he essentially memorised it. It has long surpassed its hundredth edition, and translations of the story sprang up quickly in English, Italian, Dutch, Portuguese, German, Polish, Spanish, Russian and Greek, to name a few. Its evocative language and scene-setting together with its underlying philosophy of simpler times had undoubtedly struck a chord under the darker temperate skies of Europe.

That all said, the novel unquestionably had—and still has—its vehement critics. For a start, there is absolutely no getting away from the fact that its subtle message regarding slavery—instinctively abhorrent to the modern reader—is essentially that 'Slavery is OK, as long as their masters and mistresses are kind to them.' One could also make a good case for saying that Bernardin de St Pierre's descriptions of nature and its forests outshine his characterisation, up to and including the two lovers. The island is ultimately portrayed as a heaven on earth, which—taking into account the bouts of smallpox that afflicted the population, the relentless cyclones and the prevalence of slavery—it most certainly wasn't. Yet still it undoubtedly holds a certain ineffable power that makes it read and studied today. Needless to say, although it is clearly a piece of historical fiction—and with some intriguing similarities to James Cameron's film *Titanic*—many still ask whether the story is true. Alas, it is not; but such is its ongoing allure, it has arguably added an extra dimension to the growing body of Mauritian folklore that sprang up in the eighteenth century.

Whilst the artistic scene in Mauritius was not as well developed, it would become increasingly so under British rule. Perhaps the most evocative paintings are those of Malcy de Chazal, a young girl born in Port Louis in 1804. Refreshingly free-spirited, she was enchanted by the flowers and plants pointed out to her

143

STAR AND KEY

by her father, the keen amateur botanist Antoine Toussaint de Chazal, on their frequent walks together. Indeed, it was her father who introduced silkworms to the island in 1820, with the family side-hustle of sericulture soon producing 770 pounds of silk a year. This love of nature inspired her to turn to painting watercolours, especially of potentially medicinal plants. She had an incredible natural aptitude, and the vibrancy and meticulous observation of her paintings still enchant viewers to this day.

Chazal's father was good friends with Governor Farquhar, and the family were regular visitors to his home at Le Reduit. Tragically, it was there in 1822 that her father died after accidentally taking an overdose of laudanum—a tincture of opium. Nevertheless, Farquhar insisted that the remaining family would always be welcome, and the governor's grounds became Malcy's first scientific backyard, as her paintings were to complement her growth into one of the most respected naturalists of the period anywhere in the Indian Ocean—a rarity for a female at this time when opportunities were often stifled. After she died in 1880, Chazal's stunning watercolours were essentially forgotten and kept in an archive for over a century, until interest in her was resurrected in the late twentieth century. Sixty-eight of her pictures are now displayed at the Mauritius Herbarium and remain a treasure trove for researchers, not least because many of the paintings represent endemic species that have sadly since been lost forever, or which are perilously endangered. Although little known outside Mauritius and the botanical world, she can still lay claim to being Mauritius' first great artist, paving the way for a sprouting of diverse Mauritian art forms in the decades thereafter.

The British were ever-keen not to upset the status quo of the island but to let it develop organically, without external pressure to conform to alternative ways of life; their unspoken objective was always: 'Maintain control at low cost.' Even so, within eighteen months of the British capture and Farquhar's arrival, the

THE SEEDS OF IDENTITY

new administration introduced a sport that continues to dominate Mauritian Saturdays to this day. For this, he had to thank the arrival in early 1812 of retired 36-year-old Colonel Edward Draper. An old Etonian who had gone up to Oxford before serving in the British Army in the West Indies and Egypt, Draper ticked almost every box that made him the right 'breed'. And men of his ilk liked one animal above all others: horses. Draper—who would serve in numerous posts on the island, including Chief of Police, Colonial Treasurer and Magistrate—founded the Mauritius Turf Club that very year, making it the oldest equine club in the whole of the southern hemisphere and the second oldest in the world.

Farquhar actively supported the idea, seeing it as something of an olive branch to those segments of the island's population who were still in two minds about their new masters. Wasting no time, a flat patch of ground on the then outskirts of Port Louis, known as the Champ de Mars—previously used as a French military training ground—was earmarked to be the island's first racecourse. By 25 June 1812 it was inaugurated and the first race run for the award of a gold cup presented by Lady Maria Lautour, Farquhar's francophone wife. The track itself is, by global standards, tiny: a mere 4,260-foot right-hand oval, with the shortest of finishing straights. It was intended to be the first of several. The true selling point, however, is its setting, as it nestles at the foot of the spectacular Moka Range mountains, with imposing views of Le Pouce mountain helping it remain one of the most beautiful racecourses in the world—even if the quality of its racing will likely never match that of Europe or North America.

Regardless, it kick-started a love affair between Mauritians of all creeds and backgrounds and the ancient sport of horse racing, an affair that has never abated. In 1984, an astonishing 100,000 turned up to watch the island's top race, the Maiden Cup; this surpasses the numbers that make it each day to the Cheltenham Festival or Royal Ascot back in the UK, at racetracks that offer considerably more space. Even now, it is far from uncommon to walk into any village bar on the island on a Saturday afternoon and witness several of the clientele flicking between two radio stations: one commentating on the local racing and the other on the English football Premier League.

If horse racing was the great form of mass entertainment that the British could be proud to have introduced, it nevertheless remained the preserve of the wealthy to own a horse, even if folk of all backgrounds turned up to watch. Amongst the poor slave population, there was another form of entertainment that was by then already well established, and which has played a part in shaping the Mauritian identity as much as anything else.

It is very hard to pinpoint exactly when the Séga dance and its accompanying music first became entrenched in Mauritius as its definitive musical calling card, but it is likely a form of it has been around as long as the slaves have; it is not impossible that Séga—or a progenitor of it—was being sung and danced by the slaves during the Dutch period in the seventeenth century. Around campfires if allowed, or in their huts if not, the Séga was a full musical expression, sometimes of lament, sometimes of hope, often of anger and always of passion. Its roots, unsurprisingly, lay in both East African and Malagasy musical traditions that the slaves had brought with them. Relatively proximate they may have been geographically, but Madagascar's heritage and traditions were much removed from those of the mainland. There are certainly echoes of the Famadihana death ritual found on Madagascar, while others still hear some of its origins in the Tchéga dance of Mozambique—which likely lent it its name. Either way, in Mauritius and to a lesser extent in Îsle Bourbon, the Seychelles and Rodrigues, the two original styles evolved into a blend that was unique, hypnotic and long-lasting—it remains to this day on UNESCO's Intangible Cultural Heritage list.

THE SEEDS OF IDENTITY

Séga invariably had a 6/8 rhythm, maintained by some or all of a group of percussion instruments: the *moutia* (hand drum); the *maravanne* (rattle); a triangle (or any metal that could make a clanging sound), which was said by some to represent the sound of the shackles that sometimes bound the ankles of the enslaved; and—initially at least—the *bobre* (a kind of bow). Most important, though, was the goatskin drum known as the *ravanne*, which lent the whole ensemble its distinctive timbre and heartbeat. The rhythms—even, it seems, in its early days—would be accompanied by lyrics, and tellingly the first descriptions of these suggest that the focus was very much on the singers' current plight rather than harking back to ancestral homelands. Whilst this is unsurprising given the conditions of their lives, it also offers us a glimpse into the people of Mauritius—albeit in the most dreadful of circumstances—feeling tied to their new land rather than their old one. Séga was an intense expression of emotion, with a mix of despair and heartache blended with a liberating joy—an incongruous mix almost too hard to define and yet which somehow works.

However, no true Séga was ever complete without dancing. One of the facets that again made this burgeoning tradition stand out was the insistence that during the dance the feet never left the ground: movement would come uniquely from the rocking and swaying of the hips. Needless to say, Séga—naturally unpopular with the colonial masters as being uncouth—found another enemy in the Catholic Church, which invariably saw the sexualising of life in almost everything, and the Séga dance was no exception. Although the lyrics of those first Ségas have been lost to the winds of time, we are tempted to speculate that the planting of the feet acted as a representation of the wider situation that the performers found themselves in: rooted in a new land, with little hope of being lifted out of it. Although modern tourist performances have placed greater and greater emphasis on the beautifully coloured and designed skirts worn by the dancers, there is little evidence that this was a style passed down from the eighteenth century; conversely, straw hats would have been ubiquitous.

Mauritian culture and the identity it was forging had therefore come a long way since the first arrival of settlers and slaves. That said, it still had a long journey to make, particularly during its days under British rule, when a huge influx of workers from another country would transform it further. But with the return of the name Mauritius, that was easy to turn into an adjective in English or French, it became more and more tempting—and accurate—to talk of something as being specifically 'Mauritian' without causing undue controversy.

The Séga, for all its enduring and uplifting magnificence, was a tradition originally rooted in sadness and anger at the predicament in which the wretched slaves found themselves. The French revolutionaries had quickly tried to ban slavery around French assets abroad, with mixed results: a shamefully large proportion of the island's population—fully 75 per cent—remained enslaved at the time of the British arrival. It would therefore become Farquhar's destiny to try to finally rid the island of this malevolence once and for all. And he knew it would not be straightforward.

12

TRANSITION

Amidst all the conceptual horrors of slavery, perhaps the biggest stains of all are its global reach and its sheer longevity. When, for instance, we read of the ancient Romans and their slaves, the way it is recounted by contemporaries as something so commonplace, so horribly *normal*, suggests that it was already a very well-established tradition predating history itself. Further, the fact that it occurred on every inhabited continent—leaving very few societies either totally safe or completely innocent—remains a burdensome legacy on our capricious species that must never be forgotten. To that end, the bitter reality is that it would have been surprising if those colonising Mauritius from the sixteenth to eighteenth centuries had *not* resorted to this odious practice, despite our enduring horror when we learn about it from our modern setting, where human rights remain amongst our most cherished and universal expectations.

The rationale for the near-global seismic shift away from slavery is highly complex and beyond the scope of this story. However, three drivers seem to have been morality, activism and the economy. First, a groundswell in revisiting various passages of the Bible during the Age of Enlightenment saw folk now interpreting the disciple Paul in particular as saying that slavery was against the Christian faith, and that freedom should be the default for every man, woman and child, regardless of their heritage. Second, this was backed up by organised movements of white and black activists throughout both the nations that owned and organised the trade (e.g. Britain and France) and those that provided them, of which the African continent as a whole was the most relentlessly blighted. This had been given extra impetus by the ultimately successful slave revolt in Saint-Domingue (now Haiti) from 1791 to 1804, which showed the world that inhumane treatment could not continue unabated and that organised slaves, like the famed Spartacus nearly two millennia before, could revolt with some success.

But despite these hugely important actions to move society away from the foetid evil of slavery, it is depressing to reflect that the third and biggest driver could well have been economics. The slave trade was making its investors less and less money, and a burgeoning middle class in western Europe at the birth of the Industrial Revolution saw more sense in paying their factory workers than in coping with the complexities of slavery. Indeed, some industrialists argued that in many ways slavery was now *undercutting* their ability to make a profit. Further, with many of the European landed gentry earning the bulk of their income from the slave-dependent plantations around the world, a move away from this set-up gave businessmen a fighting chance of levelling the profit-making playing field. Some of these industrialists would certainly have supported abolition for philosophical and ethical reasons, but definitely not all of them. Although there are, unsurprisingly, very few first-hand accounts of a slave's life in Mauritius during this period, we can be sure that many slave masters undertook cruel practices, and we know too that several French masters had children by their slaves. More likely than not these children were the result of sexual abuse.

TRANSITION

Although the bulk of slavery over the previous three centuries had revolved around the infamous triangle between Europe, Africa and the Americas, the rest of the world was just as affected by this horrendous trade. When the British arrived in Mauritius in 1810, it had been three years since the passing of the Abolition of the Slave Trade Act in London's Parliament, passionately supported from within—under the leadership of William Wilberforce—as well as beyond, with ex-slaves such as Olaudah Equiano publishing powerful treatises against its continuation. Crucially, although this banned the trade itself, many of the existing slaves around the world would not be freed until the 1830s or later. Indeed, from a French perspective, Napoleon's rule had specifically differentiated between sugar-producing colonies and *le métropole* regarding slavery.

Even so, it was pivotal for the recently arrived British to deal sensitively with the topic; as much as they wanted to ultimately free the slaves, it was also critical that they remained on good terms with the plantation owners who made the whole island's economy tick. The British had inherited a crushingly hierarchical system, where a tiny French elite of officials, landowners and merchants lorded over a small artisanal middle class, all of whom sat well above the 60,000 slaves of Malagasy, Mozambican and wider Indian Ocean descent. Even by the standards of the time, this wealth and power pyramid was short and squat.

Governor Farquhar was not an inherently bad man; his instincts were fair, and he did much to progress the issue despite it competing with many other priorities during his twelve-year tenure. By the same token, there were times when the British approach—driven by a desperation not to rock the boat—was half-hearted at best. On the plus side, treaties were sought with Madagascar and Zanzibar, the two slave-trade hubs that had furnished Mauritius for so long. First, Farquhar turned west to Madagascar, where a chieftain named Radama had taken over leadership of

STAR AND KEY

the Hova people in 1810. As they were the most influential of the various groups who made up the Malagasy Merina Kingdom, this in turn made him the island's most powerful man. Farquhar was at an advantage by mere dint of not being French. The former masters of Îsle de France had left a complicated and often unsavoury legacy in Madagascar, which made the door relatively easy to push open for the British.

Farquhar sent advance parties of friendship in 1816, led by trusted Mauritian Jacques Chardenoux, and then again in early 1817 under Captain Le Sage. Radama was keen for them to become blood brothers, and Le Sage was happy to oblige. Britain would also assist in Radama's claims of kingship by offering military support against any rivals. Although not a perfect set-up and with its own challenges, a treaty was nonetheless signed by each leader's representative on 23 October 1817, with four key articles set down: enduring friendship between the British and the Hova people; the prevention of sale and transfer of slaves from Madagascar into any other country; an annual British allowance of £2,000 a year for three years to Radama personally, to help ease the loss of income from the slave trade; and a commitment by Radama to stop any Malagasy piracy in the region. Radama's request that he also henceforth be acknowledged as 'King of Madagascar' was also accepted pragmatically by the British, and they threw various military materiel into the bargain too to smooth the deal. This was backed up by a further treaty the year after, permitting British warships in local waters the right to inspect any ships that they believed might be transporting illicit human cargo.

Turning their eyes northwest to Zanzibar was a more complex challenge. The small island off the coast of what is now Tanzania was under the long-term control of the Imam of Muscat, Sayyid Said. Although he had a natural affinity with the British, like Radama, having dealt with them in previous India-related squabbles, the sad reality of revenue was the crux of the issue.

152

TRANSITION

Considering only economic rather than base human imperatives, both sides were aware that stopping this horrendous trade in its tracks might be good for the people themselves, but it would destroy with one swipe the livelihood of the Imam and many that answered to him. An initial outreach in 1815 under Sir Evan Nepean, governor of Bombay, had not quite worked, being couched in words that essentially asked the Imam, 'if he were to just stop the trade like a jolly good fellow, it would be most appreciated'. Understanding the desire but having absolutely no motive to acquiesce, Said ignored it. Only in 1821 did Britain take it a step further, sending Captain Fairfax Moresby on a fact-finding mission to Zanzibar before he wrote an impassioned and better-informed plea to the Imam, hinting that the British were not going to stop annoying him until he engaged with them.

Still, tightropes needed to be walked. The British knew that in this case, requesting a treaty that demanded an immediate cessation of the trade would fall on very deaf ears. So Farquhar sent Moresby to Muscat in June 1822, to explore the art of the possible. In fact, by this stage Said was caught between a rock and a hard place. He knew that a treaty would be frowned upon by his subjects, many of whom still believed in the concept of slavery. Conversely, he knew only too well which way the Indian Ocean wind was blowing—namely, wherever Britain told it to blow—and he would much rather have them as a strategic protector than as an enemy. Further, he knew that any personal agreement with this global power would be a de facto recognition of his own prime status as the most powerful man in East Africa and its vicinity. On 22 September he eventually acceded to the Moresby Treaty, as it would be known, agreeing to the prohibition and prevention of slaves 'to any Christian nation'. As with the treaty with Madagascar, an annexe allowed the British to inspect and seize any Arab ships containing slaves within a stipulated area of the Western Indian Ocean.

153

STAR AND KEY

But it wasn't all proactive goodness by the new masters of Mauritius. Removing slavery overnight, for all its unimpeachable morality, would see Mauritius' economy destroyed in much the same time frame. Further, the plantation owners—never the most forward looking—were seemingly allergic to change, and they held much of that economic stability in their hands. It was an open secret that they carried on an illicit slave trade, smuggling people onto an island that still had plenty of remote creeks and forests. It was equally well known that the British administrators—for all their bluster—turned a blind eye to these activities. Some even went further. In the 1820s, the Chief Registrar of the island, whose task it was to keep tabs on and suppress the illicit trade, was personally involved in importing more slaves from East Africa. It has been calculated that a further 30,000 slaves were illicitly sent to the island in the 1820s alone.

Needless to say, this caused ongoing embarrassment for the British back in Europe, and their high-and-mighty pleas to their neighbours to enforce a cessation to the trade were usually rebuked with words along the lines of 'Stop being hypocritical, then you can lecture us.' Even after Farquhar left in 1822 and his successor Sir Lowry Cole arrived in June 1823, progress was glacial. The plantation owners' intransigence in ceasing the practice was proving to be powerful. Their legal mouthpiece became Adrien d'Épinay, a local lawyer whose wider contribution to civil society had also included constructing Mauritius' first steam-driven sugar mill near the town of Quatre Cocos and founding the Bank of Mauritius, as well as Mauritius' first daily independent newspaper, *Le Cernéen*, whose name harked back to those early Portuguese days. While the lack of local engagement on the abolition of slavery persisted on-island, d'Épinay twice—in 1831 and again in 1833—made his way to London to fight the case for its continuation—at least until such time as the plantation owners were properly compensated. To some extent he succeeded.

154

TRANSITION

One could make a weak case that d'Épinay, in his role as lawyer, was merely representing his clients' position: they feared ruin and there appeared little alternative. Conversely, reading extracts from his editorials in *Le Cernéen*—stipulating that slaves shouldn't own property, shouldn't be allowed to be married and that protectors of slaves were the enemy of the colony, all while using unrepentantly racist language—makes it clear that he was politically very closely aligned with the plantation owners. Very few cultures of that time could compare to modern ones when it comes to the freedoms and rights that we now believe to be sacrosanct. Even so, the prevalent views in Mauritius were strikingly antediluvian in their outlook, and this reputation was becoming increasingly well-known abroad. As historian T. V. Bulpin recounts: '[Mauritian] society seemed at its lowest ebb, rent with the most violent personal hatreds, abuses, corruptions and sentiments so pathetically backward that Mauritius remained in bad odour for many years afterwards. Few visitors save the most superficial had a good word for the place.' It was equally reflected in the British press at the time—admittedly influenced by the abolitionists—that the Mauritian plantation owners were 'the most despicable and cruel slave-owners of the British colonies'. The La Bourdonnais years of the eighteenth century suddenly felt very far away. That said, it would perhaps be wrong to tar all with the same brush. Despite their general reluctance for societal change, some of the plantation owners were also hard-working, industrious and innovative. Their adherence to tradition and family solidarity was, they felt, the most important thing they had as they developed this unique way of life which was so isolated from the world's general tumult.

Part of their ongoing resentment might have sprung from Britain choosing a succession of governors whose instinct erred on the side of strict martial discipline rather than truly listening. In the seventeen years after Farquhar left, rather disheartened, in

STAR AND KEY

1823, his post was taken up first by Sir Lowry Cole, then by Sir Charles Colville and finally by Sir William Nicolay. All three were army officers first and diplomatic administrators second. While none provoked violence or suggested armed solutions to the behaviours they encountered, neither did they seek out common ground with their subjects, or suggest viable, imaginative, strategic alternatives to the challenges they were facing. Equally, it could just have been the planters' seething resentment that their masters were no longer from France—a country that they had distanced themselves from politically, but where much of their cultural heritage still lay. By the late 1820s, although the British had been firmly in power in Mauritius for nearly two decades, there were still swathes of the population who took the French side when the choice was binary.

Never was this more obvious than in April 1828, when a ship arrived that had aboard Sir Hudson Lowe. Lowe had famously been the senior administrator of the remote British island colony of Saint Helena in the Atlantic Ocean during the period 1815–21, when it was home to the most famous prisoner in the world: Napoleon Bonaparte. Much had been said of Lowe's harsh treatment of his prisoner—some possibly true, much undoubtedly rumour—and many still believed that it was Lowe who had slowly poisoned Napoleon to his early death aged 51, even if modern evidence suggests that it is more likely he died of stomach cancer. Either way, owing to his reputation, Lowe was made to feel highly unwelcome for the mere three days he spent in Mauritius, being relentlessly jeered or having stones thrown at him. Fearing for his life, he soon fled.

Yet even the power of the mob couldn't halt the march of history. The Act for the Abolition of Slavery came into effect in the British Parliament in January 1834. Acknowledging that it had to be a gradual process, it stipulated that all slaves aged over 6 would, as of 1 February 1835, be transitioned to officially

TRANSITION

become apprentice labourers. Six years after that, they would in theory be totally free—although this had to be cut short in 1839 in the face of a revolt by Port Louis apprentices, who claimed that their lot had barely changed since they had supposedly been emancipated. The British government would in turn offer compensation for that period, which was more than long enough to set up alternative business practices. The mid-1830s therefore saw a frenzied period of counting and valuing the slaves to ensure commensurate 'reward' was received for them. A total of 68,613 slaves made it onto the official papers. While the planters claimed that this would mean a total of £4 million compensation, the British calculated it as just over half this. Either way, with the best part of £70 per slave, the already wealthy planters were hardly in dire straits.

As this momentous and overdue societal shift was carrying on in the 1820s and 1830s, two equally startling changes were happening to Mauritian topography. The first came about because the emancipated slaves were free to leave the estate camps, squalid dormitories and insanitary huts that had been their homes for far too long. Rather than all automatically migrating to the few cities, where their treatment would be unknown but could be guessed at, there was an overwhelming tendency to set up new villages across the island. Indeed, until then, villages as we recognise them were essentially non-existent on the island; the few towns were overwhelmingly separated only by farms and plantations. The founding of many of Mauritius' numerous villages therefore dates from this era.

The second and more immediate change concerned the crops those farms and plantations were growing. Up until then, a wide variety of crops had been grown—sugar, coffee, cloves, nutmeg, indigo and cotton, to name a few—with many farms also tending to cattle. Yet the cyclones were unrelenting, washing away the less hardy crops in the early nineteenth century, much as they

STAR AND KEY

had previously. Further, an unknown cattle epidemic swept the island from December 1822, with rats proliferating exponentially to make things even more miserable. Mauritian crop growers needed a break, and it inadvertently came on 27 June 1825. Having hitherto always taxed 10 shillings on every 100 pounds of sugar exported from Mauritius, the British authorities now decided it was time to let it flourish and be sold in their markets, as they had with their West Indian sugar crops. The two could now compete with each other, as it was hoped that the Mauritian plantations, like their West Indian counterparts, would soon transition to labour by free workers rather than slavery—which they eventually did, kicking and screaming.

Ever since the Dutch had first introduced the crop from the East two centuries earlier, sugar cane had been the one crop that had usually flourished in the face of Mauritius' unforgiving climate. With this huge new financial incentive, almost every farm on the island that had not grown sugar before now switched to it immediately, making the island essentially a monoculture. The speed of this change was unprecedented. In 1825, 20,000 tons were cultivated. By 1830, 55,000 acres of sugar had been processed by 160 mills into nearly 34,000 tons of sugar. This was a 113-per-cent increase in land devoted to growing the crop since the British had taken over. Even this would be dwarfed within twenty years, as by 1850 almost two thirds of the entire island's land would be ring-fenced for growing sugar. And where sugar cultivation grew, so did all the industries dependent on it, including the mills, banking and insurance, to name a few. Mauritius had taken the plunge and put all its economic prospects into one basket. Indeed, by the 1860s, Mauritius would be the British Empire's largest sugar producer, processed through an incredible 303 sugar factories by 1863.

But all this sweet-flavoured profit wasn't going to cultivate itself. Often being their own worst enemies, the planters had for

TRANSITION

years made no effort to offer the slaves a decent diet, resulting in a horrendously high mortality rate. This was exacerbated by their renting out slaves—away from their families—across to other plantations, meaning that slave birth rates dropped noticeably. With the rate of sugar production and its associated hard labour now growing fast, the planters, despite their jaw-dropping pig-headedness, realised that—slaves or no slaves—a huge amount of new labour would be needed in Mauritius at relatively short notice. Ironically, one of the first to work this out was Adrien d'Épinay. In 1825, very soon after the lifting of the sugar tax, he paid for the passage of a handful of labourers from India to work on his estate alongside the slaves. The very first had in fact arrived late the previous year from India and Ceylon (Sri Lanka), including from Calcutta (Kolkata), Madras (Chennai) and Colombo.

D'Épinay's motives were hardly altruistic: these were contractual workers who would eat less into his profits than either local workers or slaves. Although many of these workers rebelled due to the inhumane conditions that they were predictably put under and returned home a few months later, they nevertheless proved to be the vanguard of a mass immigration from India over the ensuing decades that would transform the culture and outlook of the island. In the late 1830s, with the transitional apprenticeship system introduced by the British being hideously abused by the planters, the former slaves had absolutely no desire to carry on working under these conditions for such irredeemable masters. Dockworking and fishing would be tough, but surely better than still being a slave in all but name. Such was the backdrop to the acute need for cheap labour in Mauritius from the 1830s onwards, to stave off Mauritian economic ruin.

D'Épinay's new policy would be known as indentured labour. In a rare moment of planning and to ensure that there would be no internal competition within the empire, the British authorities set up a recruiting office in Calcutta for the joint benefit of

STAR AND KEY

Mauritius, Trinidad and Jamaica. As has previously been noted by countless researchers, whilst indentured labour wasn't slavery, neither was it a million miles away from it. Initial recruitment, predictably, was targeted at young males, who were contractually bound—indentured—for five years to work on the sugar estates. Achingly empty promises were doubtless made about the paradise island—and living conditions—that awaited them. With the Indian economy in the doldrums—especially in the Bihar region, where there was a collapse in poppy growing due to a ban on opium in China—they may not have taken much persuading. In reality, though they would be paid a salary (albeit a pitiful one), conditions were still atrocious: food was always insubstantial, movement off the estate was heavily controlled and sanitation was essentially non-existent. The contract of ten-hour days, seven days a week, was a minimum that was often abused. At the end of the contract, the workers were able to return to India, yet despite most having had a horrendous time, the majority chose to stay on-island. This likely had less to do with conditions being markedly worse in India, and more to do with the promises of higher wages once they were no longer under contract. Further, there were numerous examples of former workers soon being arrested as 'vagrants' due to a legal loophole. Ultimately, many had cut off their links to India, whether they had chosen to or not.

Yet ultimately other options became available beyond the torrid life of a sugar-cane worker. Infrastructure was needed to help ship the huge quantities of sugar that were being grown, and this meant labourers were needed to build roads, railways and ports. These were by no means the first influx of workers from India—a number of skilled workers had arrived during the eighteenth century too, as reflected fairly accurately in *Paul et Virginie*. That said, by the middle of the century, the trickle of Indian arrivals had become a stream, which in turn become something of a flood—although it should be stressed that not all arrivals from

TRANSITION

India were indentured labourers; there were many skilled, middle-class traders too. In 1842, 6,000 new arrivals were greeted. Yet by the census of August 1846, the island's total population of 158,462 counted amongst them 56,245 who identified as Indian. Not all were indentured labourers; some were free traders. But by 1871, Indians would form 68 per cent of the total population, with a growing proportion of them having been born on the island, who would soon be known as Indo-Mauritians. Indeed, with the sugar cultivation proving so economically successful, the island's population would nearly quadruple between 1837 (just under 96,000) and 1891 (over 370,000). Early on, between 1842 and 1860, the recruiters were paid a lump sum if the proportion of male-to-female recruits was respected. The proportion was initially fixed as forty women to every 100 men immigrants, although that was later ditched as unsustainable.

Although not conceptually new, there seemed little doubt that the idea of indentured labour on this scale had been a success if viewed purely through an economic lens. Equally, it was a process that continued to pay lip service to personal rights and dignity. From 1835 to 1849, during the first fourteen years of labour arriving overwhelmingly from India, there was no central arrival point where they could be processed, causing administrative headaches. In 1849, an old French building on the outskirts of Port Louis in the Trou Fanfaron—named after Nicolas Fanfaron, who had once lived beside the 'Trou', or crater—was earmarked to be transformed into a much-needed hub. It continued to be added to over the years, as a greater number of arrivals meant a greater need for more processing space, and would soon be known simply as the Immigration Depot. Between 1848 and 1923, when the practice was finally ended, it has been calculated that just under half a million indentured labourers (mostly Indians but also others, including thousands of Chinese) were processed there—at a bottleneck that helped shape the future of

161

STAR AND KEY

Mauritius today. After 1923, the building was left derelict and ignored, with rampant construction work from the 1950s onwards needlessly demolishing part of this integral piece of Mauritian social history. Only from the 1970s did a groundswell of support and interest shine a new light on the remaining structure of the old depot, which from 1987 onwards was referred to as 'Aapravasi Ghat'—the Hindi translation of Immigration Depot—to reflect the origin of those who had so optimistically arrived from 1835 onwards. It was declared a UNESCO World Heritage Site in 2006.

After such an upheaval in the first half of the nineteenth century, Mauritius was finally beginning to settle. A change in the imperial leadership of the colony had shaken it violently, but it had also given it new opportunities and a chance to improve its lot internally as well as its reputation externally. As the century progressed, the British masters were able to oversee unprecedented economic growth on a small island that was now home to a raft of ethnicities, cultures, languages and religions. Such diversity would present a plethora of challenges, yet ultimately be the island's strategic trump card. What the British now needed to focus on, however, wasn't just the internal issues around Mauritius, but how this increasingly boisterous, assertive and disproportionately powerful little island would now choose to act with its neighbours—not to mention the smorgasbord of dependencies that Mauritius itself now had responsibility for.

162

13

THE NOISY NEIGHBOURHOOD

Nothing has ever really been straightforward in the Indian Ocean.

For all its immense size, Madagascar remained something of an enigma to the British in Mauritius. Whilst fully recognising that the Malagasy had provided Mauritius, and Île de France before it, with countless slaves, the interior of the vast island was still not well charted—not least because it had always been regarded as a hotbed of 'fever', or malaria. To explore Madagascar's forests was seen by some as a shortcut to illness and death. The tribal make-up remained sketchy, with the cultures on the island far removed from those of the Mascarenes, which had been uninhabited when Europeans first started landing there. Linguists in the nineteenth century had worked out that the nearest languages to Malagasy were not on mainland Africa, with which it shared no kinship, but across the Indian Ocean amongst the Austronesian-speaking peoples of Southeast Asia. Unequivocally this meant that upwards of 1,500 years previously, the original Malagasy had travelled—somehow—across the Indian Ocean and settled here, and apparently nowhere else. It remains something

STAR AND KEY

of a human mystery as to exactly how or why. Only much later did Bantu, Arab and (eventually) European settlers arrive.

As we have seen, Madagascar's indirect response to the pillaging of its people for the industry of Mauritian colonists was either to act as a base for piracy or for the Malagasy to practise piracy themselves; this seemingly timeless menace only died down in the 1810s. The Merina Kingdom was essentially an absorption of various tribes as part of a growing policy of military expansion, continued lustily by 'King' Radama with his plentiful supply of British military materiel and training. As far as the other tribes in the area were concerned, such as the Betsimisaraka and the Benzanozano, the aggressive colonials weren't the British but their own tribal neighbours. This internal warfare ultimately suited the British fine. So long as they had a healthy trading base, with the kingdom's support, and a steady supply of food provided to Mauritius, and as long as the Malagasy were only interested in attacking each other on-island, then Madagascar did not continue to pose any genuine threat to its much smaller and less-populated neighbour nearly 500 miles to its east.

Much closer to Mauritian shores lay Réunion island. It had gone through its own naming odyssey, with Île Bourbon being consigned to the dustbin after the French Revolution, the name Réunion then being applied in 1793, only for it to be renamed Île Bonaparte at the height of the Napoleonic Wars. After the 1814 Treaty of Paris, Réunion was again chosen. It was allowed to remain French, with the British aware that after the events of 1810–15, both locally and internationally, France was unlikely to mount any attempt to retake Mauritius. The British wisely chose to adopt the mantra, 'Keep your friends close and your enemies closer', in their limited dealings with their neighbour. When the French on Réunion started claiming parts of the east coast of Madagascar for themselves in 1829, they were soon repelled by Malagasy forces and returned with their tails between their sea

164

THE NOISY NEIGHBOURHOOD

legs. The revolutionary upheavals in France in 1830 had in any case cut off their funding for any more external forays.

The lack of a good natural harbour had always been Réunion's Achilles heel. As a result, despite its proximity, Réunion had never held the same cachet as Mauritius and was often more of an afterthought to the big European powers squabbling over its sister island. Even when the sixteenth-century Portuguese had regularly used Cirne as their depot on trips to and from the East, Réunion (then known as Santa Apollonia) was left virtually untouched. The Dutch had likewise paid it scant regard, not least as their official claim on Mauritius in 1638 had immediately been met by a similar claim on Santa Apollonia/Réunion by France, even though it was based on nothing more than an initial fact-finding visit that year by François Cauche and Salomon Goubert. There was not even a temporary French outpost there, although that didn't stop French sailors from using it as a deportation camp for mutinous sailors. Only in 1665 did the French East India Company properly start settling the island in a meaningful way.

Being so close to Mauritius meant, of course, that Réunion was as susceptible to the same climatic catastrophes that befell its sister island, most notably the cyclones that tore through almost every summer. The cyclone of 1806 was a particular horror, and convinced the planters that coffee—one of the mainstays of the island's economy hitherto—was simply not going to be a viable and profitable option anymore. Like Mauritius, they planted far more sugar cane—and the need was urgent. The loss of Saint-Domingue (Haiti) in the West Indies after the slave revolt left France with an acute need to source sugar from elsewhere from 1809 onwards. Cannily, though, they chose not to go 'full monoculture'. In 1841, a 12-year-old Réunion boy born into slavery, Edmond Albius, found that he had a natural skill as a horticulturalist. He worked out a technique for hand-pollinating vanilla orchids quickly, which meant that it could then

STAR AND KEY

grow abundantly, far from its native Latin American habitat. Within fifteen years, Réunion had become the world's largest vanilla producer.

Not that Réunion's overall attitude to slavery was any more enlightened than in Mauritius. It took the skilled hand of the island's administrator from 1838 to 1841, Admiral Anne Chrétien Louis de Hell, to instil a gradual hearts-and-minds change in mentality, and only in 1848 was a full abolition on the island finally recognised. Yet social progress thereafter sped up, with the first Creole governor, Louis Henri Delisle, being elected in August 1852, a post that he filled with distinction for six years. Again, the British on Mauritius saw in Réunion an island that it could trade with when needed, but that no longer posed a direct security threat to its neighbour. The greater priority at the time was to take stock of and consolidate Britain's own wider possessions that it had, almost by accident, picked up on its meandering journey.

The largest, nearest and most important of these was Rodrigues, the third of the Mascarene islands, settled in a lonely piece of ocean another 350 miles northeast. Known distantly to the medieval Arab sailors as Dina Moraze, it had led its own idyllic existence, free from human corruption, until 1507, when it was stumbled upon by the ship of Diogo Fernandes Pereira, which had been blown well off course by a cyclone. It was left alone for another twenty-one years until 1528, when another explorer, Dom Diogo Rodrigues, decided to see if it was real, and modestly offered it his name for future map-makers, who duly obliged. Being so far from the natural trade routes and reliable winds of the Indian Ocean, neither the Portuguese nor subsequently the Dutch thought it worth the effort to go there for much more than to obtain fresh supplies to try to counter the various rats rampaging through Mauritius through the sixteenth and seventeenth centuries. As with Réunion, its lack of

166

THE NOISY NEIGHBOURHOOD

a natural harbour was offset by its attractions, in particular its stunning lagoon.

But just as the pirates of Île Sainte Marie were warming up to cause carnage in 1690, along came nine French Protestant pioneers from the other side of the world in search of nothing but some peace and quiet. The nine Huguenots—all bachelors—had been persecuted in their homeland and were seeking a refuge where they could practise their faith, deep in nature. Catching wind of Rodrigues, they set sail on the undersized frigate *Hirondelle* and arrived at the lonely island on 1 May 1691. It is to our great good fortune that their leader, 52-year-old François Leguat, kept a journal of the two years that these newcomers spent on the island—a journal that was eventually published in 1708. Except for Pitcairn Island after the mutiny on the *Bounty*, it is almost unheard of in history to know the names of each and every original settler of an island. However, there is a twist to this assertion; on making land, the group saw mysterious Dutch carvings on some of the trees, with various names amongst them. Who these Dutch sailors had been—and whether they were part of the Mauritian colony or were others who had been shipwrecked and forgotten here—was unknown.

The small French group was greeted in the northwest of the island by gentle, green and fertile hills, comparatively few mosquitoes, no venomous snakes and an abundance of other wildlife that charmed them—and fed them—for the next twenty-four months. Leguat's journal captures the plants and animals of this Eden in detail. Chief amongst these were the huge land tortoises and sea turtles in their hundreds that grappled for space on the beaches—the former to feed, the latter to lay eggs. Gentle dugongs sometimes entered the reef to accompany the embarrassment of fish, and the crabs were the size of a fist. Most enigmatic of all, however, was the Solitaire, the close cousin of the Dodo (and still found at that time in decent numbers on Rodrigues),

167

STAR AND KEY

unaware that its nearest relative was on the cusp of going extinct at that very time—and that its own fate within fifty years would be similar. So named because it preferred its own company, as highly territorial birds tend to, it was described as swan-sized, light brown in colour and flightless—similar to, yet distinct from the Dodo. Its single egg in a rough ground nest echoed the approach of its cousin, although annoyingly there is no record of its call—confirmation of which might have helped us deduce how the Dodo obtained its immortal name. All these tales of Arcadian life were later read by many in Europe, amongst them Daniel Defoe, who is thought to have been equally as inspired by Leguat's story as he was by that of shipwrecked sailor Alexander Selkirk, when conjuring up his immortal *Robinson Crusoe*.

Regardless, this location on the island was considered ideal for a settlement, and the *Hirondelle* was sent away. The pioneers' experience over the following two years confirms to us, as well as any source, that an earthly paradise simply doesn't exist. Despite the abundance of food, the lack of threat from others, the time they had on their hands due to not having to farm and the lovely climate outside of the cyclone season, the men predictably became lonely and homesick—and, claimed the diary, they greatly missed 'the only joy of man', which one has to take as meaning the company of women. They yearned for home once more. First, they had to get to the nearest island, which was Mauritius. Constructing an open boat and taking little with them, they left their island home and after eight days made landfall at Black River on Mauritius' west coast, where they had spotted a few Dutch huts. Finding the Dutch governor, Roelof Diodati, who had been there less than a year, they expected something of a welcome.

Instead, with piracy at its appalling height, Diodati suspiciously thought the worst of these poor homeless refugees and promptly locked them up, initially on the mainland and later on

168

THE NOISY NEIGHBOURHOOD

an islet 'one hour off the coast'—possibly the one now known as Île aux Bénitiers (Clam Island). Despite pleading to be sent home, they were given little leeway by the Dutch and few comforts. Only after three years of wretched imprisonment did agreement arrive from the Dutch authorities, and only then to let them ride on the *Suraag* to Batavia in the Dutch East Indies—in the opposite direction from where they wanted to go. With little choice on offer they boarded, arrived in Batavia and eventually found their various ways home. Persecution, it seemed, was better than loneliness.

Such had been the first attempt at settlement on Rodrigues. It saw little human life for the next few decades, bar a British ship in 1706, surveying the northwest of the island, which was underwhelmed and promptly left. The British motive had doubtless been to see if it would be a good place from which to launch possible attacks on the wider ocean. It was very much with this in mind that the French went further in 1725, soon after arriving in Îsle de France, when they sent a party to Rodrigues to map it and set up beacons around the island to show that it was now claimed. Only transient sailors stayed overnight there, though, until the governorship of Barthélemy David in the 1750s, when the ongoing food shortages on the island meant they needed to pillage Rodrigues' huge and tasty tortoises—with the influx of these handsome, stately beasts to Îsle de France soon reaching a completely unsustainable 30,000 a year. A handful of those who collected and traded them—and therefore wiped them out— chose to stay on Rodrigues, since when the island has always had human habitation.

Those who stayed included a French officer, a corporal, a surgeon and a dozen slaves, and they met up with visiting French scientist Abbé Pingre in June 1761. The latter had arrived as he had worked out that Rodrigues would be one of the best places from which to observe the transit of Venus on 6 June. He was

STAR AND KEY

amazed at—and slightly jealous of—the simple but rather bucolic life led by these men (the free ones, at least). He was even more astonished when on 15 September a British squadron landed and claimed the island, with the tiny group of inhabitants showing no desire whatsoever to resist. However, the British had clearly been expecting reinforcements that never came, and on Christmas Day they meekly skulked away again. Rather pathetic it may have been, but it did open certain eyes to the reality that Rodrigues could be a hugely useful staging post for a future invasion of Îsle de France.

Yet as the winds of change spread in the first decade of the nineteenth century, France no longer had the desire or funds to maintain any meaningful connection with Rodrigues. Abandoning all their support, they left it to the five families who had by then made their homes there, headed respectively by Philibert Marragon, Michel Gorry, Etienne Rochetaing, Germain Le Gros and Mathurin Brehinier, as well as their eighty-two slaves. Brehinier's home and shipbuilding yard were in the northwestern corner which now harbours the island's capital, named Port Mathurin after him. When the British finally did arrive in August 1809 (see Chapter 9), this time stronger and better pre-pared, resistance was negligible. Yet even after taking over a rela-tively successful colony on Mauritius, the British found it hard to know what to do with Rodrigues, and how to persuade many people to emigrate there. The on-island defence force only needed to be skeletal, and even a decade after slavery was abol-ished, in 1834, the island's population barely hovered around 250—augmented in 1843 by its first police station. The British thought they had found another use for it in 1856 as a quarantine post for any potentially sick indentured labourers arriving from India, but the idea was quickly shelved as impractical.

What did this tiny community do all day? In essence, Rodrigues became a farm supplying food to Mauritius itself.

170

THE NOISY NEIGHBOURHOOD

Growing beans, oranges, lemons, onions, garlic and maize, producing outstanding honey and salting the plentiful fish and octopus, these would be shipped over to their mother island on a tiny 25-ton boat. The ships may now be larger, but this is still the main produce being grown on the island for wider Mauritian consumption. By this stage, Mauritius needed to import almost everything except sugar. The main distraction had been shipwrecks—lots of them: the *Queen Victoria* in April 1843, the *Oxford* five months later, the *Samuel Smith* in November 1847—these were just some of the ships that found it too hard to navigate Rodrigues' tricky reefs in that decade alone. The scant good news for those who were shipwrecked was that the culture of this isolated island had developed in a serene way, meaning that it gained a reputation for friendliness towards all visitors—a reputation that it maintains strikingly to this day.

Over 1,000 miles to the north of Mauritius lay another of its dependencies, a group of islands that most certainly were not seen then—as they are now—as the final word in paradise. Known about since 1503, and soon after being used as yet another grim base for either pirates or slave traders, the stunningly beautiful islands of the Seychelles were deceptively promising. Even so, there is a decent chance that those trailblazing Austronesian sailors of the early first millennium who eventually colonised Madagascar may well have used the Seychelles as a staging post. In 1609 they received some unplanned visitors. The English East India Company's ship *Ascension* was on its way north to India when a storm blew it sharply off course to the west. On 19 January the crew spotted the green-clad hills of land and gingerly made their way there for repairs. They were stunned by the new Eden they had stumbled upon: a millpond lagoon dripping with fish, freshwater streams plentifully skidding down the hills, ample tortoises, coconut palms and birds ... and, most importantly, no people. Restocked and repaired, they sailed off

STAR AND KEY

and reported their findings on their arrival. Amazingly, no one acted upon it.

This was odd, as the Seychelles certainly had some benefits: being equatorial rather than tropical, they missed the annual horrors of the cyclone season. Yet they were essentially uninhabited by any permanent settlement until the French East India Company, wanting to consolidate its Indian Ocean holdings, laid a 'Stone of Possession' in 1756 on the main island of Mahé, under the eye of Captain Nicholas Morphay. Formerly drifting between the names the Seven Sisters or the Admiral Islands, Morphay chose to formalise things by naming them after the then minister of finance, Jean Moreau de Séchelles.

Their profile remained relatively low for nearly forty years, save for two important events. First, in 1769, French navigator/explorers Abbé Rochon and Jacques de Grenier tested their theory that sailing to India via the Seychelles rather than the Mascarenes would be faster and safer. This would affect future trade routes. Second, a year later, French colonists were encouraged to come from Mauritius along with their slaves. This is usually regarded as the first proper settling of the islands, and more importantly, these would become the ancestors of the Seychelles' modern-day population. But the aftermath of the French Revolution, as we have seen, kick-started a hive of aggression and activity amongst the other powers, keen to pounce on France's temporary weakness and distractions. The British got there first.

Jean Baptiste de Quincy, the French administrator of the islands, had until then cannily protected himself in the 1790s by allowing French corsairs to use the islands as a safe base from which to attack anyone non-French. Described by a passing British commodore as 'a perfect Frenchman of the old school ... combining ease with pride, making him appear like a walking testimonial to the honour of *la grande nation*', Quincy was also

172

THE NOISY NEIGHBOURHOOD

no fool. Quietly having his morning coffee on Mahé on 16 May 1794, he spotted a menacing British frigate called *Orpheus* coming into view, and it was clearly not popping in to share his pot of coffee. Sure enough, Captain Henry Newcome demanded that the islands be handed quietly over to the UK, as more ships were soon to arrive and no one wanted to use force. Quincy was right to trust his instincts and believe Newcome's claim, agreeing to negotiate terms of capitulation. More British ships were indeed arriving, and Quincy's pragmatism allowed those already living there to be protected as neutrals.

It hadn't all been easy thereafter. A short but intense sea battle occurred on 15 September 1801, when the British vessel *Victor* was attacked by the French ship the *Flèche*, which succeeded in destroying almost all the *Victor's* rigging. As a last-gasp Hail Mary, the British ran broadside to the *Flèche* and unleashed all their firepower. The *Flèche* was hit hard and began sinking ... only for its captain to run it aground and burn it before leaping onto land. In a sign of changing times, the captains then shook hands and drank a toast whilst congratulating each other for the courage that each had shown during the fight. What this had shown, however, was that the Seychelles were exposed. After the Battle of Grand Port and the subsequent seismic shift in power from France to Britain in Mauritius, it was imperative that the new masters solidified and formalised their wider possessions to embed their new status and to ensure that they did not revert once more into a pirate lair. The Seychelles would now be a dependency of Mauritius, a situation that would remain until 1903. Its first overseer would be Royal Marine Lieutenant Bartholomew Sullivan.

His frustrations mounted quickly. As in Mauritius, Réunion and elsewhere, the predictable intransigence against the impending abolition of slavery was evident in the Seychelles too. Using a loophole in the law that technically allowed slave ownership, if not slave trading, settlers found a way to circumvent the limited British efforts to phase the industry out. Sullivan personally tried his hardest, on one occasion taking a rowing boat under cover of darkness from Mahé to the island of Praslin in order to confiscate an illicit new arrival he had heard rumours about. On this occasion his bravery was rewarded, and he was able to ensure that no one profited. Yet he knew he was fighting an uphill battle, and soon resigned.

Sullivan's successors hardly had better luck until the 1830s, when these dreamy islands realised that harvesting coconuts from the countless palm trees on the islands was easier and more profitable than growing crops that needed constant, back-breaking tending. Maize, rice, cotton and sugar were quietly abandoned. What annoyed those in the small colony most was that they were under the direct jurisdiction of Mauritius—itself a colony—rather than London, meaning that they often felt treated like second-hand goods. Even so, once the British had shored up their defences on the islands, there was not much more that the colonial masters needed to do, and after the abolition of slavery in the 1830s and its subsequent monitoring, the Seychelles began to trickle back down the Mauritian colonial leaders' list of priorities. Indeed, their capital only gained a permanent name (Victoria) in 1841. Until then, it was non-committally referred to as *L'Établissement*. Only the occasional famine made Mauritian authorities take much notice, as the Seychelles bumbled along.

None of these dependent islands were remotely large, yet they were still behemoths compared to another of Mauritius' offshore interests. This one, 650 miles north of Port Louis, had only been brought into the British/Mauritian fold in 1811, and it was tiny: two flat, corally islets, joined by a sandbank and barely 1.5 miles long, now known as Agaléga. We can't tell from the records if the Arab navigators ever found this minuscule out-

THE NOISY NEIGHBOURHOOD

crop, but in 1808 the French certainly knew of its existence, and Governor Decaen granted it for settlement to two businessmen, Laurent Barbé and a certain M. de Rosemond. On their arrival on this remote island they were confronted with a shipwreck and two skeletons, which they quickly buried in the shifting coral sands. These skeletons told a haunting tale, that was only pieced together later. The shipwreck had once been the *Creole*, owned by corsair Jean Dufour. In the early 1800s it had been captained by Dufour's son Robert, who was gallantly transporting his beautiful cousin Adélaïde d'Emmerez from Port Louis to Mahébourg, when it was spotted and chased by British pirate hunters, who understandably assumed it to be corsairing. Winds prevented the ship from returning, and they were chased remorselessly further and further north for two full days. In the darkness, like so many others in those waters, they too had struck the nasty reefs around the island, but they managed to scramble ashore. Whilst some of the crew tried to build a raft and sailed away for help, Robert stayed on the island with Adelaide. And help never came. Only in 1833 did one of the tiny island's later administrators find a bottle hidden in the sand. Within it lay a rough but harrowing message etched in crayon: 'I am responsible for her death, since it was I who proposed the voyage; but I swear before God before I die that that virtuous and lovely angel was always respected by me.' The little hill on the island is now known as Montagne d'Emmerez.

After the British took over Mauritius, they quickly dispatched Captain Briggs of the *Clorinde* to chart what was still a largely unmapped area. The treacherous reef around the islets made landing a challenge, yet that didn't prepare him for what he found: somehow another (unnamed) French corsair had quietly made his home there and had twelve African workers for company. It was evident that they were not slaves, as they could have overwhelmed the privateer easily. Together they cultivated the

175

STAR AND KEY

limited land with wheat and maize and none seemed particularly keen to leave. They didn't have much choice. The British finally saw an opportunity to make good use of Agaléga in 1827, when they sent over the perfect man to transform the island into something meaningful. Over the ensuing fourteen years, the industrious Auguste Leduc was to achieve on Agaléga a miniature version of what Mahé de La Bourdonnais had previously managed on Îsle de France.

Never overseeing a population of more than 127, Leduc was diligent, kind and imaginative. Planting countless coconut palms over the measly 6,000 acres of the island, he was soon producing mountains of coconut oil. He introduced a beehive and planted more maize, whilst also importing soil to grow more vegetables. More importantly, he built roads, a jetty and a mini-lighthouse for passing ships, a small hospital, some houses and a swimming pool, as well as a tiny prison that—tellingly—was hardly used. Being that rare thing—a nineteenth-century colonial leader with more than a touch of humanity—Leduc's patch may have been tiny and virtually unknown to anyone outside Mauritius, yet he showed that having a moral compass and a conscience went a long way towards being a model leader. He was sorely missed after his departure in 1841, but he left a small colony in rude health and in turn, one less patch of Mauritian turf for Port Louis to worry about.

Roughly halfway between Agaléga and Mauritius lay an even smaller islet with an even more tragic tale to tell. Tromelin had only been discovered in 1720 by the French sailor Jean Marie Briand de La Feuillée—not surprising, as it was only 1 mile long and essentially in the middle of nowhere. That he called this place Île de Sable (Sand Island) gave a fair indication of its lack of potential to support a colony. Yet four decades later, this is exactly what it found itself doing. In July 1761, the French East India Company's frigate *Utile* was doing what so many ships at

1. Although it is not proven that Portuguese explorer Dom Pedro de Mascarenhas (1480–1555) ever even set foot on Mauritius and its neighbouring islands, he gave his name in the early sixteenth century to the Mascarene Islands of Mauritius, Réunion and Rodrigues.

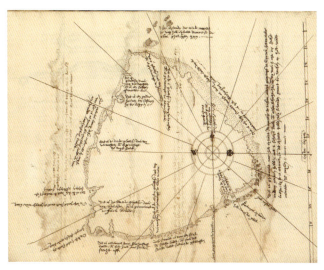

2. One of the earliest maps of Mauritius ever drawn: a 1603 rendering by Dutch sailor Reijer Cornelisz.

3. Dutch sailor Johann Theodor de Bry's early seventeenth-century sketch of life in the Mauritian colony has much to unpack, notably the deliberate portrayal of diligent hard work via fishing, barrel-making, blacksmithing, shipbuilding and receiving religious instruction. An outsized Dodo and some huge tortoises wander in the background.

4. Raouf Oderuth's rendition of the arrival of the first Malagasy slaves on Mauritius in 1640, aboard a VOC ship. Two iconic Mauritian mountains, Le Pieter Both and Le Pouce, can be seen in the background.

5. François Leguat (c.1639–1735)'s 1708 map of his pioneer colony on Rodrigues. Solitaires—Rodrigues' close cousins to the Dodo—can be seen dotted throughout the map.

6. Legendary pirate Olivier Levasseur (c.1690–1730), who made landfall on Mauritius more than once, threw an infamous cryptogram into the crowd as he walked to his hanging at the gallows in 1730, claiming that within it were details of where he had hidden a stash of booty. Despite massive efforts over the years, nothing has yet turned up.

7. Bertrand-François Mahé de La Bourdonnais (1699–1753), the man who, more than anyone, turned Mauritius from a colony going nowhere fast into a permanent settlement with a bright future.

8. A bust of Pierre Poivre (1719–1786), Mauritius' intendant for five years from 1767. The polymath Poivre was responsible for sneaking nutmeg and cloves into Mauritius, but also for nurturing and developing the gardens which would eventually be known as Le Jardin de Pamplemousses.

NAUFRAGE DE VIRGINIE.
Elle paroit un ange qui prend son vol vers les cieux.

9. Such was the popularity across Europe of Jacques-Henri Bernardin de St Pierre (1737–1814)'s novel *Paul et Virginie* that many believed it to be true and the protagonists to have been real. Here Virginie's fate is sealed in Mauritius' most famous (and romanticised) shipwreck, the *St Géran* (1744).

10. English explorer Matthew Flinders (1774–1814) was famous for giving the name Australia to that continent, but equally for his outrageous captivity on Mauritius from 1804 to 1810. This was used as one of the many pretexts for Britain to capture Mauritius from France.

11. Captain Nesbit Willoughby was the chief provocateur in the epic 1810 Battle of Grand Port but was thwarted by a dogged response. The result was victory for France and a lost eye for Willoughby, meaning that he sported a pirate-style eyepatch for the rest of his life.

12. Robert Surcouf (1773–1827), the most notorious—and successful—of the corsairs in Mauritius.

13. A late nineteenth-century poster of the various Mauritian stamps, including the legendary and vanishingly rare 1847 'Post Office' Penny Red and Two Penny Blue, the most expensive stamps ever sold at auction.

14. The Séga has evolved and has latterly become more of a staple for tourists, but its origins are interwoven with the early and darker days of slavery on the island.

15. French missionary Jacques-Désiré Laval (1803–1864), who converted thousands of Mauritians to Catholicism from 1841 onwards.

16. Sailing ships still dominated Port Louis' harbour in 1899.

17. Indentured labourers, like these photographed in the late nineteenth century, arrived in ships from India from the late 1830s onwards, and they and their descendants would change the face of Mauritius forever.

18. Old meets new. The concretising of the path around the Trou aux Cerfs volcano in Curepipe in 1937 was an ambitious modernisation project, but the methods used were still far behind Europe at the time.

19. From Malcy de Chazal onwards, Mauritius has nurtured many artists inspired by their natural surroundings. One of the most celebrated in the mid-twentieth century was Marcelle 'Didi' Lagesse, whose evocative style—as seen in this 1976 painting of Le Morne—captured Mauritius on the verge of major change.

20. Despite society changing in the mid-twentieth century, there were still families living in stunning colonial houses. This is the Piat family in the village of Moka in 1945.

21. The Champ de Mars racecourse has not only been a hugely successful hippodrome since the inauguration of the Mauritius Turf Club in 1812, but also the site of military training as well as the celebrations of Mauritian independence in 1968. Here, 'No Name' is seen winning the Maiden Cup, 1955.

22. Le Réduit has been the official home of many Mauritian leaders, be they French and British colonialists or Mauritian presidents.

23. As this Raouf Oderuth painting shows, sugar cane fields, as well as the labourers undertaking the back-breaking work of the harvest, have been the dominating factor in Mauritius' landscape for centuries. The crop was introduced to the island in the 1640s by Dutch doctor Jan Bockelberg.

24. The cyclone season has left destruction and desolation in its wake for centuries. The notorious Cyclone Carol in 1960 left many homeless.

25. The 'Father of the Nation', Sir Seewoosagur Ramgoolam (1900–1985).

26. The Chinese New Year Festival, seen here being celebrated in the 1950s. Although driven by the Sino-Mauritian community, it has long been celebrated by many Mauritians, regardless of their background.

27. A design that has barely changed in centuries: the Mauritian *pirogue*, photographed here in 1946. This staple of Mauritian fishermen is still visible off almost every shore around the island—these days with outboard motors, rather than sails.

28. The 1970s was a pivotal decade for Mauritius, when the much-predicted economic catastrophe was avoided and instead the island began to thrive. This photo shows a political gathering on Royal Road in Rose Hill.

29. The island of Diego Garcia in the Chagos Archipelago will continue to host a US military base leased out by the UK, but in 2024 the UK and Mauritius finally agreed a new way forward to return the Chagossians and their descendants. Even so, a rocky road lies ahead to draft a treaty that satisfies Mauritius, the UK and the US—not to mention the Chagossians themselves.

30. The Pink Pigeon, one of Mauritius' nine remaining endemic bird species, and one of its most iconic. Its incredible restoration from no more than ten individuals in the late 1970s to a much healthier population is a great success story, but speaks volumes about the destruction of Mauritius' natural habitat.

31. Mauritius' national park at the Black River Gorges boasts stunning landscapes, but its endemic and indigenous plants and trees are under enormous threat from invasive and exotic species.

32. Mauritius' worst ecological disaster: the bizarre shipwreck of the oil tanker *MV Wakashio* in 2020, which galvanised many Mauritians into wanting to protect their unique island's riches more than ever.

THE NOISY NEIGHBOURHOOD

the time were doing: illegally transporting slaves from Madagascar to Mauritius, in this case 160 Malagasy men, women and children. Yet Captain Jean de Lafargue had been provided with conflicting naval charts, and trying to find a middle ground, proceeded instead to go wildly off course. Although hundreds of miles north of Mauritius, he pressed on, only to crash onto the reefs of the virtually unknown Tromelin island.

Nearly 100 of the Malagasy slaves never had a chance and drowned while locked in the hold. The crew of 122 and the remaining sixty slaves did manage to find a way to the island, and soon worked as a team to catch birds and turtles, and dug a hole in which to collect water. Two makeshift camps were soon erected, each with an oven. All this industry in the face of hardship was too much for de Lafargue, who soon went mad. His lieutenant, Barthélémy Castellan du Vernet, took over and committed to building a craft to sail to Mauritius. The ship was indeed built by 27 September, but it was just for the French crew; the slaves were to remain to fend for themselves on the island, with promises that the crew would return to rescue them. Surprisingly, these pledges were in earnest. On arriving first in Madagascar, then Îsle Bourbon and finally Mauritius, after something of a perilous journey, they requested that Governor Desforges-Boucher send a rescue ship to Tromelin. They were shocked when he steadfastly refused, claiming that every ship was needed to fend off the pesky British.

It is hard today to reconcile the contradiction within Castellan du Vernet. On the one hand, he had been involved in the slave trade: this hardly made him ethically pure. Yet his few months of desperate isolation on Tromelin had showed him what the Malagasy slaves were now going through. Returning to France in 1762, he made it his sole aim in life to find a way to rescue them. He ensured that articles were written about them in the Paris press and played on all his contacts to open any door that might

177

STAR AND KEY

help. Yet their fate was quietly forgotten by everyone else. It was not until 1773—twelve years after the shipwreck—that a French ship passing close to Tromelin spotted some of the slaves and informed Port Louis. With a lull in fighting against the British, the French administration now allowed a ship to be sent there later in the year. It couldn't approach the island due to difficult weather and turned back. Another ship was sent in 1774; the same thing happened. It is almost unimaginable to know what those poor folk were going through, having somehow kept alive for so many years on a tiny, deserted islet, only for ships to approach and then leave again. Only on the third attempt, on 29 November 1776—fifteen years after the *Utile* had sunk—did the corvette *Dauphine* successfully anchor by the island. Tragically, all they found were seven women and an eight-month-old baby, showing that there had been an attritional death rate amongst these poor castaways right until the year before. How these women had managed to find the resourcefulness to keep alive with so little to hand—almost all the wood had been used to build the escape craft years earlier—remains one of the greatest survival stories in history. On arrival in Île de France, they were offered to be returned to Madagascar as free citizens. They all refused.

By the nineteenth century, circumstances had changed. Perhaps due to an oversight, Tromelin was not mentioned within the articles of the Treaty of Paris in 1814, when Île de France and its possessions were handed over to Britain. France continued to administer it from Réunion without Britain really caring much. Only in the twentieth century would this cause headaches, when an independent Mauritius would claim Tromelin for itself, only for the French to state that their sovereignty over it had been continuous since 29 November 1776—the day that the *Dauphine* rescued those poor, stranded Malagasy slaves. The two nations have now found a way to administer it jointly, although it has no permanent inhabitants.

THE NOISY NEIGHBOURHOOD

Two more atoll groups made up Mauritius' outlier possessions, both to its northeast. The first was Saint-Brandon, another group of islands that appear (unnamed) on ancient Arabic maps. Both Portuguese and Dutch sailors had stopped there for provisions on their way east during the sixteenth and seventeenth centuries, but only occasionally. Low-lying and stretched like an arc of pearls through the ocean, its total land area is barely a few hundred acres, scattered over many islets. Even a medium-sized cyclone would put most of it underwater. Although it was recognised as part of the French possessions in the 1720s, it wasn't until 1806 that Governor Decaen—rightly sensing that greater security was needed—sent the corsair Charles Mariette on a mission to the islands to report back if the British were loitering there (they weren't) and to install six men as scouts to act as a basic defence force, just in case. By the time the British took over Mauritius in 1810, the small advance guard had quietly slipped away and it remained empty.

The last of Mauritius' concerns lay further northeast still, nearly 1,250 miles away. The Portuguese again had been the first there, although likely not before 1532. They named the group of atolls 'Bassas de Chagas' (with 'Chagas' meaning 'wounds' and alluding to the stigmata of Christ on the cross). This, over time, would morph into Chagos. The larger atolls were also assigned names, including Peros Banhos and Diego Garcia—possibly the names of two of the crew members. Again though, their remoteness was unappealing, and no effort was made to colonise them meaningfully until the 1770s, when the French administration in Mauritius began to issue permits for growing coconut palms to cultivate oil. In 1793, the largest island of Diego Garcia established its first settlement, again with a focus on coconut production.

The population was always small, but despite the scope of the atolls over many miles, a new distinct culture grew up over the decades, even as the British took over Mauritius itself. The peo-

179

STAR AND KEY

ple were known as '*Les Chagossiens*', or simply the '*Ilois*' (Islanders). Britain was at this stage still in fact-finding mode, knowing comparatively little about what the islands could genuinely offer. Sixteen years after helping guide through the slave-trade related Moresby Treaty, Commander Robert Moresby was tasked with charting the atolls accurately in 1838, so that the British could ruminate further about what—if anything—needed to be done with them. The ultimate decision would come much, much later, and with huge repercussions (see Chapter 18).

By the second half of the nineteenth century, and perhaps for the first time in its eclectic history, Mauritius felt neither existentially threatened nor internally stagnant. Its wider responsibilities now stretched across the Indian Ocean, but the British felt content that the best approach was now to 'manage and maintain' rather than make changes in any particular direction. From a 'safety-first' angle they were largely right, but even they may not have properly sensed what was happening under the surface.

14

CONSOLIDATION

In the second half of the nineteenth century, something imperceptible but crucial happened to Mauritius.

Off the back of condemning slavery to the history books and introducing indentured labour as a fix, Mauritius quietly continued to develop its infrastructure and to turn into as modern a society as its isolation would allow. By extension, it was slowly but eventually turning from being a place to be wary of to being an island worth a visit.

The average length of tenure for successive governors of the island was not long at all. When Sir Henry Barkly arrived in 1863, Mauritius had seen no fewer than twelve governors or acting governors since 1840. Whilst this was hardly ideal for the continuity of longer-term projects, it didn't seem to hinder some key developments. High on the list of priorities—as it was almost everywhere else—was health. Hospitals remained predictably rudimentary affairs, but genuine efforts were made to improve sanitation, with the dawning realisation that health and sanitation were strongly interlinked. Canals and wells were dug to improve access to clean drinking water for all, not just the elite.

STAR AND KEY

Efforts were also made to improve the drainage in Port Louis, which by now, unquestionably, absolutely stank. The more superstitious-minded of the inhabitants, however, were also the most vocal, petitioning and convincing others that digging up the foul earth of the city would only unleash Balrog-like evil from the depths and thus compound their sickness. It was sheer nonsense, but it prevented progress. Meanwhile, quarantines were strictly enforced for ships arriving from areas at risk of infectious diseases. Sometimes this meant them bobbing around in the harbours for upwards of a month.

With its unhealthy history, the island was right to be wary. Despite attempts to keep all contagious diseases away, as the Star and Key of the Indian Ocean became a dropping-off point for so many ships coming from Australia, the Americas, Africa and Asia—not to mention Europe—some were bound to slip through the net. In September 1851 and then again in 1893, nearly 50 per cent of the island suffered from influenza. Just three years later, from May to July 1854, things were even worse, as cholera swept through first Port Louis and then the rest of the island. There were nearly 8,000 officially recorded deaths—the real number was very likely higher—and this included one in fourteen of Port Louis' population of 49,000. Just a year later saw smallpox catching hold in late 1855 (it would return with a vengeance in 1891), before a second bout of cholera in 1856 rounded off a miserable decade. On the latter occasion, a ship quarantined in unsavoury conditions on Ilot Gabriel and Île Plate, two islets to the north of Mauritius, had resulted in hundreds dying there, with others desperate to get away and rafting their way to the Mauritius mainland. Another 3,500 islanders soon perished, thanks to the infected newcomers. Most horrendous of all was in December 1865, when a few Indian workers on the Wolmar estate on the west coast somehow contracted malaria. Within weeks, a full-blown malaria epidemic ploughed its way Mauritius,

CONSOLIDATION

and from 1866 to 1868 it ghoulishly caused upwards of 32,000 deaths—easily a tenth of the population—including, appallingly, one in three in Port Louis. Unquestionably the outdoor labourers caught the brunt of it, although no one was immune; the desperately needed stocks of quinine were nowhere to be found and fresh ones took a long time to arrive. It wasn't just quinine that was in short supply; so were actual doctors. In 1851 there were sixty doctors for the whole island—already a very thin spread. Twenty years later, the number hadn't grown and it was barely higher, at sixty-eight, in 1909. To further rub Mauritius' face in it, nature had one final trick to play, delivering in March 1868 a cyclone of biblical proportions that dwarfed any other witnessed hitherto since the British had arrived. Crops were destroyed, half of Port Louis flattened and 20,000 homes were obliterated.

If good health remained something of a lottery, more concerted efforts were made in primary education. Transport, likewise, was improved immeasurably, with more and more roads built as well as the colony's first railway line. The main railway transecting the island, spanning the 30 miles from Port Louis to Grande Rivière Sud-Est, was opened to some fanfare in 1864, with a further 100 miles of track laid down over the ensuing two decades and a new Moka branch and Savanne line greatly reducing travel times. Mauritius' complex legal system, hybridised with both French and English influences, but overwhelmingly adhering to the Napoleonic Code, was at least being followed, with corruption not thought to be higher than in any other colony. Importantly, the establishment of clear legal processes for the adjudication of property rights, including for land ownership, surveying and registration, were accepted by all sectors of the population. Mauritius thus escaped the endless difficulties faced elsewhere stemming from the complications of land occupancy disputes. So whilst you would be hard-pushed to call Mauritius

STAR AND KEY

completely 'safe' by the 1870s, it had certainly turned the corner from the dangerous free-for-all that seemed to be endemic in the first half of the century. In parallel, as the sugar plantations continued to make sizeable profits, efforts were also made to diversify the island's output, with the introduction of rubber and tea plantations in the 1880s. The former never really got going; the latter continue to thrive via the outputs of the Bois Cheri and Corson estates in the highlands.

It was these inland highlands, in fact, that acted as a telling barometer of the island's make-up as well as its societal health. As with most islands at the time, the population of Mauritius had hitherto largely been coastal, with the obvious exception of the sugar plantation workers. But with so much disease spreading throughout the hotter, more humid coasts—notably in the ever-stifling Port Louis—from the 1860s the wealthier and more mobile inhabitants no longer saw the need to stay close to the non-stop activities of the harbours; their health was more important. After the initial setting up of villages by ex-slaves two decades earlier, there began a second steady exodus into Mauritius' Central Plateau, where the higher altitudes brought respite from the summer's oppressive heat and a better survival rate. The climate up there was far wetter, but it was a reasonable price to pay.

This saw the rapid development of Curepipe, now Mauritius' second city, where the island's top school, the *Collège Royal*, was 'temporarily' moved from Port Louis during the various epidemics, before finding its permanent home there. The city's name roughly translates as 'Pipe cleaner', although no one is really sure why. The story that French soldiers travelling between Port Louis and the southeast would routinely stop there and out of habit start cleaning their ubiquitous pipes is disarmingly charming, but conveniently forgets that French soldiers were by then long gone from the island. Not far away from Curepipe lies

CONSOLIDATION

Vacoas, which also blossomed into a bustling town at this time. Unlike Curepipe, its nomenclature is more straightforward, it being named after the Mauritian word for the endemic Pandanus tree that grew there in abundance. In 1877, Quatre Bornes, Beau Bassin and Rose-Hill were all officially recognised as new villages, and have never really stopped growing since.

Conversely, the end of the 1860s saw an unfavourable shift in Mauritius' fortunes, although the cause this time lay thousands of miles away. The opening of the Suez Canal in 1869 was transformational for the trade—not to mention the security—of ships passing between Europe and Asia. The boisterous harbour of Port Louis had hitherto usually seen as many as sixty sailing ships berthed within its ample waters on any given day—a magnificent sight captured by early photographs. Yet this seismic shift in routes was only going to impact Mauritius' external importance negatively. The shipbuilding trade declined overnight, and the city of Port Louis, already hollowed out by countless epidemics and internal migrations, saw a great deal of its lustre disappear. Fortunately, Mauritius' colossal sugar trade kept it afloat.

But with all these peaks and troughs hitting the island like the irrepressible cyclones that continue to be its bane to this day, something else had perhaps been triggered. It is sometimes said that a true culture isn't just one that can look forward to a brighter future, but one that can begin to look back, far into the past, to recognise parts of itself and appreciate how far it has come. It seems that Mauritius, instinctively, had now reached that stage, and it is the smaller, more easily overlooked developments that tell us this most clearly. To that end, a schoolteacher in Mahébourg named George Clark, who was a keen nature lover, was also fascinated by old stories about the Dodo—the bird only found in Mauritius, extinct for two centuries, and that seemed almost too ridiculous to be real. He finally decided, in

STAR AND KEY

1865, to go looking for skeletons of the mysterious bird. The recent digging to lay down the 1864 railways had looked promising but drawn a blank.

He found luck closer to home, however. A nearby plantation owner, Gaston de Bissy, had recently cleared a swamp on his land known as Mare aux Songes, and there workmen found a treasure trove of countless species—deer, tortoises, birds—that over the centuries had found a way into the marshland but no way out. Clark caught wind of this, de Bissy was helpful, and the workmen set aside all the animal bones they could find. By November, Clark had managed to find an entire Dodo skeleton's worth, that would ultimately find its way to become a chief exhibit at the British Museum.

Indeed, Mauritians of different backgrounds were now starting to tentatively care about and explore their heritage. This interest in a dead part of the island's past unlocked in some a more modern desire to protect what still remained. While being far from the globally recognised ecological movement that we recognise today, the first green shoots were nevertheless there. Barkly's successor as governor in 1871, Sir Arthur Hamilton-Gordon, had been struck early on by the sheer wilful destruction of the island's dwindling (and endemically rich) forests, with absolutely no attempt made to replace the felled trees. His early calculations suggested that only 25 square miles of forest remained on a 714-square-mile island that early archives clearly showed had been completely forested on discovery. In 1874, despite predictable protests from the plantation owners, he introduced what was essentially Mauritius' first conservation law, ensuring that rivers and woods alike would be protected from further ill treatment. One of Hamilton-Gordon's successors, Sir George Bowen, went a step further, inviting British forestry expert R. H. Thompson over in April 1880 to make recommendations. Thompson suggested tripling the minimum measurements of forest and river

186

CONSOLIDATION

'strips' from 50 to 150 feet. He also advised the government to spend Rs3 million buying up—and thus protecting—vast swathes of former forest and to start a replanting programme. Again, it was the typically obstinate planters who hated anything that represented 'change' and who had to be gradually quelled.

Despite the awful epidemics that had ravaged the island's long-suffering people over several decades, it may perhaps seem surprising that the population grew substantially during the latter half of the century. With the population already over 310,000 in 1861, the ongoing large-scale immigration, overwhelmingly from India, continued mostly unabated for the ensuing sixty years. The dark decade of the 1860s saw only minimal net growth of an extra 6,000 by the time of the next census in 1871, but the total population had surpassed 371,000 by 1901. Bearing in mind that over this period tens of thousands chose to return to India after all, and not to settle for the longer-term, it gives a fair insight into the sheer scale of incoming labour. In addition, 1901 marked the first Mauritian census where a religious stock-take was also taken. Of those 371,000, 56 per cent were Hindu, 32 per cent were Christian and 11 per cent were Muslim, with the remaining 1 per cent made up of traditional Chinese or animist beliefs. These figures would fluctuate a little over the ensuing decades, but never noticeably changed.

It would be wrong to say that tensions didn't exist. As Mauritius was a British colony, Christianity had the support of the state. However, as has been described in detail in religious historical studies elsewhere, it was often its own worst enemy, and Catholics squared off against Protestants in Mauritius in an ongoing battle to convert as many inhabitants as possible. In fact, Catholicism had a small foothold in India already, mainly under the French in Pondicherry, so a small number of the arrivals from the subcontinent were already Christian. The main target for the proselytisers, however, were the newly freed slaves. Many

STAR AND KEY

had previously been left to practise their own, largely animist, beliefs in their own (very limited) time. Now that they were free—and therefore suddenly considered and treated more like real human souls—the race was on.

The most well-known local name in this age of conversion was Jacques-Désiré Laval, or simply 'Père Laval'. This French Catholic missionary accumulated nicknames for fun during the mid-nineteenth century in Mauritius, all with a common theme: 'Apostle of Mauritius'; 'Patron of the slaves'; 'Lourdes of the Indian Ocean'. Having studied in Paris and then opened a medical practice, it wasn't until 1834, when he was aged 31, that he finally received the spiritual call to join the priesthood. After his training, he was sent on a mission to Mauritius in 1841. In the ensuing twenty-three years he worked tirelessly with the poor, drawing also on his medical knowledge to provide help beyond spiritual issues. It is hard to put an exact figure on how many folk were converted through his guidance and championing of the poor, but over 60,000 seems realistic. The date of his death in 1864, 9 September, has become a day of regular pilgrimage on the island, with worshippers coming from South Africa, Britain and France to pay their respects. Père Laval was beatified by Pope John Paul II during a visit to Mauritius in 1979.

Mauritian Hindus, meanwhile, were establishing their own sacred shrine. The volcanic lake known colloquially and unimaginatively as Grand Bassin (Big Pond) took on a new significance from 1866. A former indentured labourer, Pandit Sanjibonlal, had always been struck by the simple beauty of the highland lake. With Hindus recognising the importance of bathing in the Ganges to celebrate the main festival of Shiva, Panditji had an idea. The Mauritian lake's divine appeal could act as a representation of the Ganges to pilgrims. He obtained permission to build a temple on its shores, helped by artisan friends. He then began to undertake a small-scale pilgrimage every year. Sadly, most

CONSOLIDATION

indentured labourers who heard about this and wanted to participate were not allowed to, due to the harsh terms of their contracts; time off for religious purposes was forbidden.

Things changed in 1897, when a Brahmin *pujari* (priest) called Shri Jhummon Giri Gosagne Napal declared that he had had a vision wherein he had seen the water of Grand Bassin springing directly from the River 'Jahnvi'. The news of this holy dream spread rapidly, and by the following year, many barefoot pilgrims were finally able to trek to the lake to collect its water to offer to Lord Shiva on the occasion of Maha Shivaratri. The pilgrimage grew year on year. In the early twentieth century it was known amongst Hindus as 'Pari Talao' (Lake of the Fairies), as it was believed that fairies would come and dance there during the night. In 1972, Prime Minister Ramgoolam brought Ganga water from Gomukh and mixed it with the waters of Grand Bassin, renaming the latter Ganga Talao (Lake of the Ganges).

The British rulers, for their part, had quietly continued to practise their Church of England version of Protestantism. After initially making some efforts to convert many on the island to their branch of Christianity, they soon pragmatically recognised that leaving the overwhelmingly Catholic plantation owners to follow their own faith was the path of least resistance. Although things might have been more challenging for the Hindus and Muslims who had recently arrived from India, there is not much direct evidence of them being actively discriminated against. The first mosque had in fact been built as early as 1805, in the dying days of the French administration. Hindu temples were erected from 1834 onwards. The British, ever-pragmatic, were more concerned with developing a safe and profitable island rather than a religiously homogeneous one.

This was also the wider period of step changes in global communications, and Mauritius felt confident enough to want to be part of those revolutions too. At a more prosaic level, it started

STAR AND KEY

in 1846 with the recently inaugurated concept of postage stamps for letters. Internal letters would cost a penny (orange stamp); international letters would cost tuppence (blue stamp). It was in the following year that the island's only engraver, 31-year-old Joseph Barnard, accidentally launched himself into twentieth-century philately folklore. Engraving the words 'Post Office' up the left-hand side of the cast, and only printing a very few stamps, by the following year he had corrected the wording to 'Post Paid'. This was the first decade of stamps, Mauritius was remote, and as stamp collecting grew as a pastime, the rare 1847 'mistake' stamps were to become the holy grail of philately. Many were in fact used by the governor's wife, Lady Gomm, for a ball invitation in 1847, and over the years both used and, very occasionally, unused versions of the stamps have appeared at auction, where their value through sheer rarity is mind-blowing. An envelope written by Lady Gomm bearing one of the stamps sold in 2021 for 11 million euros—by far the most ever paid for a stamp at auction.

Even so, science was well taught at the more prestigious schools at the time on the island, and technological developments were always welcome. One of the most esteemed alumni of the *Collège Royal* was Charles-Édouard Brown-Séquard, who in the latter part of the nineteenth century became an internationally renowned neurologist and physiologist. Then September 1864 saw the first electric telegraph being demonstrated in Port Louis, whilst the first two telephones were installed in October 1883. Most importantly, Mauritius was then brought into the ever-expanding world of underwater telegraphic cables in November 1893, transforming the speed of strategic decision-making on-island when London needed to be consulted. That same year saw electricity replace oil in the street lights of Curepipe. Despite all the challenges thrown its way, Mauritius was calmly progressing and changing for the better. The true

190

CONSOLIDATION

litmus test for a mature colony, however, was always going to be how it would deal with democratic elections. Would their introduction give rise to an enlightened appreciation of the right to have a say—no matter how small—in shaping the island's future? Or would old grudges and resentments, or long-standing privileges, cloud Mauritius' progress? In 1886, the island finally had a chance to find out, and the answer was: a bit of both.

There had always been various councils and assemblies during both French and British rule, none of which could in any way be seen as representative of all the island's inhabitants. For example, the updated Council of Government set up in 1825, partly to work out how to deal with the abolition of slavery, consisted of only a handful of government officials. As most of these only ever conversed with the sugar plantation owners, it was never going to even pretend to be a real representation of the masses. This rather lily-livered outfit muddled on for a few decades alongside various other half-hearted associations. Yet the planters continued in their rambunctious ways, demanding a more direct say in decisions. It was only with the arrival of a controversial governor in 1883 that their dream would become reality. Sir John Pope Hennessy was the fifteenth British administrator since 1810, and it's fair to say that there had been none before quite like him.

Born in County Cork, Ireland, in 1834, he was both a Catholic and a supporter of Irish Home Rule. This already made him something of an anomaly in British political circles. He had shown that he sympathised disproportionately with the locals in his previous role, when as governor of Hong Kong for five years, from 1877 to 1882, he dramatically increased the rights of the Chinese to buy land and to develop new businesses in competition with ex-pats, making himself many new local friends— whilst raising a few eyebrows in London. (He was a passionate man elsewhere too, finding time to father two illegitimate chil-

STAR AND KEY

dren in the process.) This progressive attitude stuck with him after he arrived in Mauritius in 1883. Perhaps overly sympathetic to the wealthy planters, who exaggerated the hardships they had been put under by previous administrators, he was equally impressed by the emergent middle-class Creoles, who had worked cleverly with Mauritius' booming press to lay down their case that some form of wider governmental representation was now due. To that end, in 1885, Hennessy petitioned London to introduce a form of parliamentary self-government on the island. In September that year, he received his answer, which amounted to 'OK, but within reason'.

Mauritius was to be granted a brand-new Legislative Council and the majority of its members would not be elected: the governor, eight hand-picked 'officials' and nine further (British) members nominated arbitrarily by the cabinet. So far, so old-school. This time, however, there would also be ten elected members of the Council. As for the electorate itself, the voting criteria were strict: male property owners who earned over Rs50 a month. Conversely, those who stood for election could be Mauritians of all backgrounds, including the more recently arrived Indians—who were now increasingly referred to as Indo-Mauritians. In practice, this meant that the whole electorate would consist of just over 4,000 men, of whom 295—just over 7 per cent—would be from the emergent Indian middle class. Together with the introduction of an updated constitution in 1885—referred to as *Cens Démocratique*—it was an attempt to create the first steps towards a 'Mauritius for the Mauritians'. Mauritius' first elections were therefore held on 11 January 1886, although no one was kidding themselves by calling this a democracy: universal suffrage remained a long way off—as indeed it was in Britain itself.

Debates beforehand centred on issues that remain achingly familiar to this day: the economy; immigration; class misunder-

CONSOLIDATION

standings. Political parties rapidly emerged, although their differences and delineations seemed to sway like the winds of the cyclone. Predictably, those of the Franco-Mauritian plantation class were suspicious of the Indian voting element gaining a disproportionate foothold; conversely, many others suspected that the powerful and influential would form an oligarchy. In the event, reformers and anti-reformers both found their way onto the Council, including the appointment of Mauritius' first-ever Indo-Mauritian in a senior decision-making role, Gnanadicarayen Arlanda, who had himself become a successful plantation owner.

The more conservative elements of the Council, however, thought that Hennessy had gone too native. That they themselves had preferred another Indo-Mauritian, Emile Sandapa, for the post was an irony that was not lost on anyone. Four of the new members—Charles Planel of Pamplemousses, Celicourt Antelme of Plaine Wilhems, O. Beaugeard and Gustave de Coriolis of Port Louis—trumped up spurious and even fictitious accusations against Hennessy, using their new powers to make these complaints directly to London. Britain felt obliged to investigate, sending out senior diplomat Sir Hercules Robinson in November 1886 to seek the truth. There was shock when Hennessy was suspended the following month, with unprecedented scenes of locals supporting their colonial administrator outside his residence at Le Reduit as he left. The more liberal elements of the local press defended him resolutely, and after six months back in London, defended by his barrister friend William Newton, Hennessy was able to be reinstated and also gained a huge £20,000 in damages from *The Times* newspaper in London for libel. His return to Mauritius in July 1887 was welcomed as though he were a modern-day pop star. Even so, the whole debacle had been exhausting and chastising, and Hennessy kept a low profile for his last two years as chief administrator, albeit happily accepting the sheepish resignations of two of the Council members.

193

STAR AND KEY

Mauritius' first dip of its toes into electoral waters had been predictably complex, yet slowly it was shaking itself free of its unsavoury earlier reputation, and its storied history was now seeping into the wider international consciousness—amongst the intelligentsia at least. Tourism as we know it today did not really exist outside the 'Grand Tour' of the western European nations practised by the wealthy. Nevertheless, Mauritius would now welcome two well-known visitors. The first was already an established author; the second would become a world-famous catalyst for change. When celebrated US writer Mark Twain—author of *The Adventures of Tom Sawyer* and *Huckleberry Finn*—found himself in Mauritius in 1896, it was initially out of necessity. Needing to pay off his debtors, he went on a worldwide lecture tour encompassing Canada, Australia, New Zealand, India, Ceylon, Fiji, South Africa and Mauritius.

Twain would write up his journal as a highly readable travelogue titled *Following the Equator*, although latter-day Mauritians have wilfully—and repeatedly—perpetuated various myths about what Twain did or did not say about their island. Twain was no fool, and gave balanced views on the things he liked about Mauritius—its verdant mountains, its cosmopolitan make-up, its beautiful lagoons—as well as those aspects that left him underwhelmed. It was this sensible approach that earned him worldwide respect, and which features in one of his most misquoted journal entries from his stay on the island, dating from 18 April 1896. It actually reads as follows:

> This is the only country in the world where the stranger is not asked 'How do you like this place?' This is indeed a large distinction. Here the citizen does the talking about the country himself; the stranger is not asked to help. You get all sorts of information. From one citizen you gather that Mauritius was made first, and then heaven; and that heaven was copied after Mauritius. Another one tells you that this is an exaggeration; that the two chief villages, Port Louis and

CONSOLIDATION

Curepipe, fall short of heavenly perfection; that nobody lives in Port Louis except upon compulsion, and that Curepipe is the wettest and rainiest place in the world.

All of a sudden, the implication of one citizen's view—note, not Twain's—regarding Mauritius' paradisiacal claims is set against the rather less alluring views of another—and it doesn't seem quite as worthy of plastering on every tourist billboard as was once the case. Even so, it seems he enjoyed his stay there, for all the island's flaws. And the mere fact that Mauritius was on Twain's world lecture tour at all suggests that Mauritius had turned the corner regarding its previously disagreeable reputation.

Five years later, in 1901, another much younger man whose name would pass down the generations spent nearly three weeks on the island. This 32-year-old Indian Hindu lawyer was at the time a resident in South Africa, where he was experiencing racial prejudice that was understandably agitating him. He was on a trip back home to India when his ship, the steamship *Nowshera*, stopped at Mauritius, where the young lawyer stayed with his Muslim trader friend Ahmed Goolam Mohammed. The lawyer's name was Mohandas Karamchand Gandhi. Being even then incredibly charismatic, he was invited to dinner at the governor's residence, and attended other social functions where it is believed he encouraged his new Indo-Mauritian friends to 'passively resist' any discrimination that they faced to achieve their longer-term goals. The racism that had been a mainstay for Gandhi in South Africa was plainly evident in Mauritius too, but he was buoyed up by the fact that the Indo-Mauritians were engaging politically.

Irresistibly tempting though it may be to think that the first inklings of Gandhi's later powerful tool of passive resistance against British rule in India were originally conjured up during his brief stay on Mauritius, it can't be so. Despite his later *volte face*, Gandhi at the time was still a firm believer in British rule in India. That said, we know that he once referred to Mauritius as

195

STAR AND KEY

'a miniature India beyond the sea', so who knows what was going through his mind or what immediate impact his words had on his audiences? What we do know is that his visit occurred at the same time that the latest horror disease—this time, bubonic plague—was working its morbid way through the island, so we can only remain eternally grateful that it didn't take with it a man whose philosophy would have such a telling impact on world affairs in the twentieth century.

By the time of Gandhi's visit, the colony of Mauritius had welcomed the advent of the twentieth century with mild trepidation rather than overt confidence. That said, its economy was relatively stable, its ruling power far from overbearing compared to elsewhere, and it had taken its first tentative steps towards representative government. It may still have been governed by the British, but it was now populated by a growing, ethnically mixed population who now—whether they were labourers, mercantile class or wealthy and privileged—had something in common: they were calling themselves 'Mauritian'. And this unity in the face of diversity would help shape the island's future over the tumultuous century that lay ahead.

15

PROGRESS

Reverting to type, the first few years of the twentieth century saw Mauritius' fortunes at their most contradictory.

There was excitement in 1903 when the first primitive motor car in Mauritius chugged its way slowly along Port Louis' cobblestones. It was the latest hint of modernity to come to the island. Yet as though to prove that Yin had to come with Yang, in the same year a horrendous parasitic cattle epidemic known as 'surra' swept the island, thanks to an infected herd that had been imported from Bombay, with virtually every ox, mule and horse on the island dying painfully or having to be put out of its misery. That first motor vehicle (manufacturer unknown) therefore shared the streets with carts drawn not by draught animals but by men. That busy year was rounded off with the British administrators finally deciding to offload the Seychelles from the Mauritius portfolio so that they could be administered by a separate arm of the colonial infrastructure—an outcome the group of islands had yearned for over the preceding few decades. In a darkly ironic way, 1903 seemed to sum up the ongoing suspicion that there was always more than one Mauritius vying for space.

STAR AND KEY

Despite an inevitable economic hit resulting from the surra epidemic, the sheer quantity of Mauritian sugar being exported had never been higher: the annual average between 1904–06 was 182,000 tons. South Africa and India helped themselves to two thirds of this, with the other British colonies of Canada and Hong Kong—as well as the motherland herself—taking nearly all the rest. Almost all food was by now imported to the island, since, although it was not technically a monoculture—tea, aloe fibre, manioc and a few other crops were still grown in fair quantities—the fact that 95 per cent of Mauritius' total export was directly dependent on the success or otherwise of sugar meant that the industry as a whole needed to be protected more than ever and at almost all costs. The difference now was that economic circumstances had changed, and the labourers had been around long enough for them to make more assertive and organised demands of the sugar industry leaders for higher—or at least fairer—wages.

When workers chose to strike at the Beau Champ sugar estate in the east of the island, in December 1904, it was the first tentative role of the dice. When they were followed up by their colleagues at Bel Ombre estate in the south in October 1905, the genie known as 'workers' unions' was well and truly out of the bottle. Coupled with Britain's unwillingness to act as a literal 'sugar daddy' to the plantation owners and to bail them out, the situation was ripe for a burst of political activity and for new parties to appear that were not behoved to the Franco-Mauritian plantocracy—which they did. At the head of the pack was the mayor of Port Louis, 57-year-old Eugène Laurent. As a middle-class man who had studied at the *Collège Royal* before studying medicine in England, he had the education to match his political nous, and in 1907 he founded *Action Libérale* (whose members were also known as 'the Democrats') as the first organised political shot across the bows of the Franco-Mauritian community who

PROGRESS

had hegemony over the sugar trade. It felt, conceptually at least, like a genuine middle-class/working-class pact that had legs.

But Laurent, appealing to what he referred to as the 'Indo-Creole masses', couldn't do it alone. The clarity of his mission—to improve fairness in island life and to overturn the lopsidedness of the 1885 constitution, as well as to introduce electoral reform, which had hitherto been completely skewed in favour of the sugar dynasties—was attractive not just to other Creoles but also to many Indians, and even—in Anatole de Boucherville and Edouard Nairac—some less conservative-minded Franco-Mauritians. Chief amongst Laurent's wingmen was the 26-year-old Gujarati Indian barrister, Manilal Doctor. Having arrived in Mauritius in 1907, under the specific recommendation of Gandhi, Doctor would use his own brilliant mind both to defend Indo-Mauritians in court and to launch and edit *The Hindustani* newspaper, to offer more working-class insights to those who had hitherto been of more closed minds. An early affirmation of Indian identity in the local scene was Doctor's clash with the Judge of the Supreme Court, when he steadfastly refused to remove his shoes and turban before entering the court. The matter was taken before the governor, who thereafter issued an order allowing shoes and turbans to be worn in the courts of Mauritius. Every little victory mattered. Whilst Doctor's occasional calls to make Mauritius a colony of India itself may have gone too far, he unquestionably helped Laurent galvanise, for the very first time, a meaningful opposition to the plantation owners' own *Parti de l'Ordre*, led by Sir Henri Leclézio, whose members were known more prosaically and accurately as 'the Oligarchs'. Mauritian politics would never be the same again.

First blood fell to the Democrats, who successfully persuaded the Legislative Council to send a Royal Commission from London to address, amongst other things, the sheer absurdity of only 2 per cent of the island's population having any say in

STAR AND KEY

Mauritius' elections. Led by Sir Frank Swettenham in 1909, the commission equivocated over many issues and remained non-committal to either side. But at least for the short term the Oligarchs would cement their position. Council elections were scheduled for January 1911. Despite the Democrats taking the two seats in Port Louis, all the eight remaining seats, largely representing rural communities, went the way of the Oligarchs. Things then got worse when one of Mauritius' favourite pastimes to this day—gossip—went into overdrive. Soon after the election results, a notorious criminal started spreading the rumour that Laurent and his family had been murdered by the Oligarchs at his home in Curepipe.

The inter-class tensions that had bubbled menacingly under the surface for so long could not be hidden any longer. Barely three days after the election, rioting and looting broke out in Port Louis for a month, with much of it directed at the substantial city homes of the Oligarchs, as well as, for some reason, many of the shops run by Sino-Mauritians. Even Laurent showing up to prove that he was alive and well hardly put off the looters. The printing presses, which had been pivotal to the incitement on both sides before the elections, were broken into and destroyed. The home of one of the Oligarchs, M. Ducasse, was invaded, and only a handy pistol saved both him and his son. The military was finally called and restored order to a trashed capital.

Fortunately, no one was killed, but the upshot remained political intransigence: the anachronistic constitution stayed resolutely unchanged, and landowner power remained over-whelming. A disillusioned Laurent disbanded *Action Libérale* not long after. Still, it had been a stark message that the status quo would not carry on forever. The angry masses, meanwhile, con-soled themselves with a new obsession: cinema. February 1897 had seen the first cinematograph demonstrated to a goggle-eyed public at the Port Louis Theatre. Now, fourteen years later,

PROGRESS

Curepipe had its own highly popular version, and a bigger cinema still, Luna Park, would be built at Port Louis in 1915.

By then, of course, British eyes were very much elsewhere. The public assassination of Austrian Archduke Franz Ferdinand in Sarajevo in June 1914 had set off the long-positioned dominoes to their inevitable conclusion and war immersed Europe and beyond. While vast swathes of that continent would be physically wrecked, and their economies even more so, the isolation that had for so long been the bane of Mauritius was for once its saving grace. Even though a voluntary militia was assigned to help defend the island just in case, the prowling amoeba of war chose not to spread its tentacles this far and a great irony emerged: not only was Mauritius spared actual conflict on its shores, but its economy positively—and perhaps sheepishly—boomed. The desperate shortage of sugar in Europe, as trade became either slow or too dangerous, meant that its price soared. With Mauritius providing so much sugar to Britain and her colonies, this cash went straight into the Mauritian economy.

But just because the war didn't come to Mauritius did not mean that Mauritians didn't go to war. The sugar estates donated 500 tons each to both the British and French armies, whilst the women took the lead in raising thousands of rupees for the French and English Red Cross societies. Far more directly involved, however, were the many volunteers who fought for the Allies in the trenches. Mauritius initially chose to send its eight best soldiers—five to the British Army and three to its French ally. These were bolstered by many Mauritian students who had been caught up in Britain and France at the wrong time, who nevertheless all volunteered. But this was just the start. A 1,500-strong force known as the Mauritius Labour Battalion (including men from Rodrigues) was then set up to augment the Allied forces in the Mesopotamia campaign, in what is now Iraq. At this stage, they were enlisted into almost all the various Allied

201

STAR AND KEY

forces, including the Australian, Canadian, South African and American. Some even made it as pilots, fighting alongside British and French compatriots at the very birth of air warfare. Tellingly, the enlisted men were Indo-Mauritian, Sino-Mauritian, Creole and Franco-Mauritian: Hindu, Muslim and Christian. It was another litmus test that had been thrown Mauritius' way regarding its maturity and self-confidence as a nation in its own right. Despite its ongoing shortcomings, it passed admirably.

Beyond the soldiers, the volunteers also made a difference in a variety of ways depending on their experience, notably as carpenters, cooks, drivers and dockworkers. Many were highly regarded, but even so, sixty of these men sadly died either in combat or of local endemic sicknesses, with circumstances dictating that they had to be buried in Mesopotamia rather than be repatriated. In 1919, Mauritius' roll call of military awards was deeply impressive from such a comparatively small contingent. They included a Distinguished Service Cross, two Distinguished Conduct Medals, twelve Military Crosses, nineteen *Croix de Guerre*, one *Medaille d'Honneur* and three *Legion d'Honneur*.

It came as a surprise to very few that a Mauritius Sugar Syndicate encompassing 70 per cent of the estates was set up in 1919, after hostilities had ended, ostensibly to help protect their wealth. Needless to say, with sugar being so profitable, even less effort was made to explore other agricultural options. Yet the actual ownership of the sugar-cane fields had seen a huge change over the previous two decades. The estate owners realised that due to the rising labour costs brought on by the proto-unions, the biggest profit margins were to be found in the milling of the sugar rather than the growing of it. Many big owners accelerated the sale of their lands, ensuring that it would always be in small—and therefore unthreatening—parcels of land, and fully in the knowledge that the small-scale farmers wouldn't be able to process their own sugar once cultivated.

PROGRESS

The growing Indo-Mauritian middle class were happy to buy up this land; so much so that whereas in 1909, 30 per cent of sugar cultivation was owned by small-scale Indian farmers, this increased to 43 per cent by the end of the war. In turn, the number of workers living on the sugar estates decreased from 145,000 in 1881 to 73,000 in 1921. Overall, this growing body of self-employed planters would become another important political bloc. Even so, these newer, smaller farms, unsurprisingly, were less profitable, not least as small-scale farmers often had to undertake the cultivation themselves and were more at risk from the endless sicknesses that engulfed the island. That being said, things were improving on one major front. In 1908, the Nobel Laureate Ronald Ross—who first proved the link between mosquitoes and malaria—visited the island and recommended draining the remaining swamps as the next step towards eliminating the disease. By the early 1920s, malaria had almost been eliminated, although it would yet have a later sting in its tail.

One might think that all this social and economic change, against a backdrop of earth-shattering global conflict, might sow the seeds of thoughts towards independence. Yet, in fact, in the early 1920s a very different movement came about that again seemed to showcase Mauritius as the least predictable of all Britain's assets: retrocession.

Very few political ideas united the deeply opposing sides of Mauritian politics, but in the event of the 1921 elections, retrocession was one of them. An awkward word that was likely invented at the time, it represented an equally awkward concept: that Mauritius should be returned from Britain to France. The rationale was complex but drew much of its logic from what had been witnessed on the French-administered sister island of Réunion, where it was perceived by its supporters that Creole and Indian inhabitants had been better 'assimilated'—a word used often in papers at the time, although its true mean-

STAR AND KEY

ing in this context was skirted around—into the wider population. The same, they believed, should happen to Mauritius, as in theory it would offer the island greater autonomy in managing its internal affairs.

There were two main drivers for this relatively new movement. First, World War I had triggered an underlying nostalgia towards the French—'*La Douce France*' ('Sweet France'), as she started to be referred to by the more mawkish Mauritian newspapers. France had unquestionably had a profound and lasting cultural impact on the island during the eighteenth century, even if the French administration's less savoury elements now became invisible through these new sepia-tinted glasses. Second, and more tangibly, the movement was another unorthodox attempt to challenge the fortress-like authority of both the British administration and the sugar barons. A rather optimistic interpretation by its supporters suggested that reintegrating with France would automatically lead to greater social equality and better job opportunities.

Retrocession's poster boy was Maurice Curé, a 34-year-old with a profile not dissimilar to that of Eugène Laurent. Middle-class and having studied medicine in England, he had previously joined the *Action Libérale* party, before using his medical skills to help treat wounded soldiers on the Balkan battlefields of the Great War. Although retrocession became the major talking point of the 1921 elections, it was not a movement that shone brightly for long. It was vehemently opposed by the sugar syndicate, as well as the wealthier Indo-Mauritian businessmen, both of whom believed they had it good with the British status quo; again, they won Council seats in the rural areas. However, in addition, the Liberal Party—which had inherited the working-class mantle from *Action Libérale*—also believed it to be a backward step, and they took Port Louis' two seats. The two major forces had therefore formed a pincer movement to squeeze out the retrocessionists, helped by the British administration clamp-

204

PROGRESS

ing down on the press output and electioneering of the new movement. Defeat was inevitable.

For their part, having in 1921 passed off the retrocessionist movement as being 'disloyal' and Curé himself as 'mentally unbalanced', by 1922 the imaginative British began to suspect pockets of the Indo-Mauritian community of being 'sedition mongers', and of aligning themselves with 'terrorists' who had been agitating for Indian independence—the assumption being that they would try the same in Mauritius. There wasn't a shred of evidence for this, and it only added fuel to the fire that policy was being made up on the hoof to minimise the growing Indo-Mauritian influence. In turn, it only reflects again that rumour and intrigue were still alive and well as part of Britain's diplomatic strategy.

By the same token, the 1920s saw a notable shift in the staffing of Mauritius' colonial civil service, with Mauritians—mostly educated members of the 'General Population'—filling 93 per cent of the roles. Indo-Mauritians gradually entered too. The 1921 census revealed that 70 per cent of the total population was Indo-Mauritian—and perhaps more importantly that this translated to 31 per cent of the electorate, according to the rules of the time. Although Gnanadicarayen Arlanda had been elected for a five-year term in 1886, there had been no Indo-Mauritian representation in the Legislative Council since then. That situation changed in 1926, with Dunputh Lallah defeating Gaston Gebert and Fernand Morel for the Grand Port seat, and Rajcoomar Gujadhur (who himself owned two sugar estates) beating Pierre Montocchio at Flacq. There was now also greater cohesion amongst the smaller Indo-Mauritian landowners, many of whom introduced societies to their predominantly Hindu villages. These included the *baitka*, a Hindu village organisation that held community meetings, educational classes, religious ceremonies and entertainment. Most villages had at least one and usually more.

STAR AND KEY

The great sugar price boom, however, was never going to last forever. Again, Mauritius ploughed a different path during the global boom in the 1920s, since the drop in sugar prices—which continued during the 1930s Depression—saw a fair few of the sugar estates closing down altogether. This wasn't just bad news for the magnates, but also for the huge numbers of employees who were dependent on them. Economic and political change was most definitely in the air.

The mid-1930s therefore saw the return of a supposed bad penny—at least as far as the British were concerned. Maurice Curé had never lost hope of achieving better conditions for workers, a view which was only galvanised after he spent time observing the conditions on several estates. With trade unionism essentially outlawed by Britain, Curé saw it as his ongoing quest to improve salaries, healthcare and housing for the working folk, whilst also demanding that more should have a say in elections. First, Curé was elected to the Plaine Wilhems seat in the Council in a 1934 by-election. Then, to some fanfare, he founded the *Parti Travailliste* (Mauritius Labour Party—MLP) in 1936, and along with colleagues Emmanuel Anquetil and Pandit Sahadeo got to work agitating the masses to take greater ownership of their collective destiny and to demand the right to be heard. Whilst Sahadeo focused on inspiring the rural working class, Anquetil was left to rally the urban workers.

It was perhaps a bigger and quicker success than even Curé had bargained for. Within a year, the newly confident workers on three of the larger sugar estates, together with some of the small-scale planters, had begun illegal strikes and had set fire to numerous cane fields. Dockworkers had also started to strike. The police fought back, and infamously—on 13 August 1937—they fired on what they deemed to be 200 'rioters' on one estate, killing four. Later in the month, a rural police station was stoned by an even bigger crowd. All this time, the MLP's membership

PROGRESS

inexorably grew. Although there was no direct evidence that Curé had incited the crowds to violence on any occasion, his immovable socialist views—and growing power—made him deeply unpopular with the more conservative-leaning British authorities. The recently arrived new governor, Sir Bede Clifford, initially tried a charm offensive with Curé, but to little avail. Thereafter, mutual suspicion inevitably grew. Curé and the MLP saw the British as an inherent part of the problem; Clifford, in turn, could only see a born troublemaker, and he declared a state of emergency.

The governor provoked further ire by using his powers to investigate—rather spuriously—whether the MLP's fundraising was being done legally. Drawing on a slightly obscure technicality, he demanded that the fundraising organ of the MLP be dissolved and its funds confiscated. Within twelve months, Curé and Sahadeo were under house arrest, while Anquetil was exiled to Rodrigues. Things once again looked bleak. Except that they weren't; despite appearances, the message had in fact landed, although the British—understandably fearful of encouraging rioting as a starting pistol for change—would never admit as much. By 1938, recommendations had been made to set up a Department of Labour, which helped protect workers' rights immeasurably better: minimum daily wages were fixed; housing improved; and a more workable system was put in place to allow the reporting of mistreatment or non-adherence to the new rules without fear of retribution. Crucially, trade unions were no longer outlawed. Mauritius' first Labour Day celebrations that same year resulted in 30,000 workers choosing to forego a day's salary to attend celebrations and rallies at Champ de Mars racecourse in Port Louis. In essence, there was now an acceptance by the British that as long as the 1885 constitution continued to be upheld, with all its huge power reserved archaically for the Oligarchs and their allies, then society—and the order on which it depended—was never going to progress, and conflict would forever be the default.

Yet again, just as a step change off the back of the riots was in the offing, global conflict ensured that the progressives had to press pause. This time it was the Axis powers of Germany, Italy and Japan who were the instigators of war, and again the arenas of conflict were for the most part far from Mauritius.

Once more, the sparring parties that made up Mauritius' increasingly complex political web set aside their parochial differences to address the wider challenge: how could they help good conquer evil? Most Mauritians who were studying in Europe volunteered to join the British or the Free French forces in London. Several, given their proficiency in French, were parachuted into France to liaise with the Resistance or to undertake sabotage missions. Many were heroes in the truest sense, with some paying the price of capture or execution in the name of liberty. Meanwhile, a Mauritius Pioneer Corps was established which not only had the benefit of bolstering British troops abroad, but of offering a quick fix to the notable unemployment that had persisted throughout the 1930s. Again, Mauritian soldiers of all backgrounds served with distinction across the North African, East African, Middle Eastern and European fronts. This time, a more enlightened Britain recognised its dependence on the contribution made by the colonies to the war effort, and proceeded to greatly increase its cashflow to all its colonies.

However, there was to be no wartime economic boom this time—far from it. The ultra-dependence on sugar that Mauritius had developed over the previous decades had now come back to bite it. With so much of its food still needing to be imported—as virtually all the agricultural land was sugar cane—this always presupposed that there would be ships arriving from around the world to supply the island with its basic food necessities. For the first time in many decades, while Mauritius may not have been

PROGRESS

in a war zone itself, its location was unquestionably of strategic naval importance. Germany did get very close in 1943, when several Nazi U-boats prowled around the Mauritian waters, notably just off the coast near Port Louis, and succeeded in sinking a few medium-sized British vessels, both naval and merchant shipping and all easy pickings. What this meant was that almost all shipping avoided Mauritius, whether vessels from the African Cape, or ships from Burma (recently invaded by Japan) which brought in much of Mauritius' rice. This perfect storm could only result in one thing: starvation.

There are no official figures to capture how many people died, but estimates in the tens of thousands don't seem unreasonable. Compounding the horror was the fact that those who were barely making ends meet and were badly under-nourished became that much more susceptible to disease. Malaria—dormant for several decades—reared its ugly head again, as did hookworm, for good measure. The only things that thrived were the black market and corruption. In desperation, the authorities ordered large chunks of the cane fields to be replanted with potatoes, legumes and other much-needed vegetables. Civil unrest was inevitable, not least as the British had had to clamp down on the new trade unions, ostensibly for security purposes. This didn't stop the cane workers on the Belle Vue Harel estate in the north of the island from going on illegal strike in late September 1943. Again, the badly trained police only knew one way to quell strikers who threatened to riot: by shooting at them. Four workers were killed, and the event became known as the 'Belle Vue Harel Massacre'. Yet neither could the sugar itself be depended upon; in a real-life incidence of pathetic fallacy, a monster hurricane in 1945 destroyed half the island's sugar crop, and with it one of the only sources of income.

Another group of people were also to suffer in Mauritius during the war. Mauritius has never had a large Jewish population—

209

STAR AND KEY

estimates rarely put it above 100, with a sole synagogue situated in Curepipe and a cemetery in Beau Bassin. That cemetery has a dark past. With the horrors of Jewish persecution in Europe during World War II, Mauritius had to play its role. In September 1940, the *Atlantic* was one of three British ships scouting the shores of Europe specifically to pick up 3,600 Jewish refugees fleeing from Vienna, Prague, Gdansk and elsewhere, with the intention of taking them to the relatively safer haven of Palestine. Yet on their arrival in port there, the pernickety officials denied them entry based on inadequate permits, astonishingly referring to them as 'illegal immigrants'. Scrambling around for alternatives, the British decided that the two safest colonies to send them to would be Trinidad in the Caribbean and Mauritius.

After enduring bombings in Haifa Bay that sank one of the ships, killing many of the refugees, the *Atlantic* managed to dock in Port Louis on 9 December 1940, ostensibly to offer a relatively safe home for 1,584 refugees. On arrival, however, there was a bewildered ignorance about who these refugees were. With many of them speaking supposedly 'Germanic languages', it was not a great leap for the more imaginative to start assuming that there were Nazi spies amongst them. As a result, they were sent to the nearby town of Beau Basin, allegedly for 'processing'. In fact, it was nothing less than a detainment camp: food was limited, clothing poor and disease predictably rife. For reasons never officially made clear, the men and women were initially separated and kept in hot metal huts. More importantly, no excuse was ever given as to why these refugees were treated with such disdain by the power that had ostensibly gone out of its way to save them. Over four years later, at the end of the war, they were given the choice of returning either to Europe or Palestine. By this stage, however, it was too late for 128 of them who had succumbed to disease and malnutrition. Hastily, a corner of St Martin Cemetery in Beau Bassin was set aside for Jewish burials.

PROGRESS

It was another small but dark stain on history's treatment of the Jewish people.

The war was over. The world had changed, and for once Mauritius felt in lockstep with it. In anticipation of the 1948 elections, several major state reforms were made, all encapsulated within a new, long overdue constitution that was formalised in 1947. On top of the introduction of universal education and the installation of the Department of Labour before the war, 100 village councils (to be overseen by four new district councils) were now set up, as was a new Legislative Assembly. The district councils would be staffed by both colonial and Mauritian officials. Crucially, the legislative institution removed the property, income and gender suffrage requirements that had been the bane of the workers' lives since the 1885 constitution. Essentially, if you were an adult who could write your name in one of the nineteen languages spoken regularly on the island, then you now had the vote. To that end, twelve members were now appointed to the Assembly by the governor, and the number of elected representatives increased to nineteen. It wasn't full democracy as we would recognise it now, but it was slowly getting there.

The stage was therefore set for the seminal August 1948 elections. They were, as predicted, a game-changer. The MLP was now headed by trade unionist Guy Rozemont, a native Creole speaker and fiery orator, who stood and won in Port Louis. Indo-Mauritians took eleven of the nineteen elected seats; eight went to the General Population, of which a sole seat was won by a Franco-Mauritian. There was another barrier broken when Emilienne Rochecouste became the first female to be elected to the Legislative Council. The Oligarchs still held considerable wealth, but their disproportionate political power was finally waning. Even so, the governor himself, now Donald Mackenzie-Kennedy, still had the right to personally appoint a dozen members to the Council. The fact that he waited until the final results

211

were in before appointing twelve conservatives—largely Franco-Mauritians—seemed initially like a slap in the face or a backward step to some, appearing to perpetuate the very circumstances that many Mauritians were trying to move away from. In reality, it was canny diplomacy. By ensuring that the Council had some semblance of balance, Mackenzie-Kennedy was minimising the chances of quick-fire radical change that would likely have left Mauritius unready and unstable.

Mauritius was on a new path. At this stage, very few people were openly mentioning the 'I' word, but within a few years, a new breed of charismatic politicians would come to the fore and 'Independence' would become an unavoidable issue.

16

THE LONG AND ROCKY ROAD

Flippant as it may seem, to understand the dynamics of post-war Mauritian politics you could do a lot worse than simply looking at some of the banknotes in your wallet.

As with so much on the island, the currency needs to be scrupulously balanced and fair across ethnicity and belief. The Rs25 note shows one of the great Sino-Mauritians, Jean Moilin Ah-Chuen. His father, Chu-Wei Chuen, had come to the island from Guangdong in 1887, and Jean—born in 1911—followed the customary role of helping to manage the family grocery store. But he would set his sights very much higher. Establishing his own chain of stores in 1931 called ABC—'Au Bazar Central'—Jean rapidly revealed himself to be something of a polymath. He founded the *Chinese Daily News*; he helped set up the Mauritius Union Assurance; and at 31 he became the youngest president of the Mauritian Chinese Chamber of Commerce. ABC grew into a huge and diverse conglomerate under his leadership. His reputation and influence were so strong that after the 1948 elections, the British asked him to be one of their twelve Legislative Council members as a spokesperson for the Sino-

213

STAR AND KEY

Mauritian community—the first Sino-Mauritian to hold such a role. That community had by then grown to nearly 3 per cent of the total population. His influence spread further after Independence, since on his recommendation, the Mauritian ambassador to China would wherever possible come from the Sino-Mauritian community. Furthermore, his suggestion to Parliament that the Chinese New Year/Spring Festival should become one of Mauritius' public holidays was accepted; it remains the only African country where it is officially celebrated. He was always going to be the first Sino-Mauritian in any future cabinet of an independent Mauritius.

Next comes the Rs50 note, which shows Maurice Paturau. Like Ah-Chuen, Paturau couldn't be tied down to a single profession; his skills and successes were too wide. Having taken the well-trodden Franco-Mauritian path of *Collège Royal* followed by studies in England (Mechanical Engineering at Imperial College), he studied in France during the war and didn't hesitate to help in the Liberation, undertaking seventy-six missions as a pilot—some quite dangerous—before his twenty-seventh birthday, for which he was duly decorated. Born with a keen business brain, by the age of 30 he was already the managing director of Forges Tardieu, a company focused on modernising sugar-cutting techniques. He would also enter politics in 1962 at the request of the British governor at the time, Colville Deverell. Later in life, he would be described by an Indo-Mauritian colleague as 'A man of substance, a highly decorated war hero, a creative engineer, a remarkable sportsman, a prolific writer, a brilliant debater in Parliament, a no-nonsense Minister, a Private Sector dynamo, a caring family man and above all a patriot of the highest order.'

Renganaden Seeneevassen, who graces the Rs100 note, had a shorter life than most of his banknote compatriots, but a busy one, nonetheless. Born in 1910, and rapidly showing smarts, his

THE LONG AND ROCKY ROAD

Collège Royal schooling was followed by the London School of Economics, before he was called to the bar after studying law. He returned to Mauritius to combine legal work with a role as liaison officer at the Ministry of Health. Never one to sit back and relax, he joined the MLP in the 1940s and was soon elected as Port Louis councillor. He deeply impressed Governor Donald Mackenzie Kennedy as a man with a shrewd brain, sound judgement and compassion. He was elected to the Legislative Council in both 1948 and 1953, and chosen as Mauritius' representative to attend the 1953 Coronation of Queen Elizabeth II. Later appointed Minister of Education, he was beginning to soar the heights and challenge as a future leader before being cut down by illness in 1958, aged only 48. Although his Tamil origins might have later proved to be a handicap, his was a tale of what might have been, and he personified the leadership potential that Mauritius had at its disposal.

The man on the Rs200 note, Abdool Razack Mohamed, was very different from the first three. Abdool Razack was born in Calcutta in British India in 1906, only emigrating to Mauritius in 1928. Living in the inland town of Quatre Bornes, he became a well-known businessman during the 1930s, only switching to political life in 1940. By this stage, fed up with the anachronistic constraints of the 1885 constitution, he was amongst those pleading the cause that all Indo-Mauritians—whether they were the majority who were Hindu, or the minority who were, like him, Muslim—should be enfranchised. His persuasive voice added meaningfully to the cause, leading to the ground-breaking 1948 elections in which he personally stood as a candidate in Port Louis, but lost. In the 1950s, however, when he was elected three consecutive times as mayor of Port Louis for most of this decade, his position shifted away considerably from what seemed his natural home, the MLP, towards the new party *Ralliement Mauricien* (RM), set up in

215

STAR AND KEY

1953 by Franco-Mauritian Jules Koenig out of the ashes of a previous party known as the *Union Mauricienne.*

In light of the increased number of Hindu Indo-Mauritians who voted in 1948, and with the Hindu population at the time approaching 60 per cent of the island's total, Abdool Razack suddenly became nervous about Hindu hegemony. Although Mohamed and Koenig at face value seemed very unlikely bedfellows, their overarching joint message was that the RM should be the voice of all Mauritian minorities, whom they felt were at risk of being dominated by the Hindu majority—in a microcosm of the tensions between Nehru and Jinnah during the recent difficult birth of India and Pakistan. This, of course, was a mere assertion on Abdool Razack's part, as it had never been a stated aim of the political Indo-Mauritians. Eventually falling out with the RM, in 1959 Abdool Razack founded a new party, the *Comité d'Action Musulman* (Muslim Action Committee—CAM). This brought into stark light what was already well known: politics in Mauritius—from hereon in, for good or ill—would be dictated by ethnic or religious considerations above almost everything else.

Sookdeo Bissoondoyal, who adorns the Rs500 note, was different again. Born on Christmas Day, 1908, near Rivière des Anguilles in the south of the island, he was for over twenty years a primary school teacher. Yet as World War II ended, so did Bissoondoyal's appetite for teaching, and he was drawn by his brother into the tumultuous world of post-war Mauritian politics. It didn't take long for him to leave his mark. Using his long-crafted skill of speaking clearly and didactically at rallies, his messages landed more soundly than most. He was subsequently voted into the Legislative Council in 1948, representing the Grand-Port-Savanne constituency—a post he was re-elected for in 1953. Yet Bissoondoyal was clear that to obtain his desired outcome of independence, a more overt strategy was needed, and

THE LONG AND ROCKY ROAD

this led him to found the Independent Forward Bloc (IFB) in 1958. The name was a master stroke. By using the word 'Independent' rather than 'Independence', he was making it clear that his party (for the time being, at least) was separate from others in terms of its blend of seeking social reform whilst being culturally conservative; yet, at the same time, it was very obvious what their overarching desired end-state was: complete separation from the British.

One of Abdool Razack Mohamed's colleagues at the RM in the late 1950s would be another future titan of Mauritian politics: Gaëtan Duval, whose smiling face now decorates the Rs1,000 note. Duval was from a wealthy Creole family and was born on Barkly Street in Rose-Hill in 1930. Like so many other future political leaders, the *Collège Royal* was followed by further education in Europe, in his case to study law at both Lincoln's Inn in London and the University of Paris. Although still only in his late twenties, he was a successful barrister with a string of high-profile successes to his name. Perhaps more than any other Mauritian politician of the time—or even since—Duval absolutely oozed charisma. He was a populist, unashamedly flamboyant, and was proud to belong to the 'You love him or hate him' camp. To see him work a crowd at a political hustings was to watch a master communicator in action. Duval—or 'Joe', as he was almost universally known—also knew how to work the law. At the 1959 elections, standing as the RM candidate in Curepipe, he was defeated by MLP candidate Romricky Ramsamy. Undeterred, Duval coolly contested the result at the Mauritius Supreme Court, arguing that Ramsamy had included his nickname, 'Narain', as part of his registration and that this would have been too confusing for the electorate, as it may not have been clear to some of them who they were voting for. Amazingly, he won. He would continue to help shape the febrile world of Mauritian politics for decades.

STAR AND KEY

Yet when it comes to towering figures of twentieth-century Mauritian politics, there is one name that is associated with Mauritius more than any other. Unsurprisingly, it is Sir Seewoosagur Ramgoolam—often referred to as 'Chacha', or 'Father'—who adorns the Rs2,000 note in Mauritius; indeed, his name adorns a great deal else besides, including a hospital, the botanical gardens and the island's airport. Ramgoolam's origins were in fact a little more modest than those of many of his peers. Born in Belle Rive in eastern Mauritius on 18 September 1900, his father, Moheeth, had only arrived in Mauritius from India four years earlier on the ship the *Hindoostan*, and then worked as an indentured labourer on the local sugar estate. Their origins being in northern India near the Nepali border, the family spoke Bhojpuri, a widespread Indo-Aryan language commonly spoken there. Even so, Seewoosagur—who was nicknamed 'Kewal' ('Perfect') as a child—would soon converse fluently in Mauritian Creole like everyone else.

Ramgoolam was not just smart; he was thirsty for all knowledge. Although well-grounded in wider Indian and Hindu culture at home, he used to sneak out without his mother's knowledge to the local Catholic primary school so that he could learn more about history and geography, as well as English and French culture. By the time he was 12, his father was already long dead and Ramgoolam had lost the vision in his left eye after a farm accident. Undeterred, he breezed through the *Collège Royal* before being given a loan by his older brother to fund his further studies in medicine at University College London. During that time, he was deeply impressed at the rapid success of Ramsay MacDonald's relatively young UK Labour Party, which gained power in 1924. After being away in Europe for over a decade, Ramgoolam came back to a rapidly evolving Mauritius in 1935, and soon became enamoured of Maurice Curé's MLP message of social reform and universal suffrage—

THE LONG AND ROCKY ROAD

hardly surprising for the son of an indentured labourer who had never had things presented to him on a plate.

During World War II Ramgoolam wrote political pamphlets under the enigmatic pseudonym 'Thumb Mark II', and apart from a three-year break from 1953–56 he was elected from 1940–60 as a Port Louis Municipal Councillor. More importantly, he was concurrently a decades-long member of the Legislative Council, from 1940 until well after Independence in 1968. He inevitably took over the leadership of the MLP in 1959. By then, the British had long marked him out for his level-headedness, quiet leadership abilities and strategic thinking. Ramgoolam was undoubtedly proud of his Indian roots and became president of the Indian Cultural Association that sprang up after the war. But his willingness to always learn the ways of others—first seen by his sneaking into a primary school that he wasn't enrolled in—never left him. He was also a practising Freemason, joining the same lodge—*Loge de la Triple Esperance*—that had seen Robert Farquhar as its most famous son many years earlier.

These were far from being the only active and important politicians of the 1950s and 1960s, but their sheer diversity of culture, religion, upbringing and political thought would ensure that the road to independence was never going to be straightforward. Yet by the late 1950s, independence was much more openly discussed in a way that it had not been a decade earlier. Furthermore, following British Prime Minister Harold Macmillan's epoch-changing speech in 1960, in which he acknowledged and supported the 'wind of change' blowing through Africa, there was a sense of inevitability that Mauritius would get its own turn eventually.

This being Mauritius, however, it was guaranteed that sugar and the weather would play out their own 'Acts of God' to help mould that path. On the plus side, the Commonwealth Sugar Agreement of 1951 gave Mauritian sugar producers preferential

STAR AND KEY

prices and guaranteed export quotas, providing the industry with a measure of security. That said, there was no guarantee of minimum pay-out in case of massive fluctuations of international sugar prices, or if Mauritius couldn't produce the necessary quotas. Less than a decade later, that limitation was brought into sharp relief. On 27 February 1960, Cyclone Carol struck Mauritius, and she was an absolute behemoth with gusts of over 155 miles per hour making her the strongest on record at the time; the destruction she caused still features prominently in many old Mauritian family photo albums in a way that many other cyclones don't. Forty-two people were left dead, nearly 100 were seriously injured, and 15 per cent of the population was left homeless due to destroyed houses—well over 100,000 people. In addition to the human suffering was the economic one. Around 60 per cent of the island's entire sugar crop was wiped out in twenty-four terrifying hours, and no amount of clever interpretation could avoid the fact that this would mean a dramatic drop in public and private revenue.

But that wasn't the only challenge. Efforts to take advantage of new breakthroughs to eradicate some of the diseases that had plagued Mauritius for so long were successful. There were fewer adult deaths and by extension infant mortality had halved since before World War II. This latter decline was truly remarkable; it took Mauritius only five years to do what Britain had taken thirty years to achieve. These were great success stories, but they also meant that the population was snowballing, surpassing 650,000 by the end of the 1950s—and, compared to previously, it was a much younger population. Put bluntly, this meant there were not enough school places for the number of children; there was a subsequent rise in unemployment from all those early school leavers; and there were not enough jobs being created in a stagnant economy. The British authorities took note of this, trying in 1957 to introduce more formal family planning education. But

THE LONG AND ROCKY ROAD

for once, almost every community—regardless of ethnicity or religion—was of the same opinion: 'You still technically rule us, but you have no right to tell us how big our families should be.' Whilst politically expedient, this outright rejection would be quietly shelved across the board in the 1960s, when many began to see the economic advantages of smaller families.

Meanwhile, with the MLP the dominant power after the 1953 elections, they passed a motion via the Legislative Council demanding talks on constitutional reform. A case could be made that this was the opening salvo in Mauritius' ultimate quest for independence. Not that Britain did much, with some impressive delaying tactics meaning that it wasn't until 1959 that the constitution was again updated, and the new electoral process wasn't remotely straightforward. There would now be forty new constituencies and the twelve governor-nominated seats would morph into a system known as 'best loser'—an olive branch to protect the under-represented minorities, including the Sino-Mauritians, Franco-Mauritians and Muslim Indo-Mauritians. In turn, the governor conceived of an Executive Council consisting of a mere nine members, with even representation from all the parties already voted in via the Legislative Council. If that sounds confusing, then it's probably because it was meant to be. The introduction of these extra checks and balances was an effort to ensure that in a hyper-fluid political landscape, no party could suddenly grasp undiluted power. The ancient concept of 'divide and rule' was still alive, albeit barely.

By the 1959 election, the political parties were playing a game of merry-go-round, with alliances and splinter groups coming and going at an alarming speed. The CAM and MLP had joined forces, while the RM had been rebranded as the *Parti Mauricien Social Démocrate* (PMSD). The MLP won twenty-three of the forty seats, and the subsequent all-party coalition that formed gave many the false hope that stability would be the watchword in the run-up to the momentous events of the 1960s. They were wrong.

As part of the wider divesting of its colonial territories, London had promised to hold a conference in London in 1961 to 'discuss the path to further constitutional development'—which was diplomatic speak for: 'How can we deliver Mauritian independence without short-term bloodshed and long-term economic carnage?' Unsurprisingly, once there it was the MLP—now under Ramgoolam—who spoke loudest in favour of independence. Conversely, the PMSD (the natural home of the Franco-Mauritians, but also supported by many other members of the General Population, as well as some minority groups) disagreed, wanting to stay as part of Britain for three reasons. First, once Britain joined the European Economic Community (EEC), their possible sugar markets without tariffs would grow enormously; second, it would allow greater social mobility, as it would be that much easier for Mauritians to work in Europe; and third, it would—in their eyes—lessen the possibility of Hindu hegemony taking hold on the island. Britain, though, knew which way the wind was blowing—both for its empire and for the Mauritians.

By the 1963 elections, the PMSD had joined up with Sookdeo Bissoondoyal's culturally conservative Independent Forward Bloc (IFB), but splits were showing between the MLP and the CAM. Britain, under the auspices of the new governor, Sir John Shaw Rennie, pressed hard for further devolution of power to the Mauritians. Rennie had asked Maurice Paturau—hitherto not a politician—to act as a calm and steadying hand as Minister of Commerce and Industry and to take up the new post of Minister of Tourism. Paturau accepted. More important was another new policy: from now on, the head of the largest party in the Legislative Council—now known as the Legislative Assembly— would also take the title of 'Chief Minister', overseeing internal affairs via a new Ministerial Council that had cross-party repre-

THE LONG AND ROCKY ROAD

sentation. Ramgoolam, as head of the MLP, duly took that position. Unsaid at the time, but blindingly obvious later, was that this seemingly innocuous development was a step towards the passing on of power by Britain that could never be undone.

The PMSD, now with Duval as its deputy leader, took great exception to this development and boycotted the opening of the Legislative Assembly. Then things got really ugly: the increasingly Creole-influenced PMSD, as well as the predominantly Muslim CAM, convinced themselves that future independence was a Hindu-led stitch-up. Both started projecting a more explicitly anti-Hindu rhetoric, with some slogans using well-known pejorative terms for Mauritian Hindus. All this did was galvanise the Indo-Mauritian Hindus into a more militant posture, with the formation of the All-Mauritius Hindu Congress in 1964. Community tensions were by now white hot. In 1965, the pressure cooker finally exploded. Firstly, in February an MLP supporter named Rampersad Surath was set upon by a thuggish branch of the PMSD and beaten to death during a street rally just outside Quatre Bornes. Then, on 10–12 May, a full-blown race riot kicked off in the unassuming village of Trois Boutiques in the southeast, spreading quickly to the larger town of Mahébourg. Only the declaration of a state of emergency by the governor—backed up by a rapid deployment of the British Coldstream Guards from Aden—stopped the dangerous situation from escalating further.

The British realised that another conference was needed to try to sort out the mess before it became untenable. This would be the last. Held at Lancaster House in London from 7 to 24 September 1965, all the major players on the Mauritian side were there: Ramgoolam, Abdool Razack, Paturau, Duval, Bissoondoyal and more. It was a profoundly tense and complex affair, the details of which are too numerous to discuss here. In essence, however, the outcome was as follows. Only two parties were demanding immediate unconditional independence: Ramgoolam's MLP and Bissoondoyal's IFB. That said, in the previous elections of 1963, these two parties between them had secured over 61 per cent of the vote, which Britain—perhaps by now keen to offload the island as part of its broader 'wind of change' decolonisation of the previous decade, and therefore over-egging the terminology—called in the subsequent report, 'an indicator of the overwhelming support of independence'. The PMSD had made its position clear. Conversely, the CAM was caught equivocating due to Abdool Razack's longer-term concerns. However, he worked with Jean Ah-Chuen to propose a formula to safeguard the interests of minority groups in the Legislative Assembly—a formalisation of the 'best loser' process—which was accepted.

It looked very promising for the independence seekers, and to that end, they were keen to accede to extra British demands to ensure that the path would be as smooth as possible. In the event, they agreed to something that they would later bitterly regret. Britain, and many others, had seen a change in geopolitical power bases during the Cold War that had ensued since the end of World War II. They also knew that the Chagos Archipelago (see Chapter 13), almost slap bang in the middle of the Indian Ocean, would form an extremely desirable military base. Taking advantage of the obvious division within the Mauritian delegation, the British were happy to agree to subsequent Mauritian independence, including all its own offshore dependencies ... except for Chagos. Its population at the time was a sparse 1,600 and these '*Ilois*' would have to be resettled in the event of a military base being built—most likely by Britain's close ally the USA—and the islands renamed 'British Indian Ocean Territory' (BIOT). Britain then dangled a £3 million compensation incentive for that resettlement, and the Mauritian delegation, after some resistance, agreed. Would it really be that

THE LONG AND ROCKY ROAD

much of a problem? In Chapter 18, we will see that a pretty strong answer materialised: Yes.

By now, 1968 was being openly mentioned as the year that independence would happen. Ramgoolam, as head of the largest party, would in the interim assume the title of 'Premier'. It was also agreed that a further set of elections would need to be held in August 1967 to finalise the shape of the first independent assembly. Before then, the MLP, the IFB and the CAM realised that joining forces—for the near future at least—would make a lot of sense for the consolidation of power that was inevitably coming their way. Together, the three formed a coalition known as the Independence Party. Assuming all went well, this essentially guaranteed future ministerial roles for its leaders. Sure enough, the elections saw them gain 54.6 per cent of the vote, which translated into forty-three of the now seventy seats in the rejigged assembly.

But the path to freedom is never so simple. Voting had hardly finished before street fighting broke out in Port Louis between the CAM-supporting Muslims and the Creole and Sino-Mauritian supporters of the PMSD. Roadblocks and car burnings ensued, and even though riot police intervened with tear gas, the tensions bubbled and spread wider throughout the second half of the year, with protests and assaults growing that were exacerbated by a general increase in youth unemployment. The Employment Exchange in the capital was ransacked and again it was left to the special Mobile Units to restore order.

Sadly, this was merely an hors d'oeuvre to the events of January 1968. The island's Independence Day had now been set for 12 March—in a nod to the start of Gandhi's Salt March in India in 1930. Yet many locals remained deeply uneasy about future job security and Mauritius' ability to go it alone, not least as ethnic tensions were at their highest. It was also the first occasion that 'gangs' as we would now recognise them made their

225

presence felt in Mauritian political affairs. Although superficially the primary instigators appeared to be Muslim CAM-supporting youths and their Creole, PMSD-supporting equivalents in the eastern suburbs of Port Louis, these were far from the only protagonists. Notable too was the lack of much political intervention. Over several days, nearly 1,000 homes were looted or burned down and hundreds of families displaced. Most significantly, although the official figures for deaths were twenty-nine, it was abundantly clear that the true figure was likely far higher. All ethnicities were dragged in, and it was telling that officials soon started to refrain from naming those who had died in the riots, as they were understandably concerned that to do so would make it seem as though one ethnic group was being targeted more than another, and thus open the door for retribution and more violence.

The newly titled Governor-General Rennie was again forced to declare a state of emergency for 10 days, this time drawing on 150 British troops of the King's Shropshire Light Infantry, stationed in Singapore, to quickly arrive and restore peace. Only then did social and religious leaders start more vociferously calling for peace. Although the violence was contained to the urban and suburban areas of Port Louis and had thankfully not spread, it was clear that members of almost all Mauritius' diverse ethnic groups had suffered.

Such was the rather sobering backdrop to 12 March 1968. Furthermore, with tensions still high and the threat of violence lingering, the British decided that sending over Princess Alexandra to the ceremony to represent Queen Elizabeth II would be too risky; it was left to Governor-General Rennie himself to act as the senior British representative. This rather subdued context was far from what the independence-seeking Mauritians had envisaged, yet they made the most of it. At midday on 12 March at the Champ de Mars racecourse in Port

THE LONG AND ROCKY ROAD

Louis, an estimated 150,000 Mauritians turned up to see the Union flag slowly lowered, to be replaced by the newly designed Mauritian national flag, designed by retired schoolteacher Gurudutt Moher, which persists to this day: four horizontal bands in the descending order of red, blue, yellow and green.

Each colour had a primary meaning. Red supposedly stood for the struggle for independence and the blood that was shed in the process. The blue represented the beautiful Indian Ocean that surrounded the island. Yellow stood for 'the light of freedom' that would now be a beacon over the island. Green stood for the overwhelming colour that defined the island's landscape, be it the cane fields or the rapidly diminishing forests. But the colours had a secondary meaning too, and this was not coincidental. Red had always been the colour associated with the workers' parties; blue had long been the emblem of the PMSD, doubtless in a nod to the French heritage that many of them clung so tightly to; yellow had long been the colour associated with the IFB; and, of course, green was the recognised colour associated with Islam, as represented by the CAM. Thus the flag was another yearning attempt by the emerging nation to strive for unity.

As the flag ceremony unfurled, 'God Save the Queen' was sung for a final time, soon followed by Mauritius' new national anthem, 'Motherland'. Sir Seewoosagur Ramgoolam—who had been knighted in 1965—was sworn in as Mauritius' first independent prime minister. The emotional day continued with special religious services held in temples, mosques and churches around the island. As a final flourish, the first batch of passports of the newly independent state were printed, emblazoned with the nation's Latin motto: *Stella Clavisque Maris Indici*—Star and Key of the Indian Ocean.

After twenty years of see-saw politics, shifting loyalties, intrigue, violence and finally independence, Mauritius—of its

STAR AND KEY

own volition—now had to stand on its own two feet. Lingering ethnic tensions that by now were defining so many elements of the political landscape were always on the horizon, and sometimes much closer. The challenges were numerous, and the strategic action plans to combat them had not yet been thought through. Some wary Mauritians who had been in two minds about the benefits of independence quietly voiced their opinion that the island needed a miracle to survive and prosper.

Incredibly, however, a miracle is exactly what happened.

17

THE MIRACLE

In 1960, two reports were commissioned by the governor of Mauritius on its longer-term social and economic prospects, and their conclusions were nothing short of terrifying.

In that year, Professor James Meade, a world-renowned British economist who would later win the Nobel Prize in the subject, led an economic survey of Mauritius. In the introduction to the report, published in 1961, Meade boldly wrote: 'In the author's opinion, Mauritius faces ultimate catastrophe.' And it got more pessimistic from there. Concurrently, pioneering researcher Richard Titmuss led a report into social conditions, and his level of confidence in Mauritius' future matched Meade's: he predicted a government that would quickly face bankruptcy and a domino-like collapse of the welfare system. To complete a triumvirate of doom, the World Bank sent a mission to Mauritius in 1962 which did not hold back on its findings: 'This country exudes an air of hopelessness.' And just to show that it wasn't only 'men in suits' passing judgement, when V. S. Naipaul, future winner of the Nobel Prize for literature, visited around the time of independence, he described Mauritius as 'a stinky hell-hole',

STAR AND KEY

an 'overcrowded barracoon' and 'incapable of economic or cultural autonomy'.

It is hard to overstate the extraordinary strength of this wording coming from professionals and writers alike, many of whom usually preferred to couch their words in more nebulous political terminology. These dire assessments were based on a number of converging facts and beliefs. Of major concern to all these experts and advisors was the likelihood of an uncontrollable population explosion in what was already one of the most densely populated countries in the world. With the improvement in healthcare, the eradication of malaria, and fertility rates which had reached an eye-opening six children born per woman, this population increase—already described by Titmuss as 'phenomenal' in the 1940s and 1950s—meant a total of 804,000 had been reached in 1968. One model calculated by the demographers in the 1960s even envisaged the 'terrifying prospect' of 3 million by the end of the century.

Based on this devastating feedback, it is hardly surprising that fully half the population did not want independence to arrive in that decade, as it irrevocably did in 1968. Compounding this dire outlook were a few realities which, whilst hardly unique to Mauritius, were nevertheless extra obstacles to be surmounted. For instance, no country on earth could put their hand up in the 1960s and claim to be a bastion of gender equality; but in Mauritius, by 1972, only 20 per cent of women were in the labour market. Furthermore, the gender pay gap was starkly evident to all, and even by 1976 only three of the seventy National Assembly seats—a measly 4 per cent—were occupied by women. The inferior education opportunities offered to women over the years were undoubtedly a factor in this.

Concern for the quality of labour was equally high. Cronyism was rife—again, hardly a novelty—and there was further fear when in the four-year aftermath of independence 14,000

THE MIRACLE

Mauritians chose to make their homes elsewhere—with Europe, South Africa and Australia featuring highly as target destinations. Many of these were skilled employees, business owners and high-net-worth individuals, primarily Franco-Mauritian and Creole, who had taken the stark findings of the 1960 reports at face value and didn't want to be there to see the purported catastrophe unfold.

On the monetary front, with so much cash leaving the island, the authorities felt they had no option other than to suspend the earlier colonial system of a free convertibility rate with respect to the pound sterling, and to put in place strict exchange controls. Yet this restrictive measure only ended up causing difficulties in international business transactions and severely constraining foreign travel, all leading to even more significant negative economic impacts. This risked being the start of a proper brain drain, yet even with this mini-exodus, unemployment still hovered at 20 per cent in the early 1970s. It was already well known that tensions existed throughout the business sector in the 1960s. One of the accepted prerequisites of success in a mixed economy is a productive and confident working relationship between the government and the business sector. Yet in the lead-up to independence, this relationship looked anything but promising, compounded by the fact that the Mauritian face of capitalism was mostly that of the Franco-Mauritian 'elite' who had been amongst the strongest opponents of the MLP government-led independence platform.

To complete the untenable situation, Mauritius' independence had come with an understanding that all ethnicities needed to be treated with a kind of equity that manifested itself tangibly. To that end, and keen not to rock the already unsteady boat, officials drew up and introduced a set of annual public holidays that Mauritians could observe. However, with so many communities and religions to include, none with official primacy, in the first couple of years of independence Mauritius had an astonishing twenty-eight annual public holidays—by far the most of any country in the world. An impressive recognition of social and religious equality this may have been, but it was an absolute disaster for the economy.

'Gloomy' didn't begin to describe Mauritius' prognosis in 1968. Fittingly, the best word to capture the general mood was a Mauritian Creole one, recounted by a resident British economics expert at the time: 'The word "lamizer"—roughly equivalent to "hopeless poverty"—was on everyone's lips.' Yet here's the thing: by the end of the century, Mauritius would have undergone an extraordinary economic transformation almost unheard of since the birth of economics as a studied science, and completely unparalleled compared to its African counterparts that had gone through a similar process of decolonisation. In the twenty-first century, income per capita increased seven-fold between 1968 and 2020, when the World Bank—perhaps with a more optimistic culture than previously—reclassified Mauritius as a high-income country (albeit before the shock of Covid-19 in 2020). It was a resurrection that has come to be known as the 'Mauritian economic miracle', and continues to be used as a benchmark and study example from the United Nations down.

How on earth did it happen?

A plethora of foreign experts and Mauritian analysts have drilled down into the details, interpreting the data and the evidence in a variety of ways. The overall scene is complex, and the minutiae do not always add up, yet it appears at the macro level that there were five disparate factors which together delivered this economic alchemy. As some observers have pointed out, whilst far from being purely fortuitous, the transformation perhaps had an element of serendipity woven into it.

The first of these could be called 'institutional stability'. Many nations don't realise that they either have this or need it until it

THE MIRACLE

is too late. In Mauritius' case, it had been a conscious decision to tinker with the entire institutional set-up until a balance was struck that both spoke to what Mauritius needed and, as a litmus test, would not look out of place when sat beside the equivalent structures of its two previous colonial powers. Whilst Mauritius was now keen to plough its own furrow, it was equally open-minded enough to recognise that the political systems in Britain and France, as well as elements from India, remained good strategic role models in terms of a healthy, mixed economy working towards a stable and open democracy.

No one pretended that Mauritius' 'first-past-the-post' voting system was perfect—or even particularly fair in the long run. It did tend to favour the larger parties and allow them to gain an abnormal number of parliamentary seats; but, by the same token, the concept was borrowed wholesale from the British electoral system, and for all Westminster's recognised flaws it had at least delivered a sustained and stable democracy. Equally valid in the electoral process itself was the lack of vote rigging. Whilst the stuffing of ballot boxes and intimidation at voting booths had become a mainstay in many nations that had also recently achieved independence, Mauritius was notable for simply not having a culture of these practices, despite the odd exception. Overall, therefore, when an election result was called, it tended to be accepted and not to result in accusations of fraud—a process which even the USA couldn't adhere to after the events during and after the presidential election in 2020.

But a vital cog in having a stable parliamentary democracy is to have an independent judiciary, and again Mauritius had been well served. Despite more recent cracks beginning to appear, the Mauritian Supreme Court has been respected as the national arbiter, cemented by a later agreement to offer a right of appeal to the Privy Council of Law Lords in the UK. This stability, in turn, has prevented any one politician from thinking that they could quietly introduce more despotic policies.

STAR AND KEY

Two further key institutional elements are of course the media and the armed forces. Even the most neutral observer would probably conclude that Mauritius' press is far from perfect. The national broadcaster, the Mauritius Broadcasting Corporation (MBC), has for long periods been obliged to kowtow to the ruling government's point of view—whichever ruling party that was—and the media regulatory agency lacks full independence. Conversely, a free and open printed press was and is allowed, with strident political viewpoints published, often veering into sensationalism. Reassuringly, however, at election time most of the political parties are given a fair hearing and adequate coverage. The freeing of the radio airwaves for private broadcasters in the early twenty-first century was another major milestone, and the later ubiquity of the younger generation choosing to get their news online via many different channels has rendered the MBC's political posture slightly less relevant anyway.

As for the army, quite simply Mauritius chose not to have one. Its security functions to this day are carried out by 10,000 police officers on Mauritius and Rodrigues. This seems brave or even foolhardy on the face of it, but actually it was a clever and expedient decision. With ethnic tensions high at the time of independence, there was likely to be conflict about who would lead any armed forces and whether they would represent all Mauritians. Better, therefore, not to have one at all, knowing that Britain and France, as ongoing allies, would assist if really needed. More immediately, it allowed for the freeing up of a large amount in government coffers for other priorities—money that would otherwise have been sunk into the costly process of maintaining an army, navy and air force. All these factors together mattered. Mauritius has since maintained a high reputation within international circles, including the UN, as a mostly respectful adherent to both democracy and human rights. This reputation was put in context by the Economist Intelligence Unit's 'Democracy Index'

THE MIRACLE

in 2019 which placed the country eighteenth in the world—above every other African and Asian nation, not to mention France and the USA.

However, history has taught us the hard way that one can't just set up these institutions in a day and hope for the best; indeed, there are many sad examples of this accelerated approach having been tried, with tragic consequences. What Mauritius had on its side—a second crucial factor, and one perhaps not properly appreciated at the time—was patience. Its gradual pace along the road to self-government and independence stood in stark contrast to that of many other colonies, notably on mainland Africa. Since the 1948 election, and standing on the shoulders of those who had first been elected in 1886, this generation of politicians had gained considerable political expertise and appreciation of what it would take to run a nation. Power had also been subtly devolved by British officials over the years, with Mauritians first holding liaison posts and then ministerial positions—with all the scrutiny and risk-ownership that entailed—throughout the 1960s. This was complemented by the same situation in the civil service, staffed largely by Mauritians after the war. This unrushed path to independence, coupled with the patient wisdom of those politicians who were promoting it using restrained techniques, proved crucial for its success.

One thing Mauritian politicians could admit to themselves—even if not shout from the rooftops, due to it being a deeply unfashionable view—was that for all colonialism's unquestion-ably dark side, there had been some elements of this kind of rule that were a net positive. Whether this was economic or purely political, there was an understanding that Mauritius had the chance to be more secure in its new-found freedom than others. A fundamental fact underlying this was that unlike almost all other colonial situations, Mauritius had no indigenous peoples inhabiting it when European powers arrived, meaning no resent-

235

STAR AND KEY

ful indigenous population clamouring for payback. Pragmatic Mauritian leaders could hardly base their narrative on a 'Give us our land *back*' slogan, as generally happened elsewhere. In short, if there had been no French and British colonialists, there simply would have been no Mauritian society. The politicians got this.

So, what of the leaders of the time? Were they also integral in helping to make the miracle happen? In fact, despite holding a whole raft of conflicting views and continuing their flip-flopping on both alliances and actual policy, the leadership collectively counted as the third critical success factor. Sir Seewoosagur Ramgoolam—almost always now referred to simply as SSR—has cemented his place as 'Father of the Nation', and his face won't be removed from the back of Mauritian coins any time soon. Even his political opponents admitted that he unquestionably had a personal touch and more than his fair share of emotional intelligence. Whether it was complex and sensitive matters of policy or simply remembering names and faces, his understated and inclusive approach, offset by a disarmingly high-pitched voice, proved a mainstay throughout the 1970s.

For his part, Gaëtan Duval fulfilled his role well as leader of the opposition from 1967–69 by holding the government to task. Indeed, when Bissoondoyal's IFB left the three-way Independence Party coalition in 1969 due to diverging political philosophies, there was something of a stunned silence when the PMSD then joined the coalition, allowing Duval and several colleagues to hold important cabinet posts. This might have been the canny Ramgoolam playing out the tried-and-tested political mantra, 'Keep your friends close and your enemies closer'; yet they worked well enough together until 1973—when Duval was sacked from his ministerial post, reverted to leading the opposition and then lost his Assembly seat altogether three years later.

There were also two new heavyweights in town. Anerood Jugnauth trained as a lawyer at Lincoln's Inn like Duval,

THE MIRACLE

although there the similarities ended. He had previously served as Minister for Labour in 1966, but with the advent of a new political party, the *Mouvement Militant Mauricien* (MMM), he found a more natural home, and would serve first as leader of the opposition from 1976, and then for four terms as prime minister in the 1980s and 1990s, during which he founded instead the *Mouvement Socialist Mauricien* (MSM). The change from 'militant' to 'socialist' demonstrated that he too knew when to temper his stronger beliefs into something both more accommodating and electable.

One of the co-founders of the MMM in 1969 had been Paul Bérenger, offering the comparatively rare sight of a Franco-Mauritian fighting for left-wing social causes, doubtless influenced by his personally witnessing the infamous Paris riots (*'Les Événements'*) of 1968. Working closely with Jugnauth throughout the 1970s, together they delivered an astonishing sixty seats at the 1982 election. With Bérenger taking the role of Minister of Finance, the two soon fell out over the centralisation of power within the prime minister's office, Bérenger later filling the role both of leader of the opposition and, in the new millennium, finally getting a shot at being prime minister from 2003–05, as part of a pre-agreed alternation between the coalition parties. In the 1970s, Bérenger had also pushed for Mauritian Creole to replace English as the national language. Although popular amongst some, the idea was rejected and English kept on for its wider international appeal. Again, Mauritian politicians had an open goal to play the easy nationalist card, but instead chose the sensible, international path. Their decision did no harm to Creole, which is still spoken as the *lingua franca* by almost every Mauritian.

On the one hand it is true that many of these politicians often possessed a slippery approach to both policy and loyalty— though that is an accusation that could be thrown at almost any politician around the world. On the other hand all of them

STAR AND KEY

seemed to have the good sense to see when something was working, and did not merely reverse policy once obtaining power, simply to spite their predecessors. Jugnauth also had the foresight, after his crushing victory against Ramgoolam in 1982, to appoint the elderly 'Father of the Nation' to the largely ceremonial post of governor-general. Despite their fair share of bitterness and invective, Mauritian politicians also had the intelligence and common sense to grasp the issues that really mattered, regardless of their leanings. Business leaders also played their part, with Prime Minister Anerood Jugnauth stating in 1987: 'Government and the private sector are working hand in hand towards more economic growth ... Our private sector has responded marvellously well to our incentives and taken advantage of the healthy business climate we have created.'

If leadership qualities counted as a third plus mark towards the success story, the fourth was in finally addressing an economic risk that had hung over Mauritius like a sweet-toothed Sword of Damocles for centuries. For all sugar's potential profits, which had grown further as a result of both improved mechanisation as well as favourable buying rates offered by the European Common Market (later the EEC and then the EU), it still amounted to putting all the country's precarious economic eggs into one flimsy basket. In any case, the industry had reached its limits in terms of arable land and was incapable of maintaining its employment levels, let alone creating new jobs. It was imperative to transform the wider economy with either new or largely untapped initiatives.

In the early 1960s, the first inklings of Mauritius' tourism potential were beginning to be obvious. It is worth noting that until then, despite the enticing beaches, there had not been a wider Mauritian tradition of going to the beach for the sake of going to the beach. Qantas flights from Australia had been stopping over on the island since 1952, but only to refuel on the way to South Africa. A mere 1,803 tourists visited in 1954, yet a

THE MIRACLE

decade later this had grown substantially to nearly 10,000—all without any effort at meaningful marketing. Beach hotels had now started to pop up, notably on the west and north coasts. With the founding of Air Mauritius in 1967, the tourist figure had grown to 27,650 by 1970. With a new marketing push and the transformation of air travel making it more affordable for many, this number exploded in the 1970s and has grown inexorably ever since, reaching the giddy heights of 1.4 million tourists in 2018; this contributed fully 12 per cent to the nation's GDP. Another cornerstone of the economy had been firmed up.

Economic innovation continued into the 1990s, when the island set up the Mauritius Freeport in 1993. Calling itself 'a duty-free logistics, distribution and marketing hub for the region', it employed over 4,000 and had traded nearly Rs40 billion by 2017. In 1992, the path had also been laid for setting up Mauritius as an offshore financial centre, allowing international companies—including insurance, shipping, aircraft financing and more—the opportunity to set up their headquarters and be administered from the island. As with tourism, this now accounts for 12 per cent of the nation's GDP, not to mention thousands of jobs. Offshore financial activities were triggered by a special double-taxation agreement granted by India, which was in force for some thirty years and led to Mauritius becoming the main country investing in India.

All of these factors were in various ways key to Mauritius getting itself out of the economic doghouse in the late 1960s to become something altogether different. Yet none, perhaps, was as important as the fifth factor: the nation's decision in 1972 to set up and continually support an Export Processing Zone (EPZ). This initiative has been described by Paul Romer, one of two Nobel Prize laureates in economics in 2018, as 'the only obvious candidate for explaining the success of Mauritius'. Usually, an EPZ is essentially a fenced-in industrial estate within

239

STAR AND KEY

a special economic zone—a trade enclave, in other words—that imports raw materials, manufactures a product from them and then exports them, all without any trade restrictions. Dry as this concept is to the non-expert, it is worth understanding its basics if one is to fully appreciate 'the miracle'.

By the mid-1960s, unemployment was already huge and rising, and there simply weren't enough on-island industries serving the local market to create more jobs. Meade's doomsday report was looking very realistic. Another international expert had visited Mauritius in 1967 and concluded that 'conditions were not favourable' for Mauritius to set up an EPZ. But the following year, the Mauritius Chamber of Commerce Annual Report stated the obvious: 'It no longer is relevant to ask whether export industries should be set up. The important question is how best to achieve this kind of development.' Again, the true meaning was hidden between the lines: beggars can't be choosers.

By the mid-1960s, a local entrepreneur had already found a novel way to create a most unusual kind of export industry, based on imported inputs. He was producing and exporting 'holes'. José Poncini, a local jeweller and watchmaker trained in Switzerland, had started the 'Micro Jewels' factory. This imported tiny industrial jewel bearings, used at the time in watchmaking, which needed to be pierced before being inserted into watches. This piercing of holes was done by Mauritian workers and the jewels returned to Europe by air. But this very specialised 'industry' could not be replicated for other types of production. However, this factory was not in a special fenced-off zone, and it was realised that export industries, based on imported inputs, did not need to be in a specific geographic area. This was to be the inspiration—actively promoted by Poncini himself—for the innovative feature of the future EPZ: that a company granted EPZ status did not need to be located in a designated 'zone'.

240

THE MIRACLE

Even so, it needed a champion to get it off the ground, and in Edouard Lim Fat it found one. Lim Fat—known as 'Man Ten' by his Sino-Mauritian shopkeeper parents as a boy—was born in 1921 and trained as an engineer at Imperial College in London. Returning for an academic career at the University of Mauritius, he became a professor, head of the School of Industrial Technology and finally acting vice-chancellor. Yet he was so much more than an academic. Lim Fat frequently travelled for work and play to the Far East. When in Hong Kong, Taiwan and Singapore, he visited the EPZs that had been set up there and which had essentially offered rocket fuel to their respective economies, turning them from undeveloped anomalies into industrial powerhouses. In his own humble words, Lim Fat recounted: 'It struck me that if these countries could successfully industrialise despite severe local constraints, Mauritius with its political stability, low salaries and dynamic business community could do just as well.'

It was hard to fault his logic, yet it needed not just a thinker but a doer to make this a reality, and fortunately Lim Fat was both. He studied the Far Eastern EPZs' mechanisms in depth and wrote a detailed proposal to the Mauritian government explaining how it could turn things around. Crucially, he and fellow Sino-Mauritians also asserted that they had plenty of business contacts who would be prepared to move their businesses to Mauritius if the conditions were right. Labour laws would need to be tweaked to make it as attractive as possible for them. This initially worried SSR, as he was unwilling to leave workers' rights unprotected. But even he saw that the idea was more than sound and that there were very few alternatives being discussed. Mauritius, frankly, was desperate.

Mauritius' EPZ, from the start, was different. Enterprises applied for and were granted special status, and this alone allowed them to locate their businesses anywhere on the island—other

STAR AND KEY

EPZs had usually been gigantic warehouses in industrial quarters of the cities, but Mauritius simply didn't have the space to go the same way. The textiles industry rapidly took off, and with it the much wider employment of women; in fact, by 1984, 80 per cent of workers employed under the EPZ were female. To attract even more businesses, the government's careful and deliberate devaluation of the rupee made the sector still more competitive.

Initially, workers' salaries there were not as high as in the sugar-cane fields, although this gradually changed. It was therefore not all plain sailing, and strikes occurred in the early teething days. However, as the sharing of ideas and processes that were coming in grew and blended with the skills and know-how of local processes already on-island, success was assured. By the 1980s, the idea of local 'factory shops' to sell produce—especially woollen garments—to tourists further increased revenue. By the 1990s, the lines between EPZ and non-EPZ companies gradually blurred, after a succession of government acts and tax laws. But by this stage it didn't matter, because the EPZ had brought more than just economic growth to the island; it had been pivotal in bringing about a change of mindset and attitude throughout the commercial sector. The miracle was complete.

The essential role of women in achieving this is sometimes greatly overlooked, yet it acts as another vital yardstick regarding Mauritius' growing social maturity, not least when one realises how the treatment of women in Mauritian society had been a societal hindrance since the early nineteenth century. The Napoleonic Civil Code adopted in Mauritius in 1808 imposed the status of 'minor' on a married woman—this was patriarchalism on steroids. Tellingly, during the electoral shake-ups of the 1940s there is very little evidence of a women's lobby for suffrage; rather it was a movement led exclusively by wealthy, elite men to gain more votes for their communities. One lonely exception was Anjalay Coopen, a female sugar-cane labourer who was one of the four killed in the 1943 Belle Vue Harel uprising.

THE MIRACLE

This societal shift from the 1970s to the 1990s resulted in a surge in 'dual-earner' and working single-mother households, hitherto very rare on the island. Nannies were suddenly in much greater demand, as women's participation rate in the labour force rose from 20 per cent in 1972 to 36 per cent in 1995. Incredibly overdue as it was, in the 1980s Mauritian women were finally allowed to open bank accounts without the consent of their husbands.

Female political representation, however, hasn't kept up with this wider rate of change. Superficially, it doesn't look all bad. Mauritius saw its first female cabinet minister, Radha Poonoosamy, in 1975; Maya Hanoomanjee became the first female Speaker of the National Assembly in 2014; while Ameena Gurib-Fakhim fulfilled the largely ceremonial role of president from 2015 to 2018. Yet by and large, the glass ceilings are still well polished in Mauritian politics, as the pitifully small numbers of women in the National Assembly over the years attest—a situation which one respected analyst called a 'grave democratic deficit' in 2001—and all despite the constitution enshrining equal opportunities for all. While there has been very important progress in some key areas for women's rights (such as the 1998 Domestic Violence Act giving greater protection and legal authority to combat domestic abuse; or the 2008 Employment Rights Act forbidding discrimination within the workplace or unequal remuneration for work of equal value), it is still clear that the concept of female political champions challenging the male-dominated party infrastructure is one area where Mauritius is trailing behind mainland Africa.

It would consequently be very wrong to say that the youthful nation was anything like perfect. Further, if anyone asserts that there was no corruption in Mauritius during this period, they would either be being outright disingenuous or have succumbed to delusion. This was brought into sharp focus in Amsterdam's

STAR AND KEY

Schiphol airport in December 1985, when four Mauritian parliamentarians were caught with a suitcase containing over 44 pounds of heroin. It placed the spectre of drugs on the front pages more prominently than ever before, although most Mauritians had been well aware for a long time of two things: that drug addiction had been growing for a while and that the drug cartels on the island were not totally disassociated from politics. Mauritius would of course join a long list of countries facing similar problems. The closing century also had a sting in its tail with a final riot in February 1999, when local singer Kaya (Joseph Topize)—whose fusion of Séga with Jamaican-inspired reggae to produce 'Seggae' had produced huge hits during the decade, making him a nationally recognised face—died in a police cell in suspicious circumstances. Many of Kaya's fellow Creoles were outraged and accused the police—largely made up of Indo-Mauritians—of killing him illegally and of making up stories saying that Kaya's well-known use of marijuana had caused him to become (uncharacteristically) violent. There were riots in several inland towns for a few days, many of which soon developed along racial lines. It was a scary time, and hammered home once again that beneath the positive exterior there still lay long-simmering tensions that would continue to need political courage and expertise to navigate.

Even so, as economic prosperity and an optimistic future now beckoned, many of the generation of ground-breaking politicians who had served Mauritius so tirelessly over the previous decades gradually left us. Sookdeo Bissoondoyal passed away in 1977, having recently served as leader of the opposition. Abdool Razack Mohamed followed a year later. Sir Gaëtan Duval—knighted by Queen Elizabeth II in 1981—died aged 65 in 1996. Anerood Jugnauth continued to be a titan of Mauritian politics into the new century, only succumbing in 2021. Not only had he served as prime minister numerous times, but also as president, for he had helped usher in a new era for Mauritius: that of a Republic.

THE MIRACLE

The country chose to go that way on 12 March 1992—twenty-four years to the day since the new national flag was first tentatively raised on the Champ de Mars. It was more of a symbolic gesture than anything, with the president's role being largely ceremonial, and no powers being taken away from the prime minister, effectively removing the British monarch as head of state. Even so, as messages go, it was a quietly powerful one, telling both the world at large as well as former colonial powers: 'We got this.' The Father of the nation, Sir Seewoosagur Ramgoolam—'Chacha', 'SSR'—passed away quietly aged 85 on 14 December 1985, to much mourning. Yet young as the nation may still be, the concept of political dynasties is already rich. SSR's son, Navin, has since then served three times as prime minister. Xavier-Luc Duval, son of Gaëtan, has like his father served as both deputy prime minister and leader of the opposition. And Anerood Jugnauth's son, Pravind, also followed in his father's footsteps to become prime minister in 2017. Despite countless challenges, Mauritius had grown up very quickly by the turn of the millennium. Professor Meade's Malthusian prediction of a population explosion leading to the island nation's self-implosion never came to pass, leaving Mauritius to mix in international circles with a well-earned swagger.

This was just as well, because its biggest diplomatic headache, which had been festering since the mid-1960s, was now going into overdrive.

18

FRICTION

As alluded to previously, the 1965 Lancaster House conference had been exhausting, stressful, complex and emotional for all parties. Yet the issue that would end up driving the biggest wedge of all between Britain and Mauritius would not be independence, but the fate of another group of islands in the Indian Ocean and the people who had until then called it home.

As discussed in Chapter 13, the Chagos Archipelago had long been administered as one of Mauritius' 'lesser dependencies'. It was spread out over 8,100 square miles and incorporated sixty-four islands, most uninhabited but comprising nevertheless a thriving population of at least 1,600 by 1960. According to one visitor, 'each family had a house and garden to grow their own vegetables and run animals, and there was full employment for both men and women in the copra industry, together with boat building, fishing and construction'. Their main employer was a Mauritius-owned company, Chagos-Agalega, and relations between workers and managers were good. But as one judge rather heartlessly reflected years later, 'There intruded, in the 1960s, the brutal reality of global politics.'

STAR AND KEY

In the early part of that decade, a team of Anglo-American military experts were tasked to survey options across the whole Indian Ocean which could form a suitable military base in the future. The Cuban Missile Crisis of 1962 had scared the world into facing the bleak reality of nuclear Armageddon during the Cold War, and this was an attempt by the two powerful allies to try to redress the balance of power in the ever-fragile Indian Ocean, as well as secure the safe passage of much of the world's crude oil being shipped out of the Gulf. Mahé, the main island of the Seychelles, was considered, until the US military objected due to the heavy population on the island which would compromise security. Eyes then turned to Aldabra, distant from the Seychelles but still administered by them. Being a stunning coral atoll with the world's largest raised coral reef, and home to the world's biggest surviving tortoises, the nascent environmental community raised a storm at the dreadful impact this would have on the native flora and fauna, and the Anglo-American consortium backed down.

When the team looked east, however, the prospectors found what they believed to be the ideal answer: a large, isolated archipelago, far from prying eyes, hosting a small population and—in Diego Garcia, the largest island—the perfect place to act as a base for a fleet of naval ships, submarines and aircraft. There were two problems, however. First, Chagos was administered by Mauritius, and most acknowledged that Mauritius was soon going to get its independence, after which it wouldn't be in Britain's gift. Second, people actually lived there and had done so for generations. As it happened, Britain had barely enough money in its coffers at the time to set up and maintain such a huge and distant military outpost. The USA, on the other hand, most certainly could afford it.

Britain therefore had to play its cards differently. Regardless of where one stands in the subsequent legal debate that has

248

FRICTION

dominated this issue over the last decades, even most Britons, if armed with the facts, would not be impressed by the subterfuge used at the 1965 Lancaster House conference. First, the British set out openly that they wanted to amputate Chagos away from Mauritius and continue to administer it themselves—no direct mention was made at the time of any military installations. In a classic play of 'divide-and-rule', the British then led all parties to believe that they were still seriously considering acceding to the PMSD's requests for a referendum on independence, rather than simply granting it. The MLP had no desire to let go of Chagos, considering it a long-established part of Mauritius. However, their long-gestating dream of independence was so close and they were aware that kicking up a fuss now might risk the referendum option being taken, with the subsequent very real possibility of independence not being voted for. That felt like a gamble too far, and in exchange for £3 million for 'the inconvenience' caused, they agreed not to object to Chagos being detached from Mauritius—although only after a lot of diplomatic coming and going and inevitable Mauritian resistance. It was an understandable decision in the circumstances, but the devil was always going to be in the detail. Needless to say, the Chagossians themselves weren't asked for their opinion, and the issue of their forced removal was deliberately fudged by the British.

The United Nations General Assembly (UNGA) had other ideas, passing a resolution in 1965 stating that dismembering Mauritius was not acceptable. But whilst Mauritian influence in UNGA—where decisions are non-binding—has always been notable, Britain's power as a permanent member of the weightier UN Security Council (where resolutions essentially constitute international law) would always trump it. The UK thereafter leased the islands to the US in 1966 for fifty years, extendable for a further twenty years. Whilst independence celebrations were

STAR AND KEY

ongoing, the UK had already started to deport Chagossians to clear the way for the huge US military base and its 4,000 military personnel, all lubricated by US$14 million from the US. The archipelago was officially renamed the British Indian Ocean Territory (BIOT). The US had initially requested an uninhabited island, which left Britain in a bind. It overcame this by insisting to its allies that the inhabitants were all 'temporary labourers'—again, fully in the knowledge that they were not. Chagos-Agalega was then bought by the UK government and promptly shut down, meaning that hundreds were now jobless. All the inhabitants—by now approaching 2,000—had been 'resettled' by 1973. Resettlement in this case largely meant the inhabitants being shipped to Port Louis—as well as some to the Seychelles and even London—where they were provided with very basic accommodation and little support.

From the mid-1970s onwards, legal battles repeatedly chequered the progress of relations between Mauritius and the UK. The UK's position at the UN in 1973 stressed that 'the Archipelago was detached from Mauritius in 1965 *with the full agreement* of the Mauritian Council of Ministers'. By 1977, this wording had morphed a little into 'the maintenance of British sovereignty over the Chagos Archipelago was made *after full consultation* with the pre-independence government of Mauritius'. This change from 'full agreement' to 'full consultation' seems like a minor detail, but in the world of diplomacy, every word carries meaning and implication. The Mauritian authorities now made one point very clear: their delegation at the time was not from an independent 'government'; they were still a colony and held no legal power to agree or disagree with the proposal; and furthermore, they had felt pressured when presented with a loaded ultimatum.

Each side, therefore, claimed the legal upper hand, even if most neutrals believe the *morally* higher ground lay more obviously

FRICTION

with Mauritius. The sad truth was, however, that the Chagossians themselves had often been relegated to playing the role of mere pawns in a glacial and circular game of geopolitical chess. They now numbered around 8,000, although many of the older *Ilois* had of course passed away since their eviction. Many of their stories since resettlement were nothing short of harrowing—regardless of where one's political or legal sympathies lay. They had a few somewhat pyrrhic victories. A 2008 appeal to the UK House of Lords to challenge Her Majesty's Government for the legality of their expulsion found sympathetic ears. Anthropologists confirmed that, with the Chagossians having been resident and having developed their own subculture over two centuries, it was justifiable to call them an 'indigenous' population, meaning that their 'resettlement' had major implications in human rights law. This had come after a decade of appeals to the UK courts to either repatriate them, offer them meaningful compensation or, ideally, both. There seemed to be a breakthrough when the Chagossians' High Court victory over the UK government in 2000 established the islanders' legal right to return to islands other than Diego Garcia. However, the British then played their trump card: an 'Order of Council'—a relatively little-used form of legislation on specific issues which does not need to pass through parliamentary consultation and voting.

As the new century progressed, the already highly complex legal debate took on an extra dimension. After the shocking attacks on the USA on 11 September 2001, a 'war on terror' was announced by the US administration—a conflict which eventually mutated into brutal ground wars in both Iraq and Afghanistan. Due to its location, it was a given that Diego Garcia would be a crucial base for US military activities. Suspicions gradually grew that, along with the well-known detainment camp in Guantanamo Bay, American military and CIA officials were also quietly undertaking 'rendition' of untried detainees from these conflicts at

251

other locations around the world, including Diego Garcia. After many denials, US officials finally confirmed in 2008 that this had indeed occurred. Further, it was established that certain techniques that they had practised, such as water-boarding, were explicitly designated as a form of torture in UK law—which Chagos/BIOT was answerable to at the time.

The International Court of Justice thereafter declared Mauritian sovereignty over the Chagos, as did the UN. The UK remained intransigent. Challenges and counter-challenges continued, and even the most experienced of diplomats couldn't predict how things were going to pan out in the near or long term. The only thing that was perhaps incontestable was spelled out by a journalist who followed the Chagossians' plight during their plea to the House of Lords in 2008:

> In their 40 years of exile, the Chagos islanders arguably 'lost' and 'forgot' an entire way of life, as well as those mores and rhythms that sustain a community. The crisis that accompanies this loss, more irrevocable arguably than the loss of land, is one that displaced peoples everywhere are forced to contend with.

It looked like the most hopeless of impasses. There was more than a little shock, therefore, when on Thursday, 3 October 2024, in a joint statement by Pravin Jugnauth and Sir Keir Starmer, the Mauritian and British prime ministers respectively, it was calmly announced that the UK was giving up its sovereignty to Chagos. After nearly two years of secret negotiations, the unlikeliest of breakthroughs had been made. It needed to be ratified by a treaty which itself would take a while to draw up, but the willingness on both sides to complete the official handover was real enough. Although hardly considered a catch, there was agreement that the US-led military base on Diego Garcia would remain, with both parties committing 'to ensure the long-term, secure and effective operation of the existing base on Diego

FRICTION

Garcia which plays a vital role in regional and global security'—a nod, unquestionably, to the vast shifts in global power that the world had undergone since the mid-1960s. Herein lay the UK's unsaid concern, which had only materialised in the twenty-first century: if they simply handed the archipelago back to Mauritius, it would only be a matter of time before either Beijing or Delhi came to Port Louis to make an 'offer no one could refuse'. The continued operation of the base—under UK auspices but presumably still run by the US—was earmarked for 'an initial period of 99 years'.

What had brought about this extraordinary *volte face* from the UK, which had stated several times within the preceding decade that Mauritius had no legitimate claim to the islands? It seems that three unrelated factors coalesced with serendipitous timing to start forcing the UK's hand. The first was the word that had dominated UK politics since 2016: Brexit. Where once the British had the backing of the EU in international forums, forming a powerful coalition, their choice to leave the bloc that year had left the stronger European powers far less willing to defend British interests on the world stage on such sensitive issues. Second, this came at a time when many African nations—ironically via the African Union—were beginning to coordinate their efforts, against the UK in particular, concerning their legacy colonial interests, realising that speaking as a single voice made that voice that much louder. Third, Mauritius itself, bloodied by previous diplomatic interventions, had learned how to navigate the fiendishly complex international frameworks—the UN, the international courts and more—in a far more wily and sophisticated way, cornering a perhaps complacent and definitely more isolated Britain.

There was welcome wording too which committed to 'address wrongs of the past and demonstrate the commitment of both parties to support the welfare of Chagossians'. While something of a novelty to have a UK *mea culpa* on the issue in writing, it nevertheless shone a light on the wider but unchanged concern that the Chagossians had not been directly involved in the negotiations themselves, and were fighting merely to be party to the drafting of the treaty. Whilst the UK had now committed to providing a financial package to Mauritius which included annual support payments and infrastructure investments in the islands, it would be left to Mauritius to coordinate a strategy for the resettlement of the archipelago, which would exclude Diego Garcia itself. Some Chagossians—now mostly second- and third-generation—felt betrayed by their sidelining during the negotiations and it remains unclear what role, if any, they will play in drawing up the treaty. However, the mere fact of their scattered resettlement across Mauritius, the Seychelles and south London in the 1960s and 1970s meant that they struggled to speak with a single voice, further hampering their cause. Therefore while a major development had unquestionably been made on that momentous October day, at the time of writing it is clear that the next steps will be neither straightforward nor without further friction.

Further, that friction would not just be political but ecological. In May 2010, in one of their very last policy acts before losing power—and again by Order of Council rather than parliamentary act—the UK Labour Party government announced that the 250,000 square miles of ocean surrounding Chagos/BIOT would be designated a 'marine protected area' (MPA). This would make it, technically, the world's largest marine park. To the uninitiated, it seemed like proof of the government's ecological credentials; to others, it came across as little more than a cynical ploy to prevent the Chagossians from ever returning. Even the US was baffled, as it couldn't see how a protected marine zone could be reconciled with the reality of a huge military base sitting right in the middle of it.

FRICTION

From its own perspective, an independent Mauritius could not do that much to mitigate some of the devastating ecological decisions made by the colonial powers. The quiet destruction of Mauritius' unique wonders had begun even before the French settled, when Portuguese sailors had willingly introduced pigs and unwillingly introduced rats. The Dutch had been no better, felling the ebony trees in great numbers, introducing the Javan deer and macaques and, of course, seeing off the Dodo, the tortoises and more into eternal oblivion. But the mere fact that proper environmental statistics in Mauritius have only been collected since 2009 may perhaps be a sign that environmental policy was never as far up the list of any recent government's list of priorities as it should have been.

Like so many isolated islands, Mauritius was once blessed with hundreds of endemic plants and dozens of endemic animals, but deforestation and introduced species quickly ruined the balance of nature. Exotic species such as the now ubiquitous Chinese guava and privet have become so naturalised as to be displacing the small pockets of native vegetation. By the 1980s, less than 1 per cent of the island's original native forest remained, hidden away in the Black River Gorges and guarded by little more than a wooden fence. Although some have claimed that sugar cane prevents soil erosion, others have come to the opposite conclusion, stating that cumulative forest loss since the Dutch arrival in the seventeenth century has resulted in a much bigger loss of soil than if there had been no deforestation. Either way, Mauritian authorities have been aware of the threat posed to their island by alien species since before independence. The key was always to have the funding and the will to see projects through.

The challenges are diverse and very real. Like many small island states, Mauritius is by its very nature more vulnerable to even subtle environmental changes. The now universally recognised threat of climate change has already seen average tempera-

255

STAR AND KEY

tures in Mauritius rise by 1 degree Celsius since independence. The life-bringing force of water has also been taken for granted for too long, as records show that the average annual rainfall of the island is declining by 57 millimetres per decade, just at a time when the demand from agriculture, tourism and other industries is at an all-time high. One of the most telling events signalling a tropical island's fragility is coral bleaching. Having escaped this for so long, coral bleaching events suffered by Mauritius in 1998 and 2009 saw the predictable degradation of marine ecosystems, as well as tourists being unimpressed by the lack of a beautiful, teeming ocean that the brochures had promised them. Serious coastal erosion wasn't helping that aesthetic either.

Agricultural practices haven't helped the situation. Even in the early 1990s, fertiliser use was an incredible sixty times higher than the African average, and three times higher than in western Europe. Mauritius also has the dubious honour of being one of the highest pesticide users in the world. To cap it off, the cyclones that have defined so many key points in the island's history have become even more ferocious; torrential rains in 2013 caused flash floods that were as deadly as they were impressive, killing eleven people. A simple truth that was little expressed at the time was that whilst the concrete and asphalt spreading across the island was a visible sign of the nation's growing development and industrialisation, it often came at the cost of environmental concerns. Neither was this undisciplined construction, coupled with quasi-non-existent town and country planning, exactly making the country more beautiful.

What had this meant at the species level amongst those plants and animals that were found nowhere else? At the time of the Dutch arrival, more than twenty-three endemic birds, twelve endemic reptiles and two endemic fruit bats flourished on Mauritius. Fast forward to independence in 1968 and the picture was very different: nine endemic birds, four geckos, one skink

FRICTION

and a single fruit bat species were all that remained on the mainland. Rodrigues had fared even worse, boasting only two endemic birds and a fruit bat, when once there had been twelve unique bird species and four reptile species. Further, at least eighty species of endemic Mauritian plants were by then extinct, and likely many more had disappeared during the early days of colonialism that had never been scientifically described.

Perhaps it was the lingering iconic status of the Dodo that led the first proper conservation efforts of the 1970s to focus on the birds. Each one of the nine bird species found only on Mauritius has at some stage since then been the focus of dedicated conservation efforts. The most internationally high-profile of these was the island's only raptor, the Mauritius Kestrel. It came as close as any bird we know of to becoming extinct, before bouncing back thanks to huge intervention efforts. Being top of the food chain on a small island meant there were probably never that many of these small, beautiful falcons at the best of times—perhaps 500 breeding pairs. But three factors contributed to its freefall decline: the relentless deforestation that robbed it of its habitat and food source; the introduction of exotic animals like macaques and mongooses that ate its eggs; and, perhaps most aggressively, the merciless use of DDT in the 1950s and 1960s to finally rid the island of the last vestiges of malaria. By 1974, heartbreakingly, only four individuals were clinging on, only one of which was a breeding female.

A conservation effort was started, although almost everyone who cared had pretty much said their internal, quiet goodbyes. It was with the arrival of a quirky Welshman in 1979 that things changed. Inspired by the British conservationist and writer Gerald Durrell, whose book *Golden Bats and Pink Pigeons* had shone a light on the precarious state of Mauritian wildlife, Carl Jones was undertaking MSc research at Swansea University on 'Studies on the Biology of the Critically Endangered Birds of

STAR AND KEY

Mauritius' when he was given an opportunity to put his ideas into practice by the International Council for Bird Preservation (now BirdLife International). With still only a mere eight captive birds to play with, Jones introduced the concept of 'double-clutching'—removing the first clutch of eggs from a nest, rearing these by hand separately, and in turn encouraging the pair to breed a second round of eggs. He nurtured new fostering techniques and dietary supplements, all helped by Durrell himself setting up the Mauritian Wildlife Appeal Fund (later the Mauritian Wildlife Foundation, or MWF) in 1984, in an unassuming corner of the village of Rivière Noire (Black River). The results were miraculous. By 1993, Jones and his team of volunteers had reared 333 kestrels, both from captive breeding and from double-clutching those pairs that had already been returned to the wild. The success helped the MWF to become a fully funded foundation by 1996.

Similar projects were also undertaken for other iconic but desperately rare birds, notably the Pink Pigeon and the Echo Parakeet. The Pink Pigeon had a mere ten specimens in 1991, with habitat degradation the main culprit. Thirty years later, wild numbers had reached a much healthier 400, together with a back-up captive population. The Echo Parakeet, meanwhile, was the last of the seven-strong parrot family endemic to the Mascarenes to survive to modern times, and even then it was touch-and-go. Only twelve specimens were known in the mid-1980s, only three of which were female. With the team again pioneering new techniques to maximise reproduction, the intense efforts meant that numbers steadily grew, reaching a heartening 750 individuals by 2019. The situation was helped by the Black River Gorges—home to so many endemic plants and animals—being declared a National Park in 1994.

Two things were worth pointing out during all these efforts, however. One was the quiet realisation that, short of an enor-

FRICTION

mous, sustained effort to replant huge swathes of forest—which would usually mean taking away profitable sugar cane—it was likely that these birds and plants would always need intensive conservation management to carry on in healthy numbers. The other point of note was more stark: almost all the efforts to lead and fund these globally recognised efforts had come from abroad. Whilst many Mauritians in the 1970s and 1980s knew of these birds and had read about their plight and their phoenix-like resurrections, there was at the time precious little effort or funding coming from either the Mauritian people or the government—at least, not as much as the conservationists had hoped for. Fortunately, this would change as education efforts with the younger generations in particular saw a heartening new level of engagement. This was exemplified when the Mauritius Kestrel was officially announced Mauritius' national bird in 2022. For the country that had once been home to one of the most famous birds of them all, this was a huge acknowledgement that the focus now needed to be on the present and the future, and not the past.

Meanwhile, the endemics have to contend with swathes of introduced birds, such as the Mynah, Bulbul, Serin du Cap, Ring-necked Parakeet and Madagascan Cardinal, each of which adds charm, character and colour to the island, but nevertheless competes aggressively with the native species, which in turn usually lose out. This applies not just to birds. Wasps were introduced in the nineteenth century to eat the beetles that threatened the sugar cane; mongooses were brought over from India in an attempt to eat as many of the rats as possible; frogs—usually nowhere to be seen on volcanic islands—were brought from Madagascar in the late eighteenth century to help control the mosquito population, as was the tenrec—known locally as '*ti vitesse*' and resembling an albino hedgehog. As far as nature was concerned, none of these should have been here, and artificially

STAR AND KEY

introducing species to a new environment—as has been documented countless times around the world—is never a good idea in the long term.

It hasn't just been a struggle on the mainland. A huge effort has been made since the 1980s to eradicate rats on the islets that surround Mauritius, which themselves host species found nowhere else—not even on Mauritius itself. The 62-acre Île aux Aigrettes (Egret Island) off the southeast coast was declared rat-free in the 1990s, resulting quickly in the regeneration of native trees and making it a perfect home for hundreds of Pink Pigeons. The islets to the north have had positive results too, with Coin de Mire (Gunner's Quoin), Île Plate (Flat Island) and Ilot Gabriel (Gabriel Island) all boasting big success stories. The gem in that northern grouping is the 418-acre Île Ronde (Round Island), where rats never made it, which remains a world-renowned haven of threatened plant and reptile species, many endemic. Some bright spark still thought it would be a good idea to introduce goats and rabbits there in the 1960s, but they were eventually eradicated in 1978 before causing too much devastation.

Successive twenty-first-century Mauritian governments saw the way the global winds were blowing regarding ecology and green initiatives, making them rather more proactive than their predecessors. In 2008, the '*Maurice Île Durable*' ('Sustainable Mauritius') programme was launched, to some fanfare, with the confident intention of making Mauritius a global role model of sustainable development—much as it did with its economic miracle, but this time with a strategy. Green energy was also elevated to the status of a new economic pillar for the country, with a hugely ambitious aim of making the island 60 per cent sufficient on renewable energy by 2030.

In the 2020s, the government earmarked significant resources for the National Environment and Climate Change Fund (NECCF), tasked not only with coastal rehabilitation and coral

FRICTION

preservation but also with the aim of planting a million new trees—albeit with slightly scant detail on exactly which species. The legally protected forest areas have also grown to represent 7 per cent of the island's total land area. But although government programmes exist, they are not close to hitting their targets and remain very vague. Renewable energy planning is woefully behind, and the government's promotion of seemingly unbridled property development, to say nothing of its own infrastructure planning, or lack thereof, does not include much evidence of tree planting nor propagation. Accountability in this area at least is fairly non-existent. Nevertheless, by 2020 it very much felt as though the tide had turned regarding not taking the island for granted. Various success stories and well-funded programmes seemed, on the face of it, to set a path for the rehabilitation of Mauritius' land and sea.

However, there are some things that no one can predict. And in 2020 Mauritius faced its biggest environmental challenge yet.

19

HERE AND NOW

Many of us enjoy a few drinks to celebrate a friend's birthday party, and 58-year-old Sunil Kumar Nandeshwar was no different. The problem was, at that moment he was also captain of a 980-foot-long ship carrying around 4,000 tons of crude oil, and drink-driving is never a good idea.

On the evening of 25 July 2020, the *MV Wakashio*, a Japanese-owned tanker sailing from China to Brazil, was rounding the southeastern coast of Mauritius, but approaching much closer to the island—and the notorious reefs that surround it—than any other tanker normally did; the norm was to stay a minimum of 10 miles offshore. The reasoning for this itself was baffling, since a later inquiry would suggest that the crew were 'seeking a better Wi-Fi signal from the coast' so they could converse with their loved ones back in Asia. This made no sense to anyone, as there was unlimited free Wi-Fi on the ship already. The weather wasn't great, but it was hardly too taxing for an experienced captain. Yet, somehow, the *Wakashio* found itself striking those unforgiving reefs. As naval history has taught us in Mauritius and elsewhere, it really doesn't matter how big you are; if your ship hits a large coral reef, invariably the reef wins.

STAR AND KEY

The *Wakashio* ran aground off the coast of Blue Bay—a gem even by Mauritius' high standards, and the location of choice for many scenes from numerous Bollywood movies, as well as the odd Hollywood one. But its importance lay far beyond the visual impact it had on wealthy tourists and cinemagoers. It was a marine park and an area of high ecological value; a wetland biodiversity hotspot of 1,700 species, where the coral, seagrasses and mangroves formed a home to rare or endemic species including seventeen types of marine mammal and two species of turtle, not to mention 800 species of fish. Initially the oil was contained within the tanker, although it was clear to all that the tanker's deteriorating condition meant that it was only a matter of time before its structural integrity gave way and oil would start leaking.

What surprised many Mauritians, however, was that the authorities didn't seem to be acting with the swiftness of response that such an impending disaster clearly warranted. In fact, official communication was minimal for days, leaving that glorious Mauritian tradition—rumour-spreading—to go into overdrive. On 6 August, after twelve days beached on the reef, the *Wakashio*'s hull finally crumbled and the dreaded crude oil started leaking from the ship towards the shore. Only then did the government declare a state of emergency. As part of his address that evening, Prime Minister Pravind Jugnauth admitted that Mauritius, for all its strengths, simply 'did not have the skills and expertise to refloat stranded ships', and he appealed to international partners to help. This was most parochially directed towards France, administrator of the neighbouring island of Réunion, where it was hoped such expertise lay. It did indeed, and Réunion sent a military aircraft with pollution control equipment on board. Japan, India and several other nations also assisted, although there was some confusion as to why such help had not been requested earlier.

Conversely, as this story became big news all around the world, something else was noticed that sent an incredibly power-

HERE AND NOW

ful message both to the Mauritian authorities at home and equally to the wider international community. Oil spills are always horrendous and unforgiving ecological catastrophes in the making, and the Mauritian people could see that the huge slick of black doom was snaking its way inexorably towards the coast. It was unlikely that the average Mauritian on the street—as non-experts in ecological clean-up—could do much to help, but that certainly wasn't going to stop them trying. Some, such as fishermen and tour guides, obviously had existential reasons to act somehow. But the scenes being broadcast to a worldwide audience showed that this 'People's Response' went far beyond fishermen and boat operators.

Despite the eventual government instruction for people to stay away and 'leave it to the authorities', Mauritians of all backgrounds steadfastly ignored this and began to make their way towards the southeast, not to rubberneck at the unfolding disaster, but to do anything they could to minimise its impact. An amazing coordination effort swiftly and organically grew, with locals collecting as much straw as possible from nearby fields to fill and connect huge fabric sacks with which to form a cordon or barrier to prevent the slick spreading closer to shore. Most poignantly of all, local women—again representing the full, diverse spectrum of Mauritians—started queuing to have their long, beautifully kept hair hastily cut off, so that it could be stuffed into tights which were donated in an attempt to soak up the oil that had by now reached land.

The short-term outcome of this sorry episode was both predictable and emotional. Despite heroic efforts by the citizens on the ground, the 1,000 tons of oil that made it to the shore caused the death of many animals, including countless fish and dozens of dolphins and whales, and ruined the natural integrity of the bay for years to come. The toxic hydrocarbons had also bleached the reef, making it unquestionably Mauritius' worst-ever one-off

STAR AND KEY

ecological disaster. As the *Wakashio* split in two, the bow was towed well offshore to be sunk. It seems likely that the Pilot whales that had a mass beaching likely suffered from the bursting of their tympanic cavities, related to the dynamite explosions carried out during the inexpert offshore sinking of the hull ordered by the government. The stern proved more problematic, however, and one of the tugboats tasked to tow it, the *Sir Gaetan Duval*, crashed into a barge during the process, with all four crew members lost. The government focused on seeking compensation from the Nagashiki Shipping company, the primary listed owner of the *Wakashio*, while also arresting the captain for negligence. Meanwhile, many Mauritians were angry, and Saturday, 29 August 2020 saw a huge, 100,000-strong march through Port Louis where they showed their frustration at the way the whole incident had been handled. This represented one in twelve of all Mauritians on the island.

Thus, for all the horrors in the short term, the longer-term outcome left a different message: Mauritians now really cared about their environment. This is not a flippant or patronising statement, for the simple reason that there is plenty of documented and anecdotal evidence from the past showing emphatically that this was not always the case. For example, to walk through the Black River Gorges or climb Le Pouce mountain in the 1980s or 1990s, as I have done countless times, was to navigate through a stream of discarded garbage left there by previous ramblers, removing some element of joy from exploring areas of otherwise outstanding natural beauty. Likewise, when driving along Mauritius' busy town roads and motorways at that time, drivers and passengers had an unpleasant habit of simply throwing their rubbish out of the window as they sped along. Arguably, it's a habit that hasn't totally disappeared. Many tourists at the time offered similar feedback when returning to Europe: 'We had a great holiday and Mauritius is

266

HERE AND NOW

beautiful, but sometimes you wonder if the Mauritians realise it enough to care.'

The *Wakashio* incident, for all its appalling ecological results, showed that by 2020 Mauritians most certainly *did* care about the stunning vistas and environmental fragility that surrounded them, and were willing to take personal risks to preserve them. Furthermore, the oil spill had capped off 2020 as an *Annus Horribilis* for the island, for what made this organic, grassroots response even more impressive was that it had come at a time when the entire world was struggling to cope with the pernicious and remorseless spread of Covid-19.

On 18 March 2020, Mauritius had its first three cases confirmed; the first lockdown was called the following day, coupled with an overarching border closure. The first death was announced on 22 March. Although the situation looked bleak, in fact only ten people would die of Covid-19 in Mauritius during 2020, and around the same figure the following year. The *Wakashio* incident had occurred in between lockdowns. Only when zero cases were officially confirmed later in the year were tourists allowed to make their way to the island from 1 October—as well as all those Mauritians who had been caught out abroad and been unable to return in the interim. Even then, very strict quarantine protocols were put in place, many having to kick their heels alone for a fortnight in a top hotel before being released into the real world—and having to pay upwards of US$10,000 for the privilege. The vaccination programme started on 6 March 2021, headed by front-line workers and government ministers. This coincided with a second lockdown as the second wave peaked. The worst was over, at least as far as deaths and infections were concerned.

The economy, meanwhile, had taken a battering, constricting by 15 per cent—enough to cause Mauritius to officially slide from 'high-income' to 'high-middle-income' status. This translated into a loss of nearly Rs1.3 billion (US$28 million) every

STAR AND KEY

single day. Early on, the government had introduced a Wage Assistance Scheme to help offset some of the hit; tourism was the major, but not the only industry affected. This was a choice that the government felt prioritised people over money, and they stuck to it. Many Mauritians grumbled, seeing greater levels of freedom of movement abroad and wondering why they were being kept on such a tight leash. Citizens were allowed to leave their homes only to go grocery shopping or to the pharmacy, and even then only at staggered times by alphabetical order of last name. But the authorities were paying heed to early World Health Organization predictions that Mauritius, due to its very high population density, coupled with an increasingly elderly proportion of residents who were in turn highly vulnerable to chronic diseases, was 'among the African countries most at risk of a public health disaster due to COVID-19'.

Yet thanks to the hard-and-early lockdown policy this dooms-day scenario didn't come to pass, and the statistics spoke for themselves. Even accounting for unreported or suspected deaths caused by Covid-19, the death toll by late May 2021 was well under 100. Mauritius experienced a maximum infection rate of 96.1 per 100,000 people—this was 100 times lower than in the USA. Death rates reached 1.2 deaths per 100,000 population. By comparison, the USA's rate was 176.7 per 100,000 people. The United States may seem like an odd comparator, but bearing in mind their superior healthcare infrastructure (for those who can afford it) and their much lower population density, it proved that Mauritius was overachieving, despite the hard hit that society was taking (as it did almost everywhere else too). While New Zealand's was heralded worldwide as one of the most complete and successful responses to Covid, some experts thought Mauritius' reaction wasn't too far behind.

So where has all this drama left Mauritius in the second decade of the twenty-first century? Battered and bruised, undoubtedly,

HERE AND NOW

yet also tremendously resilient—a trait that it had demonstrated for generations to anyone who cared to observe. Just over 770 square miles of verdant and fertile volcanic rock, not forgetting the much bigger exclusive economic zone (EEZ) in the Southern Indian Ocean, is all that Mauritians have to play with, and they are still doing a remarkably good job. Of the 1.3 million population, 42 per cent now live in urban areas, reflecting well the wonderful dichotomy of city life and cane growing that has defined the island's outlook for so long. The 8 per cent unemployment rate before Covid-19—lower than that of almost all its nearest neighbours—was a testament to this. Investment in education has grown and the benefits duly been reaped; Mauritius' life expectancy of 74 years is ten years more than the East African average.

The fact that the majority of Mauritians are at least trilingual—be it a combination of Creole/French/English, Bhojpuri/Creole/French, Hakka/Creole/French, or something else—often bowls visitors over, yet with an idiosyncratic history like that of Mauritius, one could confidently assert that speaking just one language here was never going to get you far. Where and when one uses which language may seem like a minefield to the visitor, but not to the Mauritians; to that end, an in-depth language study by two German academics in the early 1980s offered some general but very telling insights into how their unique situation had instinctively evolved over the centuries: English is associated with 'knowledge', French with 'culture', Creole with 'egalitarianism' and other languages with 'ancestral heritage'.

Crucially, with globalisation now the default—and the wider exposure to global media that that entails—many younger Mauritians have started to develop a common culture and outlook on life. Anecdotally at least, the essence of being 'Mauritian' is starting to outweigh ancestral ties and the occasionally divisive communalism. Hand in hand with this, if the statistics are to be taken at face value, has been an ever so slight decrease in reli-

STAR AND KEY

gious adherence in the younger generation, whether their parents were Hindu, Christian or Muslim. The fact that in 2023 Mauritius scored four out of four for religious freedom according to US think tank Freedom House offers universal reassurance. There have also been recent clamours to get rid of the 'best loser' system in elections. Its inception was predicated on an assumption that ethnic minorities needed to be represented, and that by extension people tended to vote communally. Yet the fact that it is now seen as past its time, as a legacy that risks perpetuating ethnic divisions, is in itself insightful—and driven, perhaps, by the realisation that some of these ethnic categories are themselves becoming blurrier.

Even so, fewer and fewer people are fooled by the tourist brochures; Mauritius is *not* a perfect 'melting pot' of cultures. Despite the increasing number of mixed marriages, including with foreign spouses, ethnic groups are not giving up their own cultural traditions to blend into a common 'national' stew. Then again, neither is anyone asking them to. What Mauritius can boast, though, is a clear national 'melting-pot' *policy*, which helps bind the nation together—a pluralistic unity through diversity. To that end, Mauritius is best viewed as a unique 'cultural mosaic', whereby ethnicities and religions are interlocking, recognised, respected and celebrated, all of which sits alongside the often intangible feeling of 'being Mauritian'. Self-conscious this may be, but it undoubtedly helps cement a sense of uniqueness, not to mention a feeling of national pride, when interacting with others. And perhaps there lies the rub: seldom does a Mauritian feel more 'Mauritian' than when he or she is abroad, and the tug of identity expresses itself most in all the bountiful things that Mauritians have in common rather than the things they don't.

Indeed, the cultural scene has never been more vibrant. The music industry—whether Séga-related or going beyond this—continues to experiment, with some break-out hits making it big

HERE AND NOW

abroad. Fine art and crafts are now a staple of Mauritian culture, not just as a conveyor belt of tourist trinkets but as representations of what it means, here and now, to be and feel Mauritian. Restaurants serving Mauritian food—with its smorgasbord of different influences from East Africa to India, to France and China—are slowly increasing around the world as the national cuisine is gradually being discovered and recognised as something extraordinary. New and exciting authors materialise every year. Indeed, when French-Mauritian dual-national writer, Jean-Marie Le Clézio, won the Nobel Prize for literature in 2008, Mauritians were only too happy to claim him as one of their own, not least because much of his writing had been inspired by elements of Mauritian culture.

Mauritian Creole remains a gloriously rich and expressive language, ripe for puns and rich with humour. It has in turn produced countless proverbs, some of which can still be heard uttered every day while others have quietly been discarded. Two older sayings from the nineteenth century, seldom heard now, are perhaps ready for a comeback, as they encapsulate neatly the Mauritius of the present. One is '*Sa ki boudé manze boudin*', an almost untranslatable sentence which very roughly equates to 'Stop feeling sorry for yourself and just get on with it.' A second is '*Komen to tale to natte fau to dourmi*'—literally 'However you spread your mat, so must you lie', or more prosaically, 'This is how you've chosen to make your bed, so accept what you have and make the most of it.' Together, these proverbs capture an intangible essence of the fatalism, the courage, the intelligence, the humour and the sheer bloody-mindedness that has left us with the 'Star and Key' island we see today.

This extraordinary little island's story has been laced with more adventure than nations ten times its size, and all crammed into a mere handful of centuries. If the decades that follow are anything like as exciting, it will be quite the ride. That said, one suspects that most Mauritians wouldn't swap that for anything.

271

BIBLIOGRAPHY

1913 Almanac. 'Arrivals and Departures of Indian Immigrants, 1834–1912', in *The Mauritius Almanac for 1913*, Port Louis: R. de Speville, 1913.

Adler, Isaac. *Young Captain on a Broken Boat: Childhood Memories of a World War II Jewish Refugee Turned Away from British Palestine to an Island Prison in Mauritius*, Preston: Zaccmedia, 2021.

Allen, Richard B. *Slaves, Freedmen, and Indentured Laborers in Colonial Mauritius*, Cambridge: Cambridge University Press, 1999.

———. 'Suppressing a Nefarious Traffic: Britain and the Abolition of Slave Trading in India and the Western Indian Ocean, 1770–1830', *William and Mary Quarterly*, vol. 66, no. 4 (2009): 873–94.

Archives, Mauritius. 'Compagnie des Indes—Documents divers concernant la regie de la Compagnie 1731–45', Mauritius Archives.

Ardill, Nelly, ed. *Malcy de Chazal: Nature Art and Science*, Curepipe: SOS Patrimoine en Peril, 2018.

Bernardin de St Pierre, J-H. *Voyage a l'Ile de France*, Curepipe: Editions de l'Océan Indien, 1986.

———. *Paul et Virginie*, Rose-Hill: Editions de l'Océan Indien, 2007.

Boswell, Rosabelle. *Le Malaise Créole: Ethnic Identity in Mauritius*, New York: Berghahn Books, 2006.

Bulpin, T. V. *Islands in a Forgotten Sea*, Pretoria: Protea Boekhuis, 2010.

Burgh Edwardes, S. B. de. *The History of Mauritius (1507–1914)*, London: East & West Ltd, 1921.

BIBLIOGRAPHY

Carmichael, D. *Account of the Conquest of Mauritius*, Charleston, SC: Legare Street Press, 2022.

Carter, Marina. *Voices from Indenture: Experiences of Indian Migrants in the British Empire*, London: Leicester University Press, 1996.

Charles River Editors, *The Dutch East India Company*, CreateSpace Independent, 2017.

Chartrand, René. *Armies and Wars of the French East India Companies, 1664–1770*, Warwick: Helion & Co., 2024.

Chelin, Antoine. 'Origine des noms de lieux à l'Ile Maurice', *La Gazette des Îles*, no. 25 (October 1989).

Christopher, A. J. 'Ethnicity, Community and the Census in Mauritius, 1830–1990', *Geographical Journal*, vol. 158, no. 1 (1992): 57–64.

Dabee, Anjalee. 'Unfinished Business: The Journey to Women's Equality in Mauritius', UN Development Programme, Mauritius and Seychelles, 15 March 2021.

Dommen, Edouard. *Poudre d'or*, Geneva: PCL Press, 2018.

Dommen, Edward, and Bridget Dommen. *Mauritius: An Island of Success*, Oxford: James Currey, 1999.

D'Unienville, Noel. *L'Ile Maurice et sa civilisation*, Port Louis: Maxime Boullé & Co., 1949.

Eisenlohr, Patrick. 'Creole Publics: Language, Cultural Citizenship, and the Spread of the Nation in Mauritius', *Comparative Studies in Society in History*, vol. 49, no. 4 (2007): 968–96.

Electoral Institute for Sustainable Democracy in Africa (EISA). 'Mauritius: Socio-Economic Change and Political Conflict (1910–1945)', Johannesburg: EISA, 2009.

———. 'Mauritius: Sugar, Indentured Labour and Their Consequences (1835–1910)', Johannesburg: EISA, 2009.

———. 'Mauritius: The Road to Independence (1945–1968)', Johannesburg: EISA, 2009.

Emrith, Moomtaz. *History of the Muslims in Mauritius*, Curepipe: Editions Le Printemps, 1994.

Eriksen, Thomas Hylland. 'Nationalism, Mauritian Style: Cultural Unity and Ethnic Diversity', *Comparative Studies in Society and History*, vol. 36, no. 3 (1994): 549–74.

Geller, Jay H. 'Towards a New Imperialism in Eighteenth-Century India:

BIBLIOGRAPHY

Dupleix, La Bourdonnais and the French Compagnie des Indes', *Portuguese Studies*, vol. 16 (2000): 240–55.

Harris, Peter. 'Decolonising the Special Relationship: Diego Garcia, the Chagossians, and Anglo-American Relations', *Review of International Studies*, vol. 39, no. 3 (2013): 707–27.

Hazareesingh, K. *Histoire des Indiens a l'Ile Maurice*, Paris: Librarie d'Amerique et de l'Orient, 1973.

Hearn, Lafcadio. *Gombo Zherbes: Little Dictionary of Creole Proverbs*, New York: Will H. Colman, 1885.

Hein, Catherine, and Philippe Hein. *From Gloom to Bloom: The Path to the Development Success of Mauritius, 1968–2020*, Port Louis: Regent Press, 2021.

Hein, Philippe. *L'Economie de l'Ile Maurice*, Paris: L'Harmattan, 1996.

Hein, Raymond. *Le Naufrage du St Géran*, Paris: Editions de l'Océan Indien, 1981.

Houbert, Jean. 'Mauritius: Independence and Dependence', *Journal of Modern African Studies*, vol. 19, no. 1 (1981): 75–105.

Jackson, Ashley. *War and Empire in Mauritius and the Indian Ocean* (Studies in Military and Strategic History), Basingstoke: Palgrave Press, 2001.

Kasenally, Roukaya. 'Mauritius: The Not So Perfect Democracy', *Journal of African Elections*, vol. 10, no. 1 (2011): 33–47.

La Bourdonnais, B. F. Mahé de. *Mémoires historiques de B. F. Mahé de La Bourdonnais, gouverneur des Îles de France et de Bourbon*, Paris: Editions L'Harmattan, 2018.

Lagesse, Marcelle. *L'Ile de France avant La Bourdonnais, 1721–35*, Mauritius Archives Publications 12, Port Louis, 1973.

Lange, Matthew. 'Embedding the Colonial State: A Comparative-Historical Analysis of State Building and Broad-Based Development in Mauritius', *Social Science History*, vol. 27, no. 3 (2003): 397–423.

Leguat, François. *The Voyage of François Leguat of Bresse: To Rodriguez, Mauritius, Java, and the Cape of Good Hope*, Whitefish, MT: Kessinger Publications, 2007.

Lenoir, Philippe. *Mauritius: Former Île de France*, Port Louis: Editions du Cygne, 1978.

BIBLIOGRAPHY

L'Estrac, J. C. de. *Next Year in Diego Garcia* ..., Curepipe: Editions Le Printemps, 2011.

Meade, J. E. 'Population Explosion, the Standard of Living and Social Conflict', *The Economic Journal*, vol. 77, no. 306 (1967): 233–55.

Mehta, Rani. 'Ethnicity, Ethnic Relations and Development of Mauritian Society', *Indian Anthropologist*, vol. 45, no. 1 (2015): 47–60.

Miles, William F. S. 'The Politics of Language Equilibrium in a Multilingual Society: Mauritius', *Comparative Politics*, vol. 32, no. 2 (2000): 215–30.

Ng Tseung-Wong, Caroline, and Maykel Verkuyten. 'Multiculturalism, Mauritian Style: Cultural Diversity, Belonging, and a Secular State', *American Behavioral Scientist*, vol. 59, no. 6 (2015): 679–701.

Norder, S. J., et al. 'Assessing Temporal Couplings in Social-Ecological Island Systems: Historical Deforestation and Soil Loss on Mauritius (Indian Ocean)', *Ecology and Society*, vol. 22, no. 1 (2017), Article 29.

North-Coombes, Alfred. *A History of Sugar Production in Mauritius*, Oxford: African Book Collective, 1993.

Piat, Denis. *L'Île Maurice: Sur la route des épices (1598–1810)*, Singapore: Les Éditions du Pacifique/Éditions Didier Millet, 2004.

———. *Pirates and Privateers in Mauritius*, Singapore: Éditions Didier Millet, 2014.

Pitot, Geneviève. *The Mauritian Shekel*, Port Louis: Vizavi, 1998.

Polo, Marco. *The Travels*, trans. Nigel Cliff, London: Penguin, 2015.

Salverda, Tijo. *The Franco-Mauritian Elite*, New York: Berghahn Books, 2015.

Sands, Philippe. *The Last Colony: A Tale of Exile, Justice and Britain's Colonial Legacy*, London: Weidenfeld & Nicolson, 2022.

Saylor, Ryan. 'Probing the Historical Sources of the Mauritian Miracle: Sugar Exporters and State Building in Colonial Mauritius', *Review of African Political Economy*, vol. 39. no. 133 (2012): 465–78.

Scott, Ernest. *The Life of Matthew Flinders*, Sydney: Angus & Robertson, 1914.

Selvon, Sydney. *A New Comprehensive History of Mauritius*, 2 vols., MDS Editions, 2017.

Srinivasan, Padma. 'Slavery in Mauritius and the Moresby Treaty of 1822', *Proceedings of the Indian History Congress*, vol. 60 (1999): 1011–17.

BIBLIOGRAPHY

Stein, Peter. *Connaissance et emploi des langues à l'Ile Maurice* (Kreolische Bibliothek 2), Hamburg: Buske, 1982.

Surcouf, J. M. R., ed. *Histoire de Robert Surcouf, capitaine de Corsaire*, Paris: Plon Nourrit et Co., 1925.

Thacoor-Sidaya, Indira. 'Women and Development in Mauritius', *India Quarterly*, vol. 54, no. 1/2, (January–June 1998): 61–70.

Toussaint, Auguste. *Port-Louis: Deux siècles d'histoire (1735–1935)*, Port Louis: La Typographie Moderne, 1936.

Twain, Mark. *Following the Equator* [1897], Delhi: Open Books, 2023.

Vaughan, Megan. 'Slavery and Colonial Identity in Eighteenth-Century Mauritius', *Transactions of the Royal Historical Society*, vol. 8 (1998): 189–214.

―――. *Creating the Creole Island: Slavery in Eighteenth-Century Mauritius*, Durham, NC: Duke University Press, 2005.

Visdelou-Guimbeau, Georges de. *Le découverte des Îles Mascareignes*, Port Louis: Editions du Cygne, 1948.

INDEX

'Aapravasi Ghat', 162

ABC ('Au Bazar Central'), 213–14

Abercromby, Major-General John, 112, 123–4, 126, 127

The Act for the Abolition of Slavery, 156–7

Action Libérale party, 198, 204

Aden, 223

Admiral Islands, 172

Adventures of Tom Sawyer and Huckleberry Finn, The (Twain), 194

Afghanistan, 251

Africa, 12, 39, 114, 140, 151, 182

African Cape, 209

African Union, 253

Agaléga, 174, 176

Ah-Chuen, 214

Air Mauritius, 239

Albius, Edmond, 165–6

Aldabra, 248

Alexander VI, Pope, 55–6

Alexandra, Princess, 226

Alice's Adventures in Wonderland (Carroll), 28

All-Mauritius Hindu Congress, 223

Amazon, 24–5

Amboyna (Ambon, Indonesia), 122

American War of Independence, 89, 91, 97

Americas, 151, 182

Amiens, Treaty of, 98, 100

Amsterdam (ship), 22

Amsterdam, 243–4

Anatole de Boucherville, 199

Angola, 77

Anne-Marie, 71

Annus Horribilis, 267

Anquetil, Emmanuel, 206–7

Apple, 24–5

Arc de Triomphe, 120

Arlanda, Gnanadicarayen, 193, 205

Ascension (ship), 171

Asia, 182, 185

279

INDEX

Atlantic Ocean, 16, 49, 100, 156

Australia, 109, 182, 194, 231, 238

Austria, 55

Baco, René, 95

Baie de l'Arsenal, 88

Baie du Tombeau, 82, 126

Baldridge, Adam, 41

Bank of Mauritius, 154

Bantam, 23

Barbé, Laurent, 175

Barkly, Sir Henry, 181, 186

Barnard, Joseph, 190

Baroque, 141

Bart, Black, 38

Bastille prison, 78

Bastille, 78, 92

Batavia, 25, 27, 122, 169

Baudin, Nicolas, 109–10

Bay of Bengal, 102, 103–4

Bay of Grand Port, 115

beard, Black, 38

Beau Bassin, 87, 185, 210

Beau Champ sugar estate, 198

Beaver, Colonel, 129

Beijing, 253

Bel Air, 87

Bel Ombre estate, 198

Bellamy, Black Sam, 49

Belle Mare, 87

Belle Rive, 218

Belle Vue Harel estate, 87, 209

Belle Vue Harel uprising, 242

Bellone naval battle, 114–20

Benzanozano, 164

Bérenger, Paul, 237

Berkley Castle (ship), 33

Bermuda, 42

Bernardin de St Pierre, Jacques-Henri, 142

Bertie, Major-General, 125

Bertie, Vice-Admiral Albemarle, 123

Betsimisaraka, 164

Beverwaart, 35

Bhojpuri, 218

Bihar region, 160

Bissoondoyal, Sookdeo, 216–17, 222–4, 236, 244

Black River Gorges, 255

Black River, 113

Blaize de Maisonneuve, Catherine-Marie, 104

Bligh, Captain (Bounty fame), 109

Blue Bay, 264

Bockelberg, Jan, 27

Bois Cheri, 87, 184

Bois de Pomme, 4

Bois Jaune, 4

Bombay, 99, 153

Bonaparte, Napoleon, 156

Bonitos, 6

Bonne Cuisine (ship), 100

Bonny, Anne, 38

Booth, George, 43

Borneo (merchant ship), 44

Boscawen, Admiral, 81

Both, Pieter, 25

Bougainville, Louis-Antoine de, 83

INDEX

Bouvet de Lozier, Frigate Captain Jean-Baptiste, 83, 116, 119
Bowen, John, 42–6
Bowen, Sir George, 186
Brazil, 263
Brehinier, Mathurin, 169
Brexit, 253
Briggs, Captain, 175
British Coldstream Guards, 223
British India, 215
British Indian Ocean Territory (BIOT), 224, 250–4
British, 96
   governor, La Bourdonnais, 65–75
   Mauritius, culture, 141–8
   Mauritius, economy, 230–9
   Mauritius, separate identity, 121–33
   naval battle, 114–20
   parties, 221–7
   pepper and cinnamon, 81–7
   slaves, 171–80
   war, Britain and France, 98–107
   See also Dutch; East India Company; France
Brittany, 60, 62, 97
Broad-Billed Parrot, 3
Brown Palmiste, 4
Bruslys, Nicolas Ernault des, 112
Bulpin, T. V., 155
Burma, 209
Burnel, Étienne, 95
Butterflyfish, 6

Caillou, Mlle, 74–5

Calcutta (Kolkata), 159–60, 215
Cameron, James, 143
Camp Diable, 88
Campbell, Lieutenant-Colonel, 126
Canada, 194, 198
Cannily, 165
Canterbury, 122
Cape of Good Hope, 22, 28, 35, 90
Cape Verde Islands, 56
Caribbean Creoles, 136–7
Caribbean, 39–40, 42, 112, 123, 136–7, 210
Carol, Cyclone, 220
Carroll, Lewis, 28
Cartier (ship), 102
Catholic island, 128
Cauche, François, 165
Celicourt Antelme, 193
Cens Démocratique, 192
Ceylon (ship), 114, 116–17
Ceylon (Sri Lanka), 15, 26, 74, 194
Chagos Archipelago, 129, 224, 247, 248–9
Chagos-Agalega, 247, 250
Chagossians, 251–4
Champ de Mars, 94, 96, 145, 207, 226–7, 245
Chardenoux, Jacques, 152
Charles Planel, 193
Chazal, Antoine Toussaint de, 144
Chazal, Malcy de, 143–4
Cheltenham Festival, 146

281

INDEX

Chevalier du Légion d'Honneur, 104

China, 14, 67, 85, 160, 214, 263, 271

'Chinatown' ('Camp des Chinois'), 140

Chinese Daily News, 213

Chu-Wei Chuen, 213

Cirne, 18–20, 21–2, 165

Clarisse (new ship), 103

Clark, George, 185–6

Clifford, Sir Bede, 207

Clorinde, 175

Coates, Edward, 41

Coin de Mire (Gunner's Quoin), 260

Cole, Sir Lowry, 154, 156

Collège Royal, 198, 214–15, 217–18

Colombo, 159

Columbus, Christopher, 15

Colville, Sir Charles, 156

Comité d'Action Musulman (Muslim Action Committee—CAM), 216, 221, 223–7

Commodore Woodes Rogers, 39

Compagnie des Indes, 56

Conceção (Portuguese ship), 105

Conseil de Cinq Cents, 103

Conway, Thomas, 91–3

Coopen, Anjalay, 242

Copenhagen, 34

Coriolis, Captain de, 91–2

Cornish coast, 77

Coromandel Coast, 74

Corson, 184

Cossigny, David Charpentier de, 93

Cossigny, Joseph de, 63

County Cork, 191

Covid-19, 267–9

Creole (shipwreck), 175, 192

Crève Coeur, 138

Cuban Missile Crisis, 248

Cultural Heritage list, 146

Curé, Maurice, 204–7, 218–19

Curepipe. 184–5, 190, 200–1, 210, 217

Curtis, Captain, 118

d'Auteuil, Charlotte de Combault, 77

d'Emmerez, Adélaïde, 175

d'Épinay, Adrien, 154–5,159–60

Daniel Defoe, 38

Dauphin (ship), 86

Dauphine (ship), 178

David, Barthélemy, 77, 81–3, 86, 169

David-and-Goliath sea battle, 104

DDT, 257

de Bissy, Gaston, 186

de Lafargue, Captain Jean, 177

de Souillac, Viscount François, 89

Decaen, Captain-General Charles, 100, 105, 124–8, 175, 179 naval battle, 114–20

Defiant, 45

Defoe, Daniel, 168

Delhi, 253

INDEX

Delisle, Louis Henri, 166
'Democracy Index', 234–5
Denmark, 103
Depp, Johnny, 37
Desforges-Boucher, Antoine, 84, 176
Deverell, Colville, 214
Diana (ship), 102
Diego Garcia, 179, 248, 251–4
'Dina Arobi', 13, 17
'Dina Margabin', 13
Dinan, 101
Diodati, Roelof, 44–5, 168–9
DNA, 34
Doctor, Manilal, 199
Dodo, 28–34, 167–8, 185, 255, 257
Dolphinfish, 6
Domingos Fernandez, 17–18
Draper, Colonel Edward, 145
du Vernet, Barthélémy Castellan, 177
Ducasse, M., 200
Dufour, Jean, 175
Dufresne d'Arsel, Guillaume, 56–7
Dumas, Jean-Daniel, 85
Dumas, Pierre Benoît, 61
Duperré, Captain naval battle, 114–20
Dupleix, General Joseph François, 75–7
Durrell, Gerald, 257–8
Dutch East India Company, 24, 25, 27–8, 32, 169

Dutch, 21, 28, 32, 44, 46, 48, 56, 86, 122, 138, 158, 255
  spice market, 86
Dutertre, Jean-Marie, 99–101, 102
Duval, Gaëtan, 217, 223, 236–7, 244
Duval, Xavier-Luc, 245

East Africa, 153, 154, 271
East India Company, 48, 50, 103–4, 122
East Indies, 24, 27, 59–60, 86
Eastern Africa, 12–13
Eastlake, Captain, 43
Echo Parakeet, 258–9
Economist Intelligence Unit, 234–5
Edouard Nairac, 199
Egypt, 145
Elephant Bird, 13
Elizabeth II, Queen, 215, 226, 244
Emilie, 102
England, 24, 33, 46–9, 55, 72, 89, 99, 110, 123–4
England, Edward, 46, 49–50
English East India Company, 171
English football Premier League, 146
Equiano, Olaudah, 151
Erik the Red, 61
Escussot, Captain, 114
Esperance, 87
Etcheverry, Captain, 86
EU (European Union), 253
'Eureka', 141

INDEX

Europe, 11, 35, 39, 83, 97, 121, 128, 145, 151, 154, 182, 185, 208, 231

European Common Market (EEC), 238

European Economic Community (EEC), 222

Evertsz, Abraham, 27

Evertsz, Volkert, 32

exclusive economic zone (EEZ), 269

Export Processing Zone (EPZ), 239–42

Falmouth, 77

Famadihana, 146

Farquhar, Robert Townsend, 112–13, 122–3, 144–5, 151–3, 219
  Mauritius, separate identity, 121–33
  slavery, 153–9

'Father of the Nation', 236, 238

Ferdinand, Archduke Franz, 201

Fiji, 194

Flacq, 205

Flèche (French ship), 173–4

Flinders, Matthew, 109–10, 124, 127–8

Flying Fox, 3–4

Following the Equator (Twain), 194

Forest Side, 88

Forges Tardieu, 214

Fort Dauphin, 51

Fort Frederik Hendrik, 26

Fox (ship), 99

France, 24, 25, 49, 56–9, 76–9, 103, 121, 140, 141, 188, 201, 271
  French East India Company, 56–64
  governor, La Bourdonnais, 65–75
  Mauritius, separate identity, 121–33
  naval battle, 114–20
  pepper and cinnamon, 81–7
  revolution, 164–5
  slaves, 59–60, 171–80
  See also British; Dutch; East India Company

François-Gilles, 71

Frederik Haven (Vieux Grand Port), 45, 48

French East India Company, 56–64, 66, 77, 94–5, 165, 172

French Revolution, 164, 172

Fujian province, 140

Gandhi, Mohandas Karamchand, 195
  Salt March, 225

Ganga Talao (Lake of the Ganges), 189

Ganga, 189

Gdansk, 210

Gebert, Gaston, 205

Gelderland (ship), 22

General History of the Pyrates, A (Johnson), 38

General History of the Robberies

284

INDEX

and Murders of the Most Notorious Pyrates, A (Johnson), 37

Gennes, Pierre de, 78

Germany, 25, 59, 208–9

Giant Trevallies, 6

Gloucestershire, 132

Goa, 67

Golden Bats and Pink Pigeons (Durrell), 257

Gomukh, 189

Goolam Mohammed, Ahmed, 195

Gooyer, Cornelius, 26

Gorry, Michel, 169

Goubert, Salomon, 165

Grand Baie, 88, 125

Grand Bassin (Big Pond), 188, 189

Grand Port seat, 205

Grand Port, 90

Grand Port, Battle of, 121, 131, 173

Grand Turk (US ship), 90

Grande Rivière Nord-Ouest, 68, 88

Grande Rivière Sud-Est, 44, 183

Grand-Port-Savanne, 216

'Greenland', 61

Grenier, Jacques de, 172

Gros, Germain Le, 169

Guangdong, 213

Gujadhur, Rajcoomar, 205

Gurib-Fakhim, Ameena, 243

Gustave de Coriolis, 193

Haifa Bay, 210

Hamelin, Commodore, 116, 119

Hamilton-Gordon, Sir Arthur, 186

Hammerhead, 6

Hanoomanjee, Maya, 243

Harris, Benjamin, 33

Hell, Admiral Anne Chrétien Louis de, 166

Hennessy, John Pope, 191–3

Henry IV, King, 56

Hermansen, Commander, 23

Heron (ship), 101

Heureux (ship), 100

Hindoostan (ship), 218

Hindustani, The (newspaper), 199

Hirondelle (frigate), 98, 167–8

Hollanda, Cyclone, 139

Hong Kong, 191, 198, 241

Hook, Captain, 37

Horn of Africa, 37

Hornigold, Benjamin, 49

Houtman, Cornelis de, 21–2

Hova people, 152

Howard, Thomas, 45

Huge Groupers, 6

Huguenots, 167

Humboldt, Alexander von, 143

Ibn Bajjah, 12

Île aux Aigrettes (Egret Island), 32–3, 260

Île aux Bénitiers (Clam Island), 169

Île Bonaparte, 112

Île d'Ambre, 32, 73

285

INDEX

Île de la Passe, 119
  naval battle, 114–20
Île de la Passe, Battle of. *See*
  Grand Port, Battle of
Île de Sable (Sand Island), 176
Île Plate (Flat Island), 182, 260
Île Ronde (Round Island), 260
Île Sainte Marie, 22, 40, 48, 51,
  167
Ilot Gabriel (Gabriel Island), 182,
  260
Imam of Muscat, 152
Imam, 153
Imperial College, 241
Independence Party, 224
Independent Forward Bloc (IFB),
  217, 222, 224, 227, 236
India, 12, 33, 50, 62, 67, 74, 76,
  77, 81, 85, 90, 100, 121, 123–4,
  189, 194, 216, 271
  indentured labourers, 159–62
  Salt March, 225
  slavery, 159
Indian Cultural Association, 219
Indian Ocean, 1, 4, 11, 13 101, 104
  culture, 141–8
  economy, 230–9
  French East India Company,
    56–64
  governor, La Bourdonnais,
    65–75
  naval battle, 114–20
  parties, 221–7
  pepper and cinnamon, 81–7
  piracy, 38–40

slavery, 153–7, 171–80
slaves, 171–80
war, Britain and France, 98–107
See also Îsle de France
Indian Queen (ship), 49–50
Indian Sepoys, 122
Industrial Revolution, 150
Iphigenia (ship) naval battle, 114–
  20
Iraq, 201, 251
Ireland, 46, 132, 191
Irish Home Rule, 191
Îsle Bourbon (Réunion), 28, 45,
  49, 50–1, 65, 67, 111, 121–4,
  129, 178, 264
  Creole languages, 135–41
  French East India Company,
    56–64
  plantations and slavery, 164–6
Îsle de France, 76, 123
  culture, 141–8
  description, 1–9
  economy and polity, 203–12,
    230–9
  French East India Company,
    56–64
  Gandhi's visit, 195–6
  governor, La Bourdonnais, 65–
    75
  oil spills, 263–5
  parties, 221–7
  pepper and cinnamon, 81–7
  piracy, 38–40
  separate identity, 121–33
  slavery, 153–7, 171–80

INDEX

war, Britain and France, 98–107
See also Decaen, Captain-
General Charles; Madagascar
Italy, 208

Jack, Calico, 38
'Jahnvi', River, 189
Jamaica, 41, 160
Japan, 208, 264
Java, 103
Jean Ah-Chuen, 224
Jean Moilin Ah-Chuen, 213
Jenner, Dr Edward, 132
Jinnah, 216
Johnson, Captain Charles, 37–8
Jolly Roger flag, 38
Jolly Roger, 49
Jones, Carl, 257–8
Jugnauth, Prime Minister
Aneerood, 236–8, 245
Jugnauth, Prime Minister
Pravind, 245, 252, 264

Kaya (Joseph Topize), 244
Keating, Lieutenant-Colonel, 112
Kennedy, Governor Donald
Mackenzie, 215
Kent, 103–4
Kerguelen-Trémarec, Yves-Joseph
de, 83
Koenig, Jules, 216
Kunming, 14

L'Établissement, 174
L'Hermitte, Captain Sieur, 51

La Bourdonnais, Bertrand-
François Mahé de, 65–75, 85,
92, 155, 176
La Buse, 52
La Découverte des Îles Mascareignes
(Visdelou-Guimbeau), 17
La Feuillée, Jean Marie Briand de,
176
La Franquerie, Anne-Marie
Lebrun de, 65–6
la Mare, Captain de, 73
La Villeneuve, Courson de, 100
Labour Day, 207
Lallah, Dunputh, 205
Lallmatie, 139
Lambert, Captain, 119
Lammergeier, 13
Lamotius, Isaac, 28, 33
Lancaster House conference, 247,
249
Lancaster House, 223
Lapérouse, Comte de, 83
Iena, 105
Laurent, Eugène, 198–200, 204
Lautour, Lady Maria, 145
Laval, Jacques-Désiré, 188
'Le Camp', 68
Le Cernéen (newspaper), 154–5
Le Clézio, Jean-Marie, 271
Le Corps de Garde, 88
Le Jardin de Pamplemousses, 87
Le Lion, 88
Le Même, François, 97–100
Le Pouce, 88, 145
'Le Reduit' ('The Redoubt'),
82–3, 85, 141, 144, 193

INDEX

Le Sage, Captain, 152
Le Toullec, Major Duronguet, 59
Leclézio, Sir Henri, 199
Leduc, Auguste, 176
Leguat, François, 167
Leichnig, Wilhelm, 59–60
Les Trois Mamelles, 88
Levant, 66
Levasseur, Olivier, 48–51, 52
Liberal Party, 204
'Libertalia', 41–2
Liberté, 98
Lim Fat, Edouard, 241
Lincoln, 217, 236
Lincolnshire, 109
Lisboa, João de, 18–19
Lisbon, 19, 77
London, 38, 100, 123, 129, 174, 191, 217, 223
Long John Silver, 37
Lougarou, 139–40
Louis de La Caille. Nicolas, 83
Louis XV, King, 49, 56, 61, 84, 92
Lowe, Sir Hudson, 156

M25 London Orbital, 5–6
MacDonald, Ramsay, 218
Mackenzie-Kennedy, Donald, 211–12
Macmillan, Harold, 219
MacNamara, Admiral Count Henri, 93–4
Macrae, 47–8
Madagascar, 1, 3, 13, 18–19,
21–2, 27, 40, 42, 45, 51–2, 56, 74, 135, 140, 146, 152
endemics, 255–9
settlements, 163–4
slavery, 153–7
Madras (Chennai), 75–8, 159
al-Madri, Sulhiman, 13
Magicienne (ship), 114–20
Magon de La Villebague, Captain René, 83–4
Mahé, 172–4, 248
Mahébourg, 119, 130, 175, 185, 223
Mako, 6
Malagasy Merina Kingdom, 152
Malagasy slaves, 42, 136, 151, 163–4, 171–80
Malartic (ship), 100
Malartic, Comte de, 94–8, 102–3
Malaysia, 122
Malheureux, Cap, 123, 125
Malindi, 15
Mallet, Mlle, 74–5
Man, Hugh, 43
Mandinka, 136
Marbled Ebony, 4
Marco Polo, 13
Mariette, Charles, 179
'marine protected area' (MPA), 254
Marlin, 7
Marragon, Philibert, 169
Martinique, 77
Mascarene Grey Parakeet, 3
Mascarene islands, 28, 111–12, 128

INDEX

Mascarene shores, 66

Mascarenes, 68, 75, 112, 123, 163

Mascarenhas, Dom Pedro de, 19

Mathurin, Port, 169

Matthews, Commodore, 50

Maupin, Nicolas de, 62–4, 66–7

Maurès, Hippolyte de, 94

Maurice of Nassau, 22, 23

Mauritian Chinese Chamber of Commerce, 213

Mauritian Creole ('Kreol Morisyen'), 137, 140

Mauritian Wildlife Appeal Fund (Mauritian Wildlife Foundation, MWF), 258

Mauritius (ship), 22

Mauritius Broadcasting Corporation (MBC), 234

Mauritius Chamber of Commerce Annual Report, 240

Mauritius Labour Battalion, 201

Mauritius Pioneer Corps, 208

Mauritius Sugar Syndicate, 202

Mauritius Turf Club, 145

Mauritius Union Assurance, 213

Mauritius. *See* Îsle de France

Mayotte, 48

Meade, Professor James, 228, 240, 245

Merina Kingdom, 164

Minerve (ship), 116–17

Ming Dynasty, 14

Minto, Lord, 121

Modeste (ship), 99, 102

Mohamed, Abdool Razack, 215–17, 223–4, 244

Moheeth, 218

Moher, Gurudutt, 227

Moineau (ship), 95

Moka branch, 183

Moka Range mountains, 63, 141, 145

Moluccas, 86

Mon Choisi, 87

Mon Plaisir, 69, 70–1, 85, 87

Montagne d'Emmerez, 175

Montagne Longue, 126

Montocchio, Pierre, 205

Moorish Idols, 6

Morel, Fernand, 205

Moresby Treaty, 153, 180

Moresby, Captain Fairfax, 153

Moresby, Commander Robert, 180

Morgan, Henry, 40

Morphay, Captain Nicholas, 172

Morse, 76

Mouvement Militant Mauricien (MMM), 237

Mouvement Socialist Mauricien (MSM), 237

Mozambique Channel, 17

Mozambique, 102, 135, 146

Muscat, 153

MV Wakashio, 263–7

Nagashiki Shipping company, 266

Naipaul, V. S., 228

Nandeshwar, Sunil Kumar, 263

Napal, Shri Jhummon Giri Gosagne, 189

Napoleon, 98, 100, 104, 107, 116

INDEX

Napoleonic Civil Code, 183, 242

National Environment and Climate Change Fund (NECCF), 260–1

Natural History Museum, 34

Nature (magazine), 33

Navin, 245

Nehru, 216

Nepean, Sir Evan, 153

Nereide (ship), 113, 115, 116

The Netherlands, 21

New Zealand, 194

Newcome, Captain Henry, 173

Newton, Isaac, 12

Newton, William, 193

Nicobar Pigeons, 4, 5

Nicolay, Sir William, 156

Noordwester harbour area, 61

Noordwester Haven (capital Port Louis), 45

Noordwester Haven (Northwest Port), 28

Noortwyk Vlakte, 28

Normandy, 60

North America, 145

North Atlantic, 2

Nostra Signora de la Conception (Danish ship), 103

Nosy Boraha ('Island of Little Abraham'), 41

Nowshera (steamship), 195

Nyon, Denis de, 58–61

O. Beaugeard, 193

O'Keefe, Major, 126

Oligarchs, 200, 207–8

Orpheus (frigate), 173

Orry, Philibert, 68

Owen, John Ap, 42

Oxford (shipWreck), 171

Pakistan, 216

Palestine, 210

Pamplemousses, 193

Panama, 40

Paquebot No. 4 (ship), 91

'Pari Talao' (Lake of the Fairies), 189

Paris riots ('Les Événements'), 237

Paris, 27, 71, 75, 78, 90, 95, 103, 110–11, 120, 188

Paris, Treaty of, 129, 164, 178

Parrotfish, 6

Parti de l'Ordre, 199

Parti Mauricien Social Démocrate (PMSD), 221–7, 236, 249

Parti Travailliste (Mauritius Labour Party—MLP), 206–7, 211, 215–17, 218–24, 231

Passe-Partout, 100

Paturau, Maurice, 214, 222–3

Paul et Virginie (Napoleon), 142, 143, 160

Paul II, Pope John, 188

Paul, 49, 142, 150

Penguin (ship), 102

Père Laval, 188

Pereira, Diogo Fernandes, 166

Peros Banhos, 179

Persia (Iran), 68

INDEX

Peter Pan (Captain Hook), 37

Peyton, Lord, 74

Philippines, 66

Phillips Brothers, 41

Phoenix (British vessel), 100

Piémontaise, 101

Pieter Both, 138

Pingre, Abbé, 169

Pink Pigeon, 258, 260

Pirates of the Caribbean, 37

Pitcairn Island, 167

Plaine Magnien, 130

Plaine Wilhems, 59, 193

Pointe aux Canonniers, 88, 126

Pointe aux Piments, 126

Pointe aux Roches, 126

Pointe du Diable, 114

Poivre, Pierre, 89
  pepper and cinnamon, 81–7

Poncini, José, 240

Pondicherry, 56, 58–61, 66, 75, 81, 90, 97, 99, 187

Poonoosamy, Radha, 243

Port Bourbon (Grand Port), 63, 69, 124, 140–1

Port Louis church, 93

Port Louis, 61, 63, 65, 67–71, 76–7, 82, 87, 90, 94, 98, 99, 102, 103, 104, 113, 123, 126, 130–1, 140–1, 145, 174
  elections, 197–201
  health and population, 181–5
  indentured labourers, 159–61
  naval battle, 114–20
  slavery, 153–7, 171–80

Port Napoleon. *See* Port Louis

Port Nord-Ouest, 94, 103

Portugal, 18, 56
  slaves, 171–80

Portuguese East India Company, 50–1

Potier de la Houssaye, Jean-Marie, 105

Prague, 210

Praslin, 174

Pym, Captain Samuel naval battle, 114–20

Quammen, David, 34–5

Quartier Militaire, 88

Quatre Bornes, 185, 215, 223

Quatre Cocos, 154

Queen Victoria (shipWreck), 171

Quincy, Jean Baptiste de, 172–3

Radama, King, 151–2, 164

Ralliement Mauricien (RM), 215–17, 221

Ramgoolam, Sir Seewoosagur, 189, 218–19, 223, 224, 227, 236, 245

Ramsamy, Romricky, 217

Read, Captain, 43

Red Sea, 41–2

Rennie, Sir John Shaw, 222, 226

Réunion island. *See* Îsle Bourbon (Réunion)

Revenant (ship), 104–5
  naval battle, 114–20

Riche-en-Eau, 87

291

INDEX

Richelieu, Cardinal, 56
Rivière des Anguilles, 216
Rivière du Tombeau, 126
Rivière Noire (Black River), 258
Rivière Sèche, 126
Robert, 175
Roberts, David L., 33
Robinson Crusoe fashion, 23
Robinson Crusoe, 23, 38, 59, 168
Rochecouste, Emilienne, 211
Roches Noires, 88
Rochetaing, Etienne, 169
Rochon, Abbé, 172
Rodrigues, Dom Diogo, 111–12, 121–2, 124, 129, 146, 166, 169–71, 207, 234, 257
Romer, Paul, 239
Rose-Hill, 185
Rosemond, M. de, 175
Ross, Nobel Laureate Ronald, 203
Roussin, Lieutenant, 118–19
Rowley, Commodore, 112, 127
Royal and Military Order of St Louis, 58
Royal Ascot, 146
Rozemont, Guy, 211
Rue d'Enfer, 78

Sahadeo, Pandit, 206
Said, Sayyid, 152–3
Saint François, 71
Saint Helena, 100, 156
Saint-Augustin Bay, 43, 49
Saint-Brandon, 179
Saint-Denis, 112

Saint-Domingue (Haiti), 150, 165
Saint-Malo, 66, 79, 97, 101–2, 104, 105
Saint-Paul, 51–2, 112
Samuel Smith (shipWreck), 171
Sandapa, Emile, 193
Sanjibonlal, Pandit, 188–9
Santa Maria (ship), 15
Sarajevo, 201
Savanne, 62
Savery, Roelant, 31
Schiphol airport, 244
Scops Owl, 3
Séchelles, Jean Moreau de, 172
Seegar, Edward, 46
Seeneevassen, Renganaden, 214–15
Seewoosagur, 218
Séga dance, 146–8
Selkirk, Alexander, 168
Seven Years' War, 83
Seychelles, 51–2, 102, 103, 129, 146, 171–4, 197, 248, 250, 254
Creole languages, 135–41
Shapiro, Beth, 34
Shark, 6
Silver, Long John, 37
Simon, 26, 33
Simonstown, 26
Singapore, 241
Sir Gaetan Duval (tugboat), 266
Sirius (British ship) naval battle, 114–20
Slave Trade Act, 151
Solow, Andrew R., 33

INDEX

Song of the Dodo, The (Quammen), 34–5
Songes, Mare aux, 186
Souillac, 90
South Africa, 26, 124, 188, 195, 231 Gandhi in, 195
South Seas, 66
Southeast Asia, 2, 15, 29, 85, 122, 163
Southern Indian Ocean, 2, 113
Spain, 55–6
Speaker (slave ship), 43–4
Sri Lanka. *See* Ceylon (Sri Lanka)
SSR, 236, 241, 245
St Géran (ship), 73, 142
St Martin Cemetery, 210
St Thomas' Reef, 44
Starmer, Sir Keir, 252
'Stone of Possession', 172
Suez Canal, 185
Suffren, Vice-Admiral Pierre de, 90
Sullivan, Royal Marine Lieutenant Bartholomew, 173–4
Sumatra, 103, 140
Surath, Rampersad, 223
Surcouf, Robert, 101–6 naval battle, 114–20
Swansea University, 257
Sweden, 55
Swettenham, Sir Frank, 200
Sybille (English warship), 98

Table Mountain, 26
Taiwan, 241

Tanzania, 152
Taylor, 48–51
Tchéga dance, 146
Teach, Edward, 49
Terra Australis, 109
Tew, Thomas, 41
Thompson, R. H., 186
Tiger, 6
Times, The (newspaper), 193
'Tirakka Archipelago', 13
Tirakka, 19
Titanic (film), 143
Titmuss, Richard, 228
Tordesillas, Treaty of, 55–6
Tortuga, 40
Touni Minwi, 139–40
Treasure Island, 37
Tremignon, Captain, 86
Tricolore naval battle, 114–20
Trinidad, 160, 210
Triton (ship), 102
Tromelin, 176–8
Tropic of Capricorn, 5
Trou aux Biches, 126
Trou Fanfaron, 161
Twain, Mark, 194–5

UK (United Kingdom), 25, 122, 146, 173, 250
and Mauritius, 251–4
UK Labour Party, 218, 254
UN Security Council, 249
UNESCO World Heritage Site, 162
UNESCO, 146

INDEX

Unguja Island, 43

Union flag, 114–18

Union Mauricienne, 216

United Nations General Assembly (UNGA), 249–50

University College London, 218

University of California, 34

University of Mauritius, 241

University of Paris, 217

US Deep South, 141

USA (United States), 42, 178, 233, 235, 248

Utile (frigate), 176–7

Utrecht (ship), 22

Vacoas, 110, 185

van de Velde, Abraham Momber, 45

van der Stel, Adriaan, 26

van Neck, Admiral Cornelis, 22–3

van Nieuwlandt, Jacobus, 28–9

van Warwyck, Wybrandt, 22, 28, 31, 33

Vandermaesen, General, 126

Vasco da Gama, 17

Vereenigde Oostindische Compagnie (VOC), 24–6, 28, 35, 55, 86, 122, 138

Viceroy of Goa, 19

Victor (British vessel), 173–4 naval battle, 114–20

Vienna, 210

Vieux Grand Port. *See* Frederik Haven (Vieux Grand Port)

Virginie, 142

Visdelou-Guimbeau, Georges de, 17

Vlieigente Hart (slaving ship), 45

Volcan de Mascarin (ship), 99

Voyage to Terra Australis, A (Flinders), 124

Vriesland, 22

Wage Assistance Scheme, 268

Wales Island (Penang), 122

'Walghvogel' ('Tasteless bird'), 28

'war on terror', 251

Warde, Major, 127

Warwyck Haven, 26

Welsh parentage, 42

Welshman, 257

West Africa, 42–3

West Indies, 39–43, 49, 132, 145, 165

western England, 132

western Europe, 150

Western Indian Ocean, 153

'Western Ocean', 15

White Fig, 4

Wilberforce, William, 123, 151

William of Nassau, 22

Willoughby, Captain Nesbit, 113–19

Wolof, 136

Wood, Captain John, 99

Woodes Rogers proclamation, 49–50

World Bank, 228, 232

World War II, 105, 210, 216, 219, 220, 224

Wyndham naval battle, 114–20

INDEX

Xiamen, 140

Yellowfin Tuna, 6
Yemen, 56, 68
Yongle Emperor, 14
Ysbrandts, Willem, 24

Zanzibar, 43, 151–3
Zeeland, 22
Zheng He, 14–15
Zhu Di, 14
Zwarte River (Black River), 28, 168